2/08

DARK DAYS IN THE NEWSROOM

DARK DAYS

in the

NEWSROOM

McCarthyism Aimed at the Press

EDWARD ALWOOD

TEMPLE UNIVERSITY PRESS
Philadelphia

Temple University Press
1601 North Broad Street
Philadelphia PA 19122
www.temple.edu/tempress

Copyright © 2007 by Edward Alwood
Published 2007
Printed in the United States of America

Text design by Lynne Frost

⊚ The paper used in this publication meets the requirements of the American National Standard for Information Sciences—Permanence of Paper for Printed Library Materials, ANSI Z39.48-1992

Library of Congress Cataloging-in-Publication Data

Alwood, Edward.
   Dark days in the newsroom : McCarthyism aimed at the press / Edward Alwood.
      p.   cm.
   Includes bibliographical references and index.
   ISBN 13: 978-1-59213-341-3   ISBN 10: 1-59213-341-X (cloth: alk. paper)
   ISBN 13: 978-1-59213-342-0   ISBN 10: 1-59213-342-8 (pbk.: alk. paper)
      1. Anti-communist movements—United States—History—20th century.
   2. McCarthy, Joseph, 1908–1957—Relations with journalists.   3. Journalists—United States—History—20th century.   4. Journalists—United States—Political activity—History—20th century.   5. Press and politics—United States—History—20th century.   6. United States—Politics and government—1945–1953.   7. United States—Politics and government—1953–1961.
   I. Title.

   E743.5.A66 2007
   973.921—dc22   2006034205

2   4   6   8   9   7   5   3   1

In Memoriam

Margaret A. Blanchard
Teacher, Mentor, and Friend

Do the people of this land . . . desire to preserve those so carefully protected by the First Amendment: Liberty of religious worship, freedom of speech and of the press, and the right as freemen peaceably to assemble and petition their government for a redress of grievances? If so, let them withstand all *beginnings* of encroachment. For the saddest epitaph which can be carved in memory of a vanished liberty is that it was lost because its possessors failed to stretch forth a saving hand while yet there was time.

—Supreme Court Justice Owen Josephus Roberts,
Associated Press v. National Labor Relations Board,
301 U.S. 103 (1937)

Contents

Preface

WHEN THE SENATE Internal Security Subcommittee launched its investigation of Communists in the press in 1955, I was about to enter the first grade. Although I was too young to understand the fear of communism, I was keenly aware of the anxiety surrounding me. I have vivid memories of classroom drills that taught us to "duck and cover" beneath our school desks in the belief that the flimsy desks would somehow shield us from the ravages of nuclear fallout. I also remember wailing air-raid sirens that interrupted quiet days as they were being tested in anticipation of war with the Soviet Union. The frequent reminders of the dangers of the 1950s helped sustain public tensions about political conflict.

By the time I reached college age, people were less willing to accept government claims of a Communist threat. Social turmoil brought on by the civil rights movement, urban rioting, the Vietnam War, and Watergate all fed growing doubts about government policies and how those policies were being implemented. Each succeeding crisis seemed to weaken the credibility of government officials and boost public suspicions. When I began my career as a journalist in the early 1970s, skepticism was a driving force in reporting and explaining the news.

It is from this life experience that I approach the McCarthy era. While the pressures of conformity made it unthinkable for any patriotic American to question government authority during the fifties, events of the sixties and seventies provided the basis for understanding the power of government officials to define the world in a manner that fits their own interests. This was certainly true of the anti-Communist campaign that convinced society to suspend the civil liberties of innocent people during the late 1940s and 1950s in the interest of national security. It is also true of those who defined the First Amendment—publishers of newspapers, the Supreme Court, and members of Congress. Although freedom of the press is regarded as a bedrock of American democracy, this book shows that First Amendment protection is not without limits and should not be taken for granted. It must be fought for and vigorously defended, else it is lost. All the questions surrounding the hunt for Reds in newspaper newsrooms may never be answered, but I hope that reflection on its causes and an understanding of where it has led may help us to prevent it from happening again—but we can do that only if we recognize what happened the first time.

Although the investigations of teachers, lawyers, union officials, and government employees were more widespread and affected thousands of ordinary people, the investigation of journalists directly affected only a few newspapers, and only a handful of journalists lost their jobs. None served a lengthy prison sentence and none took their own lives a result—as some had in connection with other investigations. Yet, for the those whose lives were touched by it, the investigation of the press carried a heavy price, ruining careers, depleting personal savings, crushing friendships, and publicly humiliating people who had committed no crime. For journalists caught in the anti-Communist furor, the episode marked the point where the Cold War became more than a story in a distant land. It marked the point where the campaign against domestic communism crept into newsrooms. This study represents my attempt to understand this period, how it influenced journalism as a profession, and how it affected the press as a democratic institution.

To be sure, the events of 1955–56 provide a commentary on the practices of the McCarthy era and the Communist Party in the United States. I focus on the intersection of communism, anticommunism, and American journalism. What I learned has important implications for journalists—reporters, editors, and publishers—and for people who rely on journalism to understand events beyond their personal experience.

Acknowledgments

MANY INDIVIDUALS contributed thoughts, documents, and memorabilia that helped to make this book possible. I am particularly indebted to faculty and colleagues at the University of North Carolina School of Journalism and Mass Communication whose scholarship provided a guiding light for beginning this study. Individuals who generously provided personal accounts and private documents that enriched the text include Russell Baker, Michael Barnet, Joan Barnet, James Benet, Richard Burdett, Michael T. Kaufman, Albin Krebs, Anthony Lewis, Barry Lipton, Herbert Mitgang, William E. Rowley, Nora Sayre, Edgar H. Scott, Julien G. Sourwine, Victor Stewart, and Arthur O. Sulzberger Jr., and Joan Whitman. Others who patiently read drafts and offered helpful comments included John Beresford, Chris Hanson, Jarice Hanson, Daniel Leab, and James Startt.

I wish to thank many scholars of the Communist Party, anticommunism, the Newspaper Guild, and the McCarthy era for their perseverance in helping to illuminate a darkly complex period of American social and political history. Likewise, I want to thank the archivists and librarians who provided invaluable guidance to important and enlightening documents: John Earl Haynes at the Library of Congress; Charles St. Vil at the *New York Times* Archives; Barbara Samanche at the Park Library of the University of North Carolina School of Journalism and Mass Communication; Janet Greene at the Tamiment Library of New York University; Mattie Sink at the Mitchell Memorial Library of Mississippi State University; Jennifer S.

Lukomski at the Western Historical Manuscript Collection at the State Historical Society of Missouri in Columbia; Tad Bannicoff at the Seeley G. Mudd Manuscript Library at Princeton University; Richard Salvato at the New York Public Library; Harold L. Miller at the State Historical Society of Wisconsin; Paula P. Hinton, Riddley R. Kessler, Maureen St. John-Breen, and Becky Breazeale at the Walter Royal Davis Library of the University of North Carolina; Larkie Gildersleeve at the Newspaper Guild; William LeFevre at the Walter Reuther Library of Wayne State University; Alysha Black, Katherine Mollan, and Charles E. Schamel at the National Archives; Janet Linde at the American Civil Liberties Union Archives; Carmen Hendershott and Leslie Meyers at the Fogelman Social Science and Humanities Library of New School University; the Special Collections staff at the Duke University Library; and Debbie Falvey at the Yale University Library. I also wish to thank members of the FBI public affairs staff, particularly Linda Kloss and Tina Mavin, who patiently processed numerous Freedom of Information Act requests.

Research support came from the Roy H. Park Foundation, Minnie S. and Eli A. Rubinstein Foundation, Quinnipiac University Research Committee, and David Donnelly. Lisa Burns, William Dunlap, and Carol Marro provided valuable editorial assistance. Students who provided comments on early drafts were Tom Ballou, Patricia Bennett, Matthew Lissauer, and Susan Shultz. Colleagues and friends who encouraged and assisted me along the way include Jim Anderson, Michael Barnett, Robin Gallagher, Brian James, Kathy Olson, John Plank, and Larry Reynolds.

This book would not have been possible without the encouragement and patience of my editor, Micah Kleit, whose enthusiasm and unwavering support brought the idea to life. I also wish to thank Janet Francendese and the other members of the Temple University Press Editorial Review Board. It was a pleasure working with copy editor Polly Kummel, who edited my first book and again worked wonders on this one by smoothing the rough edges and identifying gaps that needed to be filled. David Wilson and Lynne Frost of the production department magically brought all the pieces together. I also wish to thank Jana Dluhosová, Magdalena Nušlová, Markéta Pokorná, and Martin Váňa in Prague for providing me with a peaceful environment where I could think and retool. Finally, I wish to thank Daniel Saar for his companionship, inspiration, and steady encouragement and for teaching me the language of the heart.

Washington, D.C.
January 2007

Introduction

O N WEDNESDAY, June 29, 1955, the Senate Internal Security Sub-committee met in the Caucus Room where the flamboyant Wis-consin senator Joseph McCarthy had held his most sensational hearings in 1953 and 1954. Led by Mississippi Democrat James Eastland and undeterred by McCarthy's political downfall, the subcommittee began an unprecedented investigation of American journalism by delving into alleged Communist infiltration of some of the nation's most prominent newspapers. Committee members saw the daily press as a prime Soviet target for propaganda and infiltration because journalists could often access sensitive information and because they influenced public opinion.[1]

The Eastland committee, as the subcommittee was popularly known, intended to ask selected reporters and editors about any involvement they may have had with the Communist Party, but the actual questioning went much further. The committee asked about their political interests and their personal thoughts and beliefs. Members questioned newspaper editorial policies and hiring practices, areas that were thought to be sacrosanct under the First Amendment.

That McCarthy-era inquest reverberated in the summer of 2005 when a federal prosecutor ordered several journalists to identify the sources whose disclosures had led to the publication of a CIA agent's name. *New York Times* reporter Judith Miller refused but others complied. She spent eighty-five days in jail and briefly became a symbol of courageous com-mitment to protecting First Amendment rights, as the media defined them.

The core issue was the same as it had been fifty years earlier: government power, exercised in the name of national security, to compel journalists to testify and reveal confidences.

Miller and several other reporters became entangled in a partisan feud over the Bush administration's Iraq policy and faced government pressure to identify the sources who had leaked the name of a CIA agent. The uproar initially focused on syndicated columnist Robert Novak after he named Valerie Plame as a CIA "operative on weapons of mass destruction." Novak questioned the State Department's wisdom in sending Plame's husband, Joseph Wilson, to investigate claims that Niger had supplied uranium to Iraq. Since it was a crime in some circumstances for government employees to disclose the name of a CIA agent, Novak's column stirred debate, but it was not clear whether the naming of Plame qualified as a crime under the 1982 law. Wilson, a former diplomat, complained that the Bush administration had leaked his wife's name in retaliation for his criticism of the war, destroying her ability to operate as a covert agent and endangering her contacts abroad. Novak's column triggered a lengthy government inquiry into who leaked her name and to whom.[2]

Miller's entanglement was particularly troublesome for the press because she had not written any story naming Plame. Several journalists who were snared by the investigation, presumably including Novak, ultimately divulged their sources to a federal grand jury after those sources agreed to be named, but Miller was not among them.[3] After she was convicted of contempt of court and the Supreme Court refused to hear her appeal, she went to jail for eighty-five days before naming her source, I. Lewis "Scooter" Libby, an adviser to the vice president, after Libby released her from their secrecy agreement. After two years of investigation, the special prosecutor did not bring charges on the leak itself but charged Libby with perjury, obstruction of justice, and making false statements after he gave conflicting testimony before a grand jury. His indictment then entangled journalists even deeper by subpoenaing them to testify at his trial.[4]

Although the public may have viewed the clash as insignificant, at base the argument really was about the press's role in a democracy, enshrined in the First Amendment, to keep the public informed without government interference in the process. Some journalists viewed Miller's jailing as an egregious violation of the First Amendment protection and a disturbing expression of the government's ability to intimidate the press. Debate within the media focused narrowly on a long-standing issue concerning journalists' ability to protect their sources.[5] However, I argue that the Miller episode resurrected other issues that have haunted American journalism since the McCarthy era: the government's power to compel testimony from journalists, especially where there is no clear evidence that any crime has been committed. During the 1950s the government tried to compel journalists to name friends and colleagues who were thought to have been members of the Communist Party, although membership was not a crime. As it did a half-century later, the Supreme Court refused to recognize any First Amendment protection for these journalists. Moreover, in both 1955 and 2005 the newspaper industry stood divided on whether constitutional protection extends beyond the publishers' office to include the journalists who gather the news and serve as a check on the government.

In order to understand better how little has changed in the last fifty years, it is necessary to revisit the 1950s and those journalists who got into trouble when McCarthyism was aimed at journalists and the First Amendment failed to protect them.

T HE EASTLAND COMMITTEE was not the first congressional committee to question journalists but it would conduct the most probing inquiry of its kind, delving into areas many considered off-limits. Such probing questioning directed at journalists had not been seen since the colonial era, when the British confronted printers and threatened prosecution if they dared to criticize the government.[6] Eastland and his colleagues put the newspaper industry on the defensive on some of the most important issues of the day: the rights of the accused to face their accusers and cross-examine witnesses (a public issue since 1938 when the House Un-American Activities Committee [HUAC] was established), and the powers of Congress to hold witnesses in contempt or charge them with perjury if they refused to answer questions. The Eastland investigation, in particular, focused attention on the meaning and scope of freedom of the press and reporters' rights to resist government pressures.[7]

Between 1952 and 1957 the three primary investigative committees—HUAC, McCarthy's Subcommittee on Government Operations, and Eastland's Senate Internal Security Subcommittee—are believed to have subpoenaed more than one hundred journalists to testify, many of them publicly, to answer questions about suspected ties between the newspaper industry and the Communist Party.[8] During this period fourteen journalists were fired by newspapers, including the *New York Times,* after they refused to comply.

Of the three congressional committees bent on rooting out Communists, the Eastland committee conducted the most extensive inquiry of the press. Its staff culled a list of more than five hundred journalists before calling more than seventy witnesses—journalists and employees of the Newspaper Guild—to testify in both open and closed hearings. Journalists who refused to answer questions faced substantial penalties. The *New York Times* fired four who refused to cooperate with the committee. Four more journalists—three from the *Times*—were convicted of contempt of Congress and faced fines and prison sentences. Many in the newspaper industry, whether they were directly involved or not, would have agreed with Arthur Gelb, the former *Times* managing editor, who called those days "a dark and scary period" that "haunts those of us who lived through it."[9]

The McCarthy era was a dramatic and fascinating period, but its complexities defy simple explanations or generalizations. Moreover, deceptive practices used by both Communists and anti-Communists make establishing the truth especially difficult. What happened to the press during the 1950s demonstrates the vulnerability of journalists to government pressure both then and now, despite the constitutional protection of the First Amendment. This is not to suggest that journalists possess special rights beyond those afforded the average citizen; however, the Constitution expressly protects the press from government intimidation. This study also examines how journalists themselves contributed to the political climate that made it dangerous for anyone to challenge McCarthyism during the 1940s and 1950s: they became allied with anti-Communists, based on the flimsiest of evidence, in a campaign to identify and purge Left-leaning colleagues from newspapers and the Newspaper Guild.

B Y THE TIME Senator Joseph McCarthy came to personify the anti-communism campaign in the early 1950s, HUAC had been exposing suspected Communists in various sectors of American society for more than a decade. Created in the late thirties as a temporary investigative committee chaired by Rep. Martin Dies, a Texas Democrat, HUAC was supposed to find and publicly expose subversives in federal agencies and labor unions. From its inception the committee had the markings of a veiled attempt by Republicans and conservative Democrats to embarrass the White House and shake public confidence in Roosevelt's New Deal, a proposition that resonated with business interests that regarded Roosevelt's initiatives to combat the Great Depression as an infringement upon free enterprise.[10]

HUAC quickly perfected public exposure as a form of punishment as it generated headlines that took Communists, who were regarded as devious and dangerous after they began promoting unionism, and turned them into political pariahs who threatened national security. News coverage of HUAC's hearings quickly established the committee as the most visible symbol of the anti-Communist movement in America—and presaged the tactics that McCarthy would use in the early 1950s. By the late 1940s HUAC was a powerful permanent committee that helped move the anti-Communist campaign into high gear.[11] McCarthyism, as practiced by HUAC beginning in the late 1930s and later by McCarthy himself, became the practice of leveling accusations of disloyalty, subversion, or treason publicly with little regard for the niceties of providing evidence or protecting civil liberties. Moreover, anti-Communists typically relied on devious methods of investigation and interrogation that were designed to legitimize their tactics and suppress opposition.

By the 1950s conservatives were joined by other groups in their fear of communism and the desire to root out domestic Communists. The American Legion, the Daughters of the American Revolution, Catholic War Veterans and Catholic unionists, state governments, private industry (most prominently the Hollywood studios), and even labor unions were eager to purge suspected Reds from their midst and adopted some of HUAC's most intrusive tactics. Since there was no unified campaign against Communists, McCarthyism itself took several forms. The federal government required its employees to take a loyalty oath beginning in 1947, a measure adopted after Truman became eager to counter criticism that he was soft on communism.[12]

Although the postwar era produced economic prosperity for Americans, international events brought a sense of foreboding as the "grand alliance" of the United States, Great Britain, and the Soviet Union crumbled. Americans viewed the Soviets as aggressors who sought to establish puppet governments across Central Europe. Russia's development of an atomic bomb and the fall of China in 1949 only exacerbated the public's fears of communism. Coupled with this was a growing concern about domestic espionage after sensitive State Department records were found in June 1945 in a raid at the editorial offices of *Amerasia,* a scholarly journal on international affairs, and a Communist spy ring was uncovered in Canada that September. For many Americans the victory over tyranny during World War II appeared to be short-lived, and the public became preoccupied with domestic communism. The term *democracy,* which in the 1930s had conveyed a sense of action in domestic politics, became identified with maintaining the conservative status quo in the 1940s. HUAC became the engine room of the anti-Communist crusade, fueled by the

FBI, which had assembled dossiers on allegedly subversive organizations and suspicious individuals since the 1920s despite the absence of any clear statutory authority. By the early 1950s McCarthy's Subcommittee on Government Operations and the Eastland committee had joined the hunt for Communists, using the investigative apparatus and legal procedures pioneered by HUAC. Most of their attention was focused on the labor movement, government employees, and higher education, where Communists were thought to be most entrenched.[13]

Between the mid-1940s and the late 1950s thousands of suspected Communists, including journalists, were humiliated before the committees, hounded by the FBI, fired from their jobs, and forced to abandon their careers.[14] Ironically, the press played an important role in promoting McCarthyism by reporting questionable committee procedures in an uncritical manner, thereby legitimizing them.[15] Conservative newspapers, particularly those owned by the media baron William Randolph Hearst and the Scripps-Howard chain, generated additional attention by conducting and publicizing their own witch hunts during the early fifties.[16] Hearst, for example, assigned staff members to pose as students and spy on professors on college and university campuses in Boston, Chicago, Syracuse, New York City, and Madison, Wisconsin, establishing a model for other conservative newspaper owners. Newspapers in Seattle, where anti-Communist sentiment rode strong, published an average of three stories on local Communists each week during 1947.[17] The upper Northwest had been a haven for radical immigrants and a pocket of "subversive disloyalty" since the early 1900s.[18] After World War II the State of Washington became one of several states that created its own un-American activities committee.

By the 1950s allegations about Communist penetration of newspapers had been kicking around for some time. They were first leveled in the late 1930s as the Newspaper Guild began to organize newsrooms and demand higher wages and better working conditions for journalists. Indeed, the guild, like other labor organizations, welcomed Communist members in the late 1920s and early 1930s when the Communist Party was an organization dedicated to helping the working class and the poor.[19] As newsroom employees began to voice their demands, headstrong publishers were quick to assert that the unrest in newsrooms was Communist inspired; the allegation was a popular tactic during the 1930s and 1940s because it allowed conservative business owners to cow recalcitrant workers and avoid addressing the underlying economic issues. The FBI monitored suspected journalists throughout the 1940s as part of its preoccupation with subversive individuals and organizations, and the newspaper industry briefly caught the attention of HUAC after the committee was established in 1938.[20] Both HUAC and the McCarthy committee questioned journalists intermittently as the Korean War further inflamed the anti-Communist sentiment that had developed after World War II. A full-fledged investigation of the press became inevitable after HUAC's clamorous Hollywood investigation in 1947 and its publication of a blacklist for the broadcast industry in 1950, but the hunt for Reds in the nation's newsrooms did not begin in earnest until the Eastland hearings in 1955.[21]

Historical descriptions of McCarthy-era investigations have ranged from "inquisitions" to "degradation ceremonies" that were specifically orchestrated to stigmatize uncooperative witnesses and portray "friendly" witnesses as superpatriots.[22] Witnesses were expected to demonstrate their patriotism by naming friends and colleagues as party members. Those who found the choice untenable faced a moral dilemma that forced them to inform on friends and colleagues or risk being held in contempt. If they invoked the Fifth Amendment, they would be seen by many Americans as unpatriotic. Moreover, they faced prosecution if they tried to use the Fifth Amendment to protect another person since it only protects witnesses from incriminating themselves, not someone else. The Hollywood writers had assumed they would be protected by their First Amendment rights of free association and speech when they appeared before HUAC, but the Supreme Court steadfastly refused to recognize their constitutional claims, and they were jailed for contempt when they refused to testify.[23] The 1955 investigation of the press played out in a similar vein—wildly irresponsible accusations based on rumor, innuendo, and outright lies that were consistently upheld by courts that placed domestic security above the constitutional protection of witnesses' civil liberties. Journalists' refusal to answer questions raised additional issues about freedom of the press, and here too the courts placed security concerns above the First Amendment.

Since the late 1950s historians have wrestled with how to interpret the McCarthy era. Some have described it as a rational response to a genuine threat posed by Soviet expansionism and have focused primarily on Soviet espionage in the United States during the 1940s. Others have characterized McCarthyism as an irrational response to a largely imagined danger, arguing that any threat posed by domestic Communists was "largely contained by the time the anticommunist furor escalated in the late 1940s."[24] Americans have traditionally reacted irrationally in periods of major upheaval, such as the shift from the delirium of the Roaring Twenties to the Depression and the shift from a wartime footing to the period of economic prosperity that followed World War II.[25] Since the colonial era the

American psyche has held that good must be defended and that anything that threatens the goodness of life must be confronted and destroyed. Because public opinion responds to the perception of the threat rather than to reality, Americans traditionally focus their attention on the aliens in their midst—shunning Germans during World War I, confining Japanese Americans to camps during World War II, and, five years after terrorist attacks on the World Trade Center, seeking to erect a fence along the border with Mexico.[26]

Although Communist Party membership never attracted more than a small fraction of the nation's population, the anti-Communist campaign pressed forward, triggering a period of political hysteria that began in the mid-1940s and did not subside until the late 1950s.[27] Despite the Communist Party's marginal role in American politics, it was instrumental in the formation of the labor movement during the late 1930s, helping to establish the Congress of Industrial Organizations (CIO) and building white-collar guilds in a variety of professions, including screenwriting and journalism.[28] To be effective in the 1930s party members laid aside the fiery revolutionary rhetoric that had characterized the party's founding in 1919 after the Bolshevik Revolution. In the early 1920s the party went underground to escape the repressive atmosphere of the Red scare, then emerged as an organization dedicated to workers' rights and the plight of the poor, gaining considerable legitimacy during the late 1920s and early 1930s. Its membership also changed, from overwhelmingly immigrant at its inception to a majority of native-born Americans by the late 1930s. Recent scholarship shows that the party operated on two levels. It publicly championed social causes and the rights of the unemployed during the Great Depression when many Americans became disillusioned with capitalism, while the party secretly maintained an underground network that engaged in espionage. Both levels were directed by party leaders in Moscow.[29] Although Elizabeth Bentley, an American who spied for the Russians before publicly renouncing communism, and Whitaker Chambers, a journalist and Community Party member, claimed that Reds had infiltrated the U.S. government, allegations that captured the public's imagination during the late 1940s, the sustainable evidence to support their claims was scant until the National Security Agency's 1995 release of the Venona cables. The transcripts were of communications between party officials in Moscow and the Communist Party in the United States that had been intercepted by a top-secret government project, the Venona Project, during the 1940s.[30] Although the deciphered cables represent a small percentage of the cable traffic exchanged, they show that the Communist Party USA was a fertile recruiting ground for Soviet intelligence.[31]

Concern about Communists in newspaper newsrooms was not without basis. Journalists had belonged to the Communist Party, although they, like most party members, kept their affiliation secret lest they find themselves under scrutiny and professionally marginalized. Some, like Alden Whitman and Seymour Peck at the *New York Times,* and James Wechsler at the *New York Post,* had joined the Young Communist League as college students before embarking on careers in journalism. Others joined the party after they became journalists, enlisting in party branches in San Francisco, Milwaukee, Detroit, and St. Louis, to name a few, but the large branches in Los Angeles and New York attracted the most attention from Congress in the 1950s. Many journalists viewed party work as an extension of their dedication to the Newspaper Guild, where they battled skinflint publishers for higher pay and better working conditions. As many as a dozen early guild leaders may have been party members or so-called fellow travelers, individuals who did not hold formal membership in the party but followed party policy and directives.[32] Radicalized journalists of the 1930s shared the idealism that had characterized the muckraking journalists at the turn of the century who had viewed their profession as a way to right social and economic wrongs.[33] Upton Sinclair, for example, campaigned for governor of California in 1934 on a platform that promised to end poverty. Similarly, he urged formation of a journalists' union that would resemble a short-lived union that had grown out of the International Typographical Union in the 1920s.[34] The Communist Party lured large numbers of Americans into its ranks during the thirties by touting the vision of a Soviet Union that fostered industrial development, the optimism of its youth, and social and cultural achievement. Many Americans, including a number of journalists, dropped out of the party after only a year or two, either because they found the demands of membership overbearing or because they realized that the dream promoted by the party was indeed an illusion.[35]

O F THE THOUSANDS of books and articles written about the McCarthy era, none has presented an in-depth examination of McCarthyism aimed at the press. Leading journalism history texts pay little, if any, attention to the Eastland investigation.[36] One explanation may be the overwhelming emphasis that historians have placed on the flamboyant senator from Wisconsin.[37] The few scholars who have examined

Eastland's inquiry relied exclusively on hearing transcripts. Most accounts have characterized it as an isolated incident aimed at the *New York Times,* a view fostered by the *Times* itself.[38] This book reveals a much more complicated and disturbing story. To research how the press became a target for a Communist witch hunt in the 1950s and how the newspaper industry responded, I drew on public and private archives, FBI files obtained under the Freedom of Information Act, private papers, personal interviews, and the transcripts of the investigative committees. But even this examination may be incomplete because some records remain restricted and FBI files are routinely censored extensively to protect sources, even dead ones. Moreover, the Venona intercepts cover a relatively brief period during the 1940s and represent only a fraction of the estimated one million cables exchanged between Moscow and the United States, making it difficult to assess the extent of Communist involvement in the press and the degree of journalists' involvement in Soviet espionage. Because party officials and operatives used code names in their communications, some individuals mentioned in the cables remain unidentified. The Venona cables indicate that eighteen journalists, among the hundreds of Americans who have been identified as Soviet contacts, may have been targets for recruitment into the Soviet network.[39] Some of their contacts with Soviet agents may have been merely routine newsgathering but others may not.[40] It is doubtful that any of the investigative committees of the 1950s had direct access to these transcripts because their existence remained a closely guarded secret until 1995. However, the committees may have received information based on the files at the FBI and Justice Department from contacts who did not identify Venona as their source.[41]

The McCarthy era was a fascinating period in journalism history and revealed the vulnerability of journalists who became suspect when the nation was in the grips of a Red scare. The targeting of journalists and the prosecution of those who refused to answer questions about their personal thoughts and political beliefs are a powerful commentary on the scope and meaning of freedom of the press. Several dozen journalists suffered the most direct consequences, but the clash over the First Amendment's protection of journalists would affect the entire profession for decades to come. Debate surrounding governmental power to compel journalists to testify became especially contentious in the 1970s when the government jailed growing numbers of reporters who refused to name their sources, usually in connection with criminal investigations, and the journalists refused. The debate grew even more pronounced in 2005 when Judith

Miller of the *New York Times* was jailed. As I show in this book, the constitutional issues raised by such episodes are rooted in the 1950s, when congressional investigative committees confronted journalists about their thoughts and beliefs. The McCarthy era was not only a grim period in American political history but a dark and haunting episode in the history of American journalism. To understand the problem confronting journalists in the 1950s and today, and the threat to the Constitution, it is necessary to understand the circumstances that prompted journalists to join the Communist Party in the 1930s and consider the political atmosphere surrounding the 1950s witch hunt for Reds in the newsroom.

CHAPTER ONE

Awakening the Newsroom

A S THE NATION struggled with the economic catastrophe of the Great Depression in the spring of 1933, reporter Frances Rockmore donned a simple dress and brushed back her hair so that she could blend into the legion of blue-collar women who worked in the needle industry. In journalism's muckraking tradition Rockmore worked undercover for two weeks at one of New York's dingiest dress factories, where she stitched by hand and toiled at a rickety sewing machine for less than three dollars a week. "The real cost of the bargains the depression has wrested for you is not listed on the price tag," she wrote in the *Brooklyn Daily Eagle,* one of New York City's most important newspapers in that era. "It is written in the gaunt faces and branded on the weary bodies of countless women and girls who work for starvation wages for ten and twelve hours a day in sweatshops."[1] But as she crafted a series of articles on the conditions, she suddenly realized that the money she made at the sweatshop amounted to more than her Depression-era salary at the *Eagle.*[2]

Rockmore was not alone in confronting the stark realities faced by many working in the newspaper industry when the nation's economy collapsed. Even before the Great Depression struck in 1929, some newspapers were feeling the pressures of declining advertising and increasing competition from other newspapers and radio. Publishers faced little choice but to cut salaries or merge with competitors. Between 1911 and 1930 more than one thousand daily newspapers went out of business or became weeklies, which translated into fewer jobs for journalists who were struggling to survive. In the spring of 1923 they watched six hundred people lose their jobs in New York City when the *Globe* merged with the *Sun*. The Great Depression only worsened the situation. "Newspaper publishing had become a branch of big business, obedient to the economic law which concentrated power into fewer and fewer hands," Frederick Lewis Allen wrote in *Harper's*. "The 'profession of journalism' had become one of the most crowded and ill-paid of all white-collar occupations."[3]

As joblessness became an everyday threat at all levels, journalists suffered repeated pay cuts and worked longer workdays—the contracting job market made it nearly impossible to find a new job. Many earned less than the average filing clerk while working ten to twelve hours a day, six days a week.[4] Severance pay and paid vacations were foreign concepts. Cash-starved reporters sometimes resorted to taking bribes to slant the news or kill a story. Unionized typesetters and press operators, on the other hand, were protected from pay cuts and job cutbacks by their labor contracts.[5]

In the meantime wealthy newspaper publishers continued a postwar buying spree, expanding their holdings by gobbling up their weaker competition. By 1933 the six largest newspaper chains claimed 70 percent of the nation's daily circulation. The Scripps-Howard chain, for example, grew to fifty-two newspapers. The media empire of William Randolph Hearst grew to twenty dailies, along with two wire services, a features syndicate, six magazines, a newsreel, and a motion picture production company. Hearst lived in grandeur on a 127-acre estate, with acres of gardens, terraces, and pools. San Simeon, his 165-room castle, housed the art treasures he collected from around the world. The castle became legendary for lavish, star-studded parties at which Hearst entertained the powerful and wealthy before his empire began to collapse in the late 1930s. Like most publishers of his era, Hearst did not translate his financial success into higher pay and better working conditions at his newspapers.[6]

A glimmer of hope for cash-starved journalists came in the summer of 1933 when President Franklin Roosevelt established the New Deal, which encouraged unionization and collective bargaining. The National Industrial Recovery Act prodded the leaders of industries of all kinds, including newspaper publishers, to adopt voluntary fair practice codes as a way of stimulating the economy by setting minimum wage scales and maximum work hours. Although publishers initially welcomed Roosevelt's initiative, they backed away when they were called upon to adopt industry-wide standards, claiming a First Amendment exemption from having to comply. The public didn't buy it, and faced with increasing public pressure, publishers ultimately submitted a plan that set a five-day, forty-hour workweek and minimum pay standards. But they exercised a loophole that allowed them to exempt editorial workers by classifying them as "professional" employees. The publishers' proposal provided a modest boost in pay for many journalists but did nothing to improve working conditions, leaving them with long hours and none of the job security benefits provided to the unionized workers who ran printing presses and typesetting machines.[7]

The ambivalence among publishers particularly annoyed the popular *New York World-Telegram* columnist Heywood Broun, although he was among the highest-paid journalists in the nation. "After some four or five years of holding down the easiest job in the world I hate to see other newspaper men working too hard," he told readers of his syndicated column, "It Seems to Me," in August 1933. "It embarrasses me even more to think of newspaper men who are not working at all. Among this number are some of the best."[8] Broun's celebrity status came after a struggle of many years that had begun in 1910 after he received an F on an elementary French examination that kept him from graduating from Harvard. He joined the *New York Telegraph,* where he had worked during his college summers, earning $28 a week to write sports stories. When he asked for a two-dollar-a-week raise two years later, the *Telegraph* fired him and he moved to the *New-York Tribune,* where he again covered sports and also wrote drama reviews. In 1917 the newspaper sent him to cover the war in Europe.[9] The military hadn't wanted his flat feet, but he recognized the war as an event no journalist could miss, and he welcomed the opportunity to become a war correspondent.

After his return to New York, Broun wrote theater and book reviews, along with occasional commentaries on life and the arts. A physically imposing figure at six feet three and 225 pounds, his rumpled appearance and easy-going manner made people feel at ease and willing to talk about personal problems that Broun translated into consciousness-raising commentaries. "Those casual pieces of yours are getting better than your book reviews," his managing editor told him in 1920.[10] After he landed a better position at the *World* a year later, he wrote a string of impressive theater reviews, including one that helped launch the acting career of Paul Robeson when the All-American football star turned to the Broadway stage. "It seems to me that it might be a good idea if I were to write about what I think, maybe a column that appeared every day in the same place," he told his editor one day. The newspaper instituted "It Seems to Me," a regular column that Broun wrote for the next eighteen years.[11]

Broun's outspoken liberalism also brought trouble, especially after 1927 when he joined a crusade that supported Nicola Sacco and Bartolomeo Vanzetti, two Italian anarchists who had been convicted of a Massachusetts murder.[12] Broun joined a chorus of defenders that was led by the Communist Party, which claimed the men's trial reflected public animus toward immigrants. Broun and others pointed to their death sentence as a glaring example of oppression aimed at the working class. When Broun's editors refused to publish two of his columns, he threatened to quit, explaining that he had become "too indiscreet to fit pleasantly into the *World*'s philosophy of daily journalism."[13] His diatribe soon became an empty threat when he realized that his contract contained a noncompete clause that barred him from writing for another newspaper for three years if he left the *World* before his contract expired.[14]

In the late 1920s Broun began writing occasional commentaries for the *Nation* and the *New Republic*, but trouble erupted when he criticized the *World* after the newspaper opposed a public exhibit on birth control. Broun interpreted the newspaper's opposition as a concession to the Catholic Church. "There is not a single New York editor who does not live in mortal terror of the power of this group," he wrote in the *Nation*.[15] His caustic admonition was the last straw for the *World*. "The *World* has decided to dispense with the services of Heywood Broun," the newspaper announced a few days later. "His disloyalty to this paper makes any further association impossible."[16] At the age of forty he returned to the *Telegram* at an annual salary of $30,000 and convinced the *World* to let him retain "It Seems to Me" as the standing headline for a column that the *Telegram* would syndicate to newspapers across the nation. "We don't care what he writes as long as it is not libelous and as long as it is interesting," said Albert Scripps, president of the Scripps newspaper chain.[17]

Broun again tested the journalistic limits in 1930 when he decided to run for Congress on the Socialist ticket to represent New York's Silk Stocking district. He had joined the Socialist Party, admitting he knew little of its standing beyond what he had learned at Socialist Club meetings while he was at Harvard. Although he never formally became a member of the student organization while in school, he enthusiastically embraced the organization's belief that the federal government should work to relieve surging unemployment. He assured his editors that his run for Congress would not harm his column but would improve it. Realistically, he had little chance of winning but he reveled in the public spotlight.[18] As he promoted his campaign, the *Telegram* ran full-page advertisements, telling readers, "He Writes and Does as He Pleases."[19] By the mid-1930s he was one of the best-known and highest-paid columnists in the nation, but he never lost touch with the struggle and sacrifices of the poor and underprivileged, especially during the Depression, when he consistently championed the unemployed and railed against racial discrimination and ethnic bigotry.

Broun broke with the Socialists in the spring of 1933, when the case of the Scottsboro Boys became a cause célèbre for Communist Party. The case involved nine black teenagers who had been convicted of raping a white woman in the deep South and were sentenced to death. Broun, like the Communist Party, defended the Scottsboro Boys to the hilt, which gave the Socialists the opportunity to criticize Broun for carrying the Communist Party line. Broun accused the Socialists of being out of touch with reality and quit. "In getting out of the Socialist Party, one should leave by the door to the left," he wrote, indicating that his defection did not signal surrender of his basic principles.[20]

The Genesis of the Newspaper Guild

In early 1933 Broun received an anonymous letter expressing concern that publishers were attempting to exclude newspapers from the wage and work standards of Roosevelt's New Deal.[21] That August he used his newspaper column to take the newspaper industry to task. At the same time he challenged his newspaper colleagues to seize the initiative. "It is a little difficult for me, in spite of my radical leanings and training and yearnings, to accept wholeheartedly the conception of the boss and his wage slaves," he said. He urged his colleagues at newspapers across the nation to organize a labor union that would fight for higher wages and better working conditions. "Beginning at 9 o'clock on the morning of October 1 I am going to do the best I can to help in getting one up."[22]

Many journalists did not wait for formal organizing to begin. The earliest groups began meeting in Cleveland and Philadelphia. In New York reporters and editors vividly remembered the *Telegram*'s 1931 merger with the *World* that left hundreds unemployed. Broun broached the idea of creating a reporters' union but the proposal stirred little interest.[23] But by late 1933 the tide of opinion had shifted, and a groundswell of support began to sweep into newsrooms in large cities and small towns. Journalists began to meet in private homes and in the back rooms of neighborhood bars to organize a united front. They called for a five-day, forty-hour workweek, a $30 minimum weekly salary for journalists with more than one year of experience—$20 for the less experienced—and discharge notices. A delegation representing fifteen groups in fourteen cities presented the journalists' proposal at public hearings before Roosevelt's National Recovery Administration in Washington, D.C., the agency that was charged with accepting or rejecting the fair practice codes submitted by industry.[24]

When it became clear that the Roosevelt administration would adopt the wage-and-hours plan submitted by newspaper publishers, New York journalists became vocal advocates for an organization to represent the concerns of journalists nationwide. On December 15, 1933, representatives from forty-four groups met at the National Press Club in Washington, D.C., to form the American Newspaper Guild (in 1970 it became the Newspaper Guild) and pledged themselves to improving working conditions and raising the standards of journalism.[25] The group adopted a decentralized structure that left decision making to the guild locals, and, although some members expressed reservations, they elected Broun as their first president. "The men behind this movement are all young, most of them in their early thirties or younger. Most of them are the new type of newspaperman, college trained, stable, solid citizens. The older type, itinerant and ne'er-do-well, already has passed from the picture," wrote Robert Bordner in the October 1933 issue of *Quill,* the magazine of the journalism society Sigma Delta Chi.[26]

Newspaper publishers remained ambivalent, remembering attempts by the International Typographers Union to organize journalists in the early 1920s that failed to attract apathetic news workers. Publishers speculated that this latest effort would waste away under Broun's leadership.[27] The newspaper trade magazine *Editor and Publisher,* however, described the guild as "the most powerful spontaneous organization ever seen in newspaper circles in this country."[28] In early 1934 the Roosevelt administration adopted the publishers' code with only minor changes, sending a clear signal that the president did not want to alienate publishers by siding with newspaper employees.[29] Journalists were most concerned that the code placed no limits on work hours and provided none of the job protections enjoyed by blue-collar newspaper employees. The code was also silent on the "closed shop," a provision that would have bolstered the guild's clout at the bargaining table by requiring publishers to limit newsroom hiring to members of the guild. Such a "closed shop" requirement would have assured the guild a reliable stream of dues and membership large enough to use as leverage in contract negotiations. Within a short time this would become the most contentious issue between newspaper management and the guild.[30]

Organizing Newsrooms

Although journalists were united in their concerns about wages and working conditions, they were divided on how they should achieve their goals.
Some viewed the guild as a professional organization along the lines of the
medical and bar associations. Others saw it as part of the struggling labor
movement, which had been invigorated by the New Deal. Young leftists saw
the conflict with publishers as a battle against worker exploitation. In time
they would become the guild's most enthusiastic and most energetic com-
batants in trying to wrestle contracts from obstinate publishers.[31]

The first newspaper contract came in the spring of 1934 when J. David
Stern, the liberal publisher of the *Philadelphia Record* who was an outspoken supporter of the New Deal, agreed to much of what the guild sought.
Not only did he meet their wage demands, he permitted a "guild shop"
arrangement, which allowed the publisher to make hiring decisions but
required eligible employees to join the guild. But Stern quickly proved to
be the exception in the newspaper industry. Other publishers held the
guild at bay, either refusing to negotiate or agreeing to contracts that met
few, if any, of the guild's terms. Some fought the guild by firing guild
members based on a trumped-up charge that the worker had breached
some newspaper policy. After the *Long Island Daily Press* fired nine from
its newsroom in July 1934, the guild launched its first protest, setting up
picket lines outside the newspaper and appealing to advertisers to drop
their ads. The *Daily Press* blamed Reds in the guild, an accusation that
became a mantra among publishers. Like many employers in other industries, publishers found Red-baiting to be an effective strategy—it allowed
them to combat organized labor without having to address the underlying
issues surrounding compensation and job security.[32] Since the turn of the
century newspapers had increasingly identified with the conservative
interests of big business as they became reliant on advertising revenue.[33]
Echoing that conservatism, *Editor and Publisher* noted in September 1934
that the guild had become "a radical trades union, at least insofar as its
national officers are concerned."[34]

The guild called its first strike four months later after the *Newark Ledger*
fired eight workers who were trying to organize its newsroom. When the
walkout forced the newspaper to shut down, its reactionary publisher ran
full-page advertisements in other newspapers describing the guild as a
"Communist-dominated" labor union that was trying to control his newspaper.[35] Other publishers, who had been ambivalent about negotiating
with a labor union as recently as late 1933, soon became recalcitrant in

contract negotiations. In one case guild negotiators at the *Cleveland News* found the publisher unwilling to spell out the terms of their agreement in writing.[36] In San Francisco Hearst's *Call-Bulletin* fired a copy editor who took time off to serve as a delegate to the guild's annual convention.[37] Federal labor officials initially supported the man's reinstatement but backed down when the White House became concerned that a ruling against Hearst might undermine Roosevelt's tenuous voluntary code arrangement.[38] Although Hearst and other conservative publishers had supported union organizing among blue-collar newspaper workers in an effort to build readership, the publishers vowed never to negotiate with the guild. "We are not only going to have trouble with the guild interfering with the efficient conduct of the newspapers, but we are going to have eternal difficulty in keeping radical propaganda out of the papers, because every newspaperman as soon as he joins a radical guild becomes a radical propagandist," Hearst told his newspaper division.[39]

The overall climate for the fledgling labor movement improved somewhat in 1935 following passage of the National Labor Relations Act (known as the Wagner Act), as it reaffirmed and strengthened government support for collective bargaining by establishing appeals procedures. An early test came when the Supreme Court ruled, in a case brought by New York attorney Morris Ernst, a long-time friend of guild founder Heywood Broun's, that Associated Press writer Morris Watson had been fired unfairly and ordered the wire service to reinstate him.[40] The landmark decision put publishers on notice that the First Amendment would not exempt them from complying with federal labor laws. "The publisher of a newspaper has no special immunity from the application of general laws," the Court ruled. "He has no special privilege to invade the rights and liberties of others. He must answer for libel. He may be punished for contempt of court. He is subject to the anti-trust laws. Like others, he must pay equitable and nondiscriminatory taxes on his business."[41] Outraged publishers saw little distinction between the "closed shop" and the "guild shop" because, in their view, both represented outside meddling in newspaper business affairs. The American Newspaper Publishers Association officially proclaimed the "guild shop" to be inimical to a free press. An undercurrent of Red-baiting swirled around the guild when it called its strike against the *Long Island Daily Press* in the summer of 1934. Vigilant police officers referred to the picketers as "those Reds."[42] As publishers aimed their vexation at the guild, attention outside the industry increasingly focused on Broun. Elizabeth Dilling, a Chicago housewife, published *The Red Network* that spring, naming him among hundreds of individuals who "contributed in some measure to one or more phases of the Red movement in the United States."[43] His reputation followed him as he traveled across the nation to support journalists who were battling stubborn publishers. The charismatic columnist galvanized angry journalists as he walked their picket lines. When he was arrested during a protest in Toledo, a police officer referred to him as "one of those rich New York Communists." "Uh-uh," Broun quickly corrected him. "That's, rich New York *columnist*."[44]

Rising Storm

In the summer of 1935 the New York Newspaper Guild led a campaign to tie the national guild more closely to the burgeoning organized labor movement by affiliating with the American Federation of Labor (AFL). Although the AFL was tame compared with the radical industrial unions of the early twentieth century, it represented the growing influence of organized labor that had been triggered by Roosevelt's New Deal. Some guild members saw affiliation as a means of gaining bargaining clout. "I believe that the past year has clarified the issues and that the newspaper men and women of this country are ready formally to take their place in the ranks of organized labor," said Jonathan Eddy, the chapter's executive secretary and a former *New York Times* reporter.[45] But the membership was not ready to jump so quickly and defeated the affiliation proposal by a slim margin.[46]

Four months later supporters of affiliation began to gain the upper hand during a strike against Hearst's *Wisconsin News* when the guild called for a nationwide boycott of Hearst publications. Labor organizers from New York oversaw the campaign to pressure local businesses to drop their advertisements. Rallies supporting the guild drew as many as fifteen hundred people after the AFL agreed to lend a hand. Police arrested Broun and several guild members during an angry clash, charging them with inciting a riot.[47] The conflict tipped the balance, convincing the holdouts that the time had come for the guild to join the AFL.[48] Conservative members, on the other hand, interpreted affiliation as further evidence that New York–based leftists had seized control of the guild.[49] Even so, the affiliation won by an overwhelming 83–5 vote and the "loose association," as it had been regarded at its founding two years earlier, joined the ranks of organized labor.

The effects could be seen two months later when the guild called a strike against a second Hearst-owned newspaper, the *Seattle Post-Intelligencer*, after it fired two veteran journalists who were active in the guild. Energetic strikers used sound trucks to prod readers to cancel their subscriptions.

Volunteers telephoned more readers, asking them to stop buying the *Intelligencer*. The guild appealed to longshoremen, loggers, and other unionized newspaper workers to honor their picket lines, and when mechanical workers stayed away, the newspaper was forced to shut down for 108 days before Hearst agreed to minimum wages and maximum hours, plus sick leave and paid vacations.[50] The agreement also pressured Hearst to settle the Milwaukee strike. "Seattle Strike Is Won; Big Gains Elsewhere," roared the *Guild Reporter*.[51]

Newspaper strikes were only one sign of the guild's radicalization. At the guild's annual convention in the summer of 1937, delegates adopted a series of resolutions with a leftist bent, including one supporting Roosevelt's ill-advised attempt to "pack" the Supreme Court with justices supportive of his New Deal policies. Another resolution expressed the guild's support for Spanish loyalists. Both paralleled positions promoted by the Communist Party and opposed by conservatives.[52]

The most glaring symbol of the guild's leftward shift came when Broun called for a switch to the more militant Congress of Industrial Organizations (CIO) and to expand the membership base beyond newsroom employees to include workers in the advertising and business departments. "Nowadays, if a reporter walks out on strike, they can replace him with some more boilerplate," Morris Watson, the guild's vice president, told the convention after he won his legal battle against the Associated Press. "But when the elevator boy quits and the publisher has to lumber up five flights of stairs, he'll know a strike is on."[53] After lengthy and sometimes heated debate, the proposal won 86 percent of the votes, led by a large bloc from the New York affiliate of the guild.[54] The New Yorkers also convinced the membership to require future contracts to include a "guild shop" requirement and a five-day, forty-hour week, a negotiating position that assured heightened conflicts at the bargaining table. As militant members became increasingly assertive, conservatives began to drop out of active participation in guild affairs or dropped out altogether.[55]

With the guild agreeing to align itself with the most radical voices in organized labor, newspaper publishers hastily arranged an emergency meeting at which they characterized the guild as a menace to press freedom. "There has never been a time in our history when uncolored presentation of news was as vitally important as today," they declared.[56] The McClure syndicate was even more outspoken, blaming Communists for pushing the guild to the left. "Reds have been active in Guild circles, especially around New York," it told subscribers to its news service. "In several Guild centers they have been successful in seizing the machinery of control."[57]

The most blistering denunciation came from AFL President William Green, who characterized Broun as a stooge who was "inspired by some very astute Moscow-trained revolutionaries." He claimed Broun had "sold down the river a lot of earnest, sincere, hardworking newspapermen, who now see their organization, which had succeeded in making better working conditions, torn to shreds."[58]

The guild's shift to militancy had begun at an unprecedented time in labor history—the mid-1930s, when the CIO was beginning to take root. The organization sprang from the AFL's refusal to organize unskilled workers in mass production and its decision to oust militant unionists in 1936. John L. Lewis, head of the United Mine Workers, and several other union leaders then formed the CIO. Unlike the AFL, the CIO was receptive to a wide variety of trades, from auto- and steelworkers to needleworkers.[59] Because of the Communists' impressive organizing skills, work ethic, and experience in organizing workers, Lewis quietly invited them to help build the fledgling CIO into a viable force. Party members had been active in organizing workers during the 1920s and 1930s in their own attempt to establish a Communist-led labor movement, which the party ultimately abandoned upon the formation of the CIO.[60] Even as the Newspaper Guild debated CIO affiliation, the AFL was in the throes of expelling several CIO-allied unions, the move that would produce a permanent industrial union movement.[61]

Communists and the Guild

By the late 1930s Communists had made deep inroads at several CIO unions, particularly among fur workers, under a party policy of "boring from within" to gain influence and establish control. Most rose through the ranks through hard work without divulging their party affiliation. They had been trained to argue and cajole at union meetings until they won the measures they favored.[62] Several officers and most of the paid staff of the Newspaper Guild were either Communists or fellow travelers, individuals who did not officially belong to the party but followed party policies.[63] Broun recognized that the party had bored into the guild's structure, although he rarely addressed the subject openly. He knew that Earl Browder, the American Communist Party's general secretary, had rented a suite of rooms in the hotel where the guild held its 1936 convention.[64] Broun was startled a year later to learn that Communists might oppose his candidacy for guild president, and one source claims that he offered to step down if the party offered its own candidate.[65] Broun suspected that one guild offi-

Congress of Industrial Organizations (CIO) when a series of sit-down strikes began in the winter of 1936. More than one hundred strikes rocked the auto industry, for example, with walkouts and picketing that would not have been tolerated before the New Deal.[3]

After a single session on propaganda the committee turned to Communist influence in organized labor and called John Frey, the vice president of the American Federation of Labor (AFL), who offered a sweeping indictment of the CIO. "The sit-down strike and mass picketing had been used by Communists as front line trenches in which to train members for the day when the signal for revolution is given," he said. He named 248 individuals as Communists and sixty others as supporters of Communist causes, including a journalist, Julius H. Klyman, a *St. Louis Post-Dispatch* reporter who was instrumental in establishing the St. Louis Newspaper Guild and later became a national guild vice president.[4]

The hearings continued the next week with several days of testimony from J. B. Matthews, a leader of several Communist front organizations during the early 1930s before he became an outspoken anti-Communist. Although he never was a party member, Matthews was touted as an expert on domestic communism, a status that would soon land him a post as the committee's research director and chief investigator. He fed an increasingly popular notion that the party constituted a subversive "fifth column," drawing on the image of the small band of Bolsheviks that successfully toppled the Russian tsar in 1917.[5]

When his testimony began on Saturday, August 20, Matthews described a schism between the Communists and the Socialist Party in the early 1930s that involved Heywood Broun, the founder of the Newspaper Guild.

MATTHEWS: Broun called me aside one day at a Socialist meeting and informed me that he was resigning from the Socialist Party in order to have greater freedom to work with the Communists.
DIES: Who was that?
MATTHEWS: Heywood Broun.
DIES: The columnist?
MATTHEWS: Yes.[6]

The following Monday, Matthews gave the committee a long and detailed description of party activities and named a variety of organizations and institutions. "In Communist Party circles it is a matter of pride and boasting that the party has its friends and sympathizers situated strategically at every important institution in the land—newspapers, magazines,

churches, women's clubs, trade unions," he told committee member Joe
Starnes, an Alabama Democrat.[7]

> STARNES: Do you have any idea as to what extent they have friends and
> sympathizers on the newspapers and magazines in this country?
> MATTHEWS: I can tell you from experiences which have come to me
> indirectly that it is considered good business to have even a routine
> person who opens the mail to undertake the business of censorship
> or destruction of mail at the request of the Communist Party. . . . The
> *New York Times,* for example, has enough Communists or Communist
> sympathizers on it to bring out a little paper known as *Better Times,*
> on the mast head of which it is frankly stated that this is published by
> the Communist members of the staff of the *New York Times.*[8]

Heywood Broun attended the hearing a few days after Matthews named
him as a Communist, and the committee called Broun to the witness table
to defend himself. "Just what Mr. Matthews would regard as a private conversation, I do not know, but neither under the seal of secrecy nor publicly
did I ever tell him that I was drawing out from the Socialists to work for
the Communists," Broun said. "I am against fascism and I am for peace
and democracy. I am not a Communist and I have never been a Communist."[9] His remarks triggered a brief commotion in the spectators' gallery,
prompting Dies to begin pounding his gavel and abruptly cut Broun's testimony short. Investigative committees routinely guarded against permit-
ting controversial witnesses to use the hearings to grandstand, and Broun
was no exception.[10]

As the hearings progressed throughout 1938 and 1939, witnesses spo-
radically cited Broun and the Newspaper Guild as examples of how communism had become a sinister force in the United States. A representative
of a patriotic organization claimed that the columnist had a sideline writing for a Communist newspaper.[11] A witness representing the American
Legion warned that the Communist Party wanted to "establish nuclei in
the various newspapers so that they could control the presentation of news
by the papers at the time of the calling [of] a general strike."[12]

In testimony three months after his initial appearance Matthews again
referred to Broun, explaining that the journalist had shared public plat-
forms with known Communists, including at a rally two years earlier at
Madison Square Garden. "Everyone of those persons is a well-known Communist Party member or a fellow traveler," Matthews said.[13] The following
year, in testimony before the committee, Benjamin Gitlow, former general
secretary of the Communist Party, identified Broun as someone who could

be relied upon to carry out Communist Party policies.[14] A garment worker who identified himself as a Communist said he knew Broun. "I think the first time he was a party member was back in 1928," he testified.[15] Another witness described Broun as "one of those Party members who never came to Party headquarters, because he did not want it known that he was a member of the Communist Party."[16] Despite the repeated allegations, the committee never launched a full-fledged investigation of the columnist, the Newspaper Guild, or any specific newspaper, turning instead to industrial unions and organizations tied to the New Deal, including the Federal Theater Project.

Guild members took the accusations in stride, comparing them with the Red-baiting tactics of publishers. "[Broun] did not try to hide from the committee's supposedly pitiless probing for the facts," said the *Guild Reporter*. "In the midst of the endless recitals by witness of gossip about his and a myriad of other individuals' activities, he walked in and demanded to be heard."[17] Scripps-Howard columnist Raymond Clapper characterized the committee as "the joke of Washington, the laugh of the press gallery, and a useful tool through which Republicans on the committee could ask questions smearing the Roosevelt Administration."[18] In its annual report the committee said only that as many as a dozen CIO unions were "more than tinged" with communism, but the report made no mention of Broun or the guild.[19]

Broun contracted pneumonia eighteen months after his HUAC appearance and died at the age of fifty-one. Tributes arrived at the *New York World-Telegram* from many quarters, including the White House. President Roosevelt said of Broun, "Neither slander nor calumny nor thought of personal consequences ever deterred him, once he had entered a fight in the cause of right and justice as he saw it."[20] The *New York Times* praised Broun's contributions in a front-page story, saying, "When Heywood Broun stepped out of a crowd he left a sizable hole." More than three thousands mourners jammed New York's St. Patrick's Cathedral, where Monsignor Fulton J. Sheen of Catholic University eulogized the late columnist. "Heywood Broun lived a full life and leaves a noble heritage," said Sheen. "Some of his friends who were loudest in shouting for freedom were the loudest in protesting against him because he acted freely."[21] Sheen also related some of Broun's comments when the columnist converted to Catholicism seven months earlier. "While I have been assocated with radical movements, I have never been a Communist and never will be a Communist," Sheen said Broun told him. He said Broun felt he had "too much intelligence to be one."[22]

Upheaval at the Guild

With Broun's death the guild lost an important stabilizing influence. Under his leadership the guild had grown from a handful of founders to more than nineteen thousand members, representing nearly one-fourth of all newspaper employees.[23] Broun had been a resident saint, the wise man who found ways to harmonize the diverse viewpoints that had threatened to divide the young organization, and his death opened the door for the underlying tumult to spill into the open. Even as Broun lay gravely ill in a New York hospital, the conservative columnist Westbrook Pegler warned that Communists would attempt to seize the guild. "I have long sensed a strong pull toward Communism in its official list," he wrote. "The masthead, so to speak, includes two officers out of five who are, to my satisfaction, either Communists or determined fellow travelers."[24] Broun and Pegler had known each other since early in their careers when both worked as sportswriters. During World War I they were assigned to Paris at the same time. In 1933 the Scripps-Howard Syndicate hired Pegler to write commentaries on social issues. Some observers speculated that conservative publisher Roy Howard had hired him to keep Broun and the guild at bay.[25] Although Pegler had joined the guild at its inception, he dropped out and distanced himself from Broun after leftists insisted that a "guild shop" provision be incorporated in all newspaper contracts, a position Pegler viewed a strident.[26]

Pegler continued to trumpet the Communist issue as the guild began considering candidates to replace Broun. "The New York guild is dominated by Communists and ... [the Communist Party] dominates the affairs and policies of the American Newspaper Guild," Pegler wrote in June 1940.[27] A week later he called the guild "a transmission belt of the Communist Party."[28] His rancor subsided somewhat after the guild appointed Kenneth Crawford to Broun's unexpired term, although the guild's constitution specifically called for elections within a month after a position became vacant.[29] A Washington correspondent for the *New York Post,* Crawford attempted to focus the guild on economic issues. "It is my opinion that the Guild's primary function is to protect and improve the wages, hours and working conditions of newspaper people; ... that it is not the Guild's business to reform the world or the world's newspapers," he said.[30]

At the guild's convention in Memphis that summer battle lines were easily distinguishable.[31] The New York Guild, home to a sizable contingent of politically radical members, held considerable influence in choosing national officers, setting the operational structure, and directing overall policies of the national organization.[32] As New York–based leftists haggled with guild conservatives, the syndicated columnists Drew Pearson and Robert Allen picked up Pegler's anti-Communist drumbeat.[33] "This union of reporters and business-office employes is in the throes of a head-on clash between anti-Communist and fellow-traveler elements," Pearson and Allen wrote. "The latter see the guild as a useful instrument to pursue 'Party-line' tactics."[34]

At the 1940 convention Communist infiltration became an undercurrent of every conversation and every vote. "Time has come to clean house," read one campaign flyer. "Tomorrow you will receive your ballot in the Union election. That ballot is your weapon against the little Red termites who have eaten their way into the Guild. It is your job tomorrow to begin the work of cleaning those termites out."[35] Conservatives criticized "paid officers and functionaries of the ANG [American Newspaper Guild] who actually control the machinery of the Guild," accusing the top leaders of "incompetence."[36] Their campaign received a boost when former first lady Eleanor Roosevelt endorsed the anti-Communist slate. She had become a guild member after she began writing her "My Day" newspaper column for United Features Syndicate in 1935.[37] But internal bickering left the conservatives divided, allowing the more disciplined, better organized radicals to gain the upper hand.

Boston Globe reporter Donal Sullivan was elected president, while Milton Kaufman took over as the new executive vice president, replacing Jonathan Eddy, who had handled day-to-day guild affairs as Broun's chief lieutenant. Kaufman, a former fashion writer at *Women's Wear Daily,* had been the executive secretary of the New York Guild and had helped organize the guild's walkout at Hearst's *Wisconsin News.* In an effort to unite the splintered membership, Sullivan and Kaufman characterized their selection as "an unprecedented opportunity for unity" and denied they were "controlled or influenced by any outside organization."[38] The dwindling conservative faction viewed the radicals' election as further evidence that the left wing had put the guild on a radical path.[39]

Another dispute erupted when the convention considered a resolution condemning "communism, Nazism, and fascism."[40] In the face of strong leftist opposition, the membership ultimately adopted a weaker version that did not name communism specifically. Although the decision may have represented backlash against Pegler more than true sentiment among guild members, it fed allegations that the guild had fallen into dangerous hands. "That is along the line of past guild resolutions and it gives new support to the charge that many prominent guildsmen are either Communists or sympathetic to Communism," said *Editor and Publisher.*[41] "The red firecracker didn't explode at the Memphis convention of the American Newspaper Guild," Mississippi newspaperman Hodding Carter wrote in the *Nation,* "but it sputtered enough to burn Guildsmen's fingers."[42]

In the fall of 1940 members considered the resolution again and adopted a clarification 986–481 by mailed ballots the next February approving a resolution proposed by the Youngstown (Ohio) Guild. "Communism, Nazism and Fascism are not indicative of the Newspaper Guild," the national resolution declared, pledging to prevent "any attempt by these organizations to control the policies" of this organization.[43] The members also adopted a resolution saying the guild "rejects any proposal or insinuation that it is, or has been, subject to outside control."[44] The passage of these resolutions represented an early sign that an anti-Communist backlash had begun to coalesce within the guild and that the left-wing bloc centered in New York, Boston, and San Francisco had begun to crumble. Meanwhile conservatives continued to press for changes, including a modified election process that would replace the delegate system with a popular vote for national officers, a switch that threatened to undermine the leftists' remaining leverage and would lead to the ouster of Communists from the guild's leadership.[45]

The conflict between the two factions smoldered for months before it burst into the open at the guild's annual convention. Conservatives produced an affidavit signed by the author Ferdinand Lundberg claiming that Kaufman had belonged to the Communist Party for more than eight years and had written under a pseudonym for the Communist newspaper, the *Daily Worker.*[46] Kaufman called the allegations "an utter, complete lie."[47] When the votes were counted, he had been resoundingly defeated by Sam Eubanks of San Francisco, who became the new executive vice president. Milton Murray of Detroit replaced Sullivan as president, marking the first time in the guild's history that none of its top leadership came from New York. "This convention represented the high-water mark of opposition to the Guild leadership, which has long been accused of following the Communist Party line," according to James Wechsler, a writer at the Left-leaning New York newspaper *PM.* He had been a party member until the late 1930s when he became a liberal ex-Communist who sided with conservatives in the late 1940s to shift the New York Newspaper Guild to the right. In essence, conservatives had amassed enough votes to purge Communists from leadership at the national level, making the guild the first CIO union to do so.[48]

The Guild and the FBI

The guild's political machinations held little interest for most Americans but caught considerable attention at the FBI. Director J. Edgar Hoover's concern with radicals went back to 1917 when he joined the Alien Enemy Bureau (later known as the General Intelligence Division) of the Justice Department and worked toward registering hundreds of thousands of German immigrants in the United States.[49] In the fall of 1919 he became the head of the General Intelligence Division as the government investigated a string of bombings that were blamed on radical aliens, including one bombing that had damaged the home of Attorney General A. Palmer Mitchell. In the early 1920s Hoover coordinated government efforts to round up radical aliens for deportation, leading raids on meeting halls of the Union of Russian Workers in twenty-three states; more than four thousand radicals were arrested and herded into detention centers. By the early 1920s the bureau would hold dossiers on about 200,000 organizations and residents, with information gleaned primarily from radical newspapers. Hoover would become the government's foremost authority on domestic communism.[50]

In 1924 the newly appointed attorney general, Harlan Fiske Stone, named Hoover to head the Bureau of Investigation (*Federal* was added to the name in 1935). But because of the bureau's habit of disregarding civil liberties during the Palmer raids in 1920, Stone restricted its investigations to violations of federal statutes. Hoover continued to identify and monitor individuals tied to radical groups despite Stone's admonition, and he focused particular attention on the Communist Party and its defenders, including the American Civil Liberties Union, which had been one of the chief critics of the bureau's violations of civil liberties during the Red scare of the 1920s.[51]

As the world began to grapple with the rising Nazi threat in Europe, President Roosevelt expanded the bureau's role in 1936 by asking Hoover to track any Nazi activities in the United States, essentially ending the ban that Stone had imposed on domestic political surveillance in 1924. When Roosevelt expressed concern that radicals might sabotage defense industries during an emergency, Hoover informed him that Communists were "boring from within" important trade unions involved in shipping, mining, and U.S. newspapers. Hoover specifically named the West Coast Longshoremen, the United Mine Workers, and the American Newspaper Guild. When Roosevelt authorized him to systematically monitor "subversive activities . . . particularly Fascism and Communism," Hoover neglected to mention that he had been conducting surveillance since the early 1920s with no statutory authority to do so and that in doing so he had also violated the attorney general's directive.[52]

Roosevelt expanded the FBI's role again after the Nazis and Soviets signed a controversial nonaggression pact in 1939.[53] As Congress enacted a series of laws that bolstered federal defenses against infiltration, Roosevelt authorized the FBI to "handle all cases involving allegations of espionage, sabotage and related matters as pertaining to persons in the United States." Moreover, Roosevelt ordered the Military Intelligence Division and the Office of Naval Intelligence to forward to the FBI "any data, information, or material" they might obtain "bearing directly or indirectly on espionage, counter-espionage, or sabotage," thus consolidating the bureau's authority to monitor subversive activities.[54]

Hoover seized the opportunity to expand the FBI's surveillance activities to include U.S. citizens. He would build upon the information collected by the bureau during the 1920s to assemble a "Custodial Detention Index" of individuals whose "interest may be directed primarily to the interest of some other nation than the United States," though the bureau lacked statutory authority. He directed agents to identify all "persons of German, Italian, and Communist sympathies," regardless of whether they were resident aliens or citizens. From the information collected the bureau would determine which individuals "would be dangerous to the public peace and safety of the United States Government" in the event of war.[55] Roosevelt expanded the bureau's authority again in May 1940 by secretly ignoring a 1937 Supreme Court decision prohibiting wiretaps and electronic surveillance. As a safeguard against abuse, Attorney General Stone directed Hoover to coordinate such operations with the newly established Neutrality Laws Unit of the Justice Department.[56] The unit was set up to oversee and coordinate a variety of war-related Justice Department activities involving detection of "espionage and other subversive activities.[57]

Concern with the Guild

A few days before Christmas 1940, Edward Tamm, an assistant director at the FBI who later became a federal judge, alerted Hoover that several "labor union type" groups were considered to be Communist-front organizations. Tamm listed a dozen groups, including the Newspaper Guild, as examples.[58] Hoover forwarded Tamm's advisory to the Neutrality Laws Unit and indicated that he was considering launching an investigation of the guild.

"From time to time newspaper dispatches indicate that the several organizations named hereinafter are Communist-dominated or controlled," Hoover told Lawrence M.C. Smith. "In view of these allegations I would appreciate being advised whether the Bureau should conduct [an] investigation for the purpose of determining the foundation of these charges."[59] Smith responded that newspaper articles alone were an insufficient basis for the bureau to begin surveillance. "Of course, I do not mean to indicate that you should not take such measures as you may deem necessary and advisable in connection with the investigative matters within the jurisdiction of the Bureau," Smith added.[60]

With Smith's tacit approval Hoover began monitoring the *Guild Reporter,* the Newspaper Guild's biweekly newspaper, and directed agents to develop "confidential sources" to learn the level of Communist influence. A New York agent obtained the official proceedings of the guild's tumultuous 1940 convention at which suspected Communists had seized power. Hoover's agents also obtained a guild manual containing the organization's constitution, collective bargaining program, and other official documents.[61] Other agents gleaned details of the guild's tumultuous 1941 Detroit convention from "confidential sources," including one source at the *Detroit News* who described "two strong factions" inside the guild. The FBI also gathered a variety of guild documents from either cooperative guild members or members who were unaware that they were dealing with the FBI. The documents included lists of elected officers and staff, campaign flyers, circulars, postcards, and other material distributed by the guild to its members.

In late November 1941, less than a month before the United States entered World War II, FBI headquarters distributed to field offices a list of more than one hundred suspected Communists in guild units in forty cities and towns. "This is the official Red list, so file it away for reference, as these boys are not licked for all time," the document said.[62] Among the names were those of former guild president Donal Sullivan and Victor Pasche, a former *New York Times* reporter who had been the guild's paid secretary-treasurer. Both had been defeated in the guild's leadership purge four months earlier. The largest group on Hoover's list was comprised of members of the New York Guild, including Milton Kaufman, the national guild's new executive vice president.[63]

Two weeks later the Japanese attack on Pearl Harbor gave Hoover further justification for monitoring labor organizations and the Communist Party with undercover agents and electronic surveillance. In 1941 an informant had told the FBI that the guild, in particular the New York local, was dominated by "a Communist element." Even so, the agent advised headquarters, the New York office had investigated and was closing the case.[64]

In January 1942 Hoover received a tip from the War Department's Military Intelligence Division, which tracked dangerous radicals overseas, that "a group of newspaper leaders" had taken control of the New York Guild. "Time and time again this Communist mob has taken matters into their own hands and on several occasions they have called unjustified strikes," military intelligence reported.[65] However, the memorandum showed that the FBI and the Military Intelligence Division were more concerned with journalists' politics than with any Communist attempts to influence newspaper content. The memorandum from military intelligence named six suspected Communists, including Nat Einhorn, a founder of the New York Guild who had been its executive secretary since 1938. "There are two other leaders in the group that are supposedly anti-communists but their actions at times would indicate that they may be secretly working with the Communists," military intellligence reported.[66] Documents released in the mid-1990s, when the "Venona" intercepts became public, indicate that Einhorn was indeed a party member.[67] The highly classified Venona Project at the National Security Agency during the 1940s decrypted thousands of cables between the United States and the Soviet Union. The cables show that Soviet intelligence used the Communist Party USA as a recruiting ground and sought to enlist journalists into its spy network.[68]

A twenty-page report in March 1942 described an informant at a New York newspaper who claimed the New York Guild was dominated by "a Communist element"; the FBI redacted the names of both the informant and the newspaper before releasing the report to me under the Freedom of Information Act. The report speculated that in New York City, where one-third of the guild members worked, Communists comprised "a very high percentage" of the guild's membership. Secrecy among party members, including the use of "party names" to obscure their true identities, makes it virtually impossible to determine the FBI's accuracy in identifying party members. The New York informant told the FBI that few guild locals outside New York City were involved. However, the report concluded that "no active investigation" would be conducted unless additional information came to the FBI's attention.[69]

Even so, FBI agents continued their surveillance of journalists, with Hoover cautioning them about how to fill out their reports. "For your guidance in the future, you are instructed that the title of a report, unless advised to the contrary, should not include merely the name of a labor organization," he said. "To designate a labor organization as the subject of an investigative report is misleading and suggests that the Bureau is investigating a labor union which you, of course, know the Bureau does not do." Donald M. Ladd, who in the spring of 1942 became assistant director of the Domestic Intelligence Division of the FBI, added that "various groups and individuals are constantly endeavoring to find bases upon which they can charge the Federal Bureau of Investigation with violations of civil liberties."[70]

The following summer Hoover again contacted Smith at the Neutrality Laws Unit and attached an article in which Pegler referred to strong ties between the guild and the Communist Party. "In view of the foregoing information, it would be appreciated if you would advise as to whether an investigation should be undertaken to determine the extent of Communist infiltration and control of the American Newspaper Guild," Hoover asked without mentioning the investigation that had already been under way for a year.[71] "There is no objection to the proposed investigation within the limits indicated," Smith responded. "In my opinion the inquiry into the activities of these organizations at the present time should be restricted to the acts of individuals and should in no manner be an investigation of either organization as such. Further, it is understood that such investigation will be conducted in a discreet manner."[72]

Hoover recognized that the guild was torn by an internal schism about the merits of strikes. Radical members saw them as a necessary tool for gaining clout at the bargaining table. Conservatives, on the other hand, viewed them as a counterproductive tactic that often triggered job cuts because of the expense of higher wages.[73] Hoover occasionally forwarded information from FBI reports on the guild to the Office of Naval Intelligence, once including a list of twenty-four candidates in guild elections.[74] The names included those of Communists, non-Communists, anti-Communists, liberals, and moderates.

In late 1942 an incident in Michigan at the *Ludington Daily News* threatened to expose the FBI's activities. Field reports provide few details of what happened, but it is clear that the FBI became concerned that the incident might compromise its investigation. "Why was lead assigned to Agent [name deleted]?" Hoover asked. "Was Agent [name deleted] instructed regarding discreet nature of inquiry?"[75] The FBI summarily transferred the agent from Detroit to the Cleveland field office, and the Ludington incident faded. "I shall expect you and every employee of the Federal Bureau of

Investigation connected with your office to be keenly alert at all times to protect the Bureau from being charged with improper activities or subject to smear campaigns," warned Ladd.[76]

Throughout the 1940s the FBI found only scant evidence of any attempts to influence newspaper content. In one case an informant claimed that "whenever Communist Party members want to put editorials in the *Milwaukee Journal* they are told by Party functionaries to contact John Kykyri." But that FBI report did not cite any example of an editorial that had been altered. In fact, the report pointed out that there was "no definite information that Kykyri is a Communist" and described him as "a very good reporter."[77] The name of Kykyri, who was president of the Milwaukee Guild, was among those on the "Official Red List" that the FBI had circulated to its field offices in 1941. The report said that Kykyri, along with other guild members, had participated in the "Citizens' Committee to Free Earl Browder" after the head of the Communist Party was jailed for making a false statement on his passport application in 1939. (Roosevelt granted Browder's release in 1942.)[78] In another instance an informant accused guild organizer Jack Ryan of trying to pressure the *New York Post* to cast the Soviet Union in a favorable light in an editorial endorsing Roosevelt's war effort. The party wanted to exploit the German invasion of the Soviet Union in 1941 to build public support for the war. Ironically, the editorial change was blocked by Communists secretly working in the newspaper's newsroom. "The Post unit [of the Communist Party], although agreeing with the edit, felt that it would be out of step to meddle with a newspaper's policy," a field office reported. "It also felt that an endorsement would establish a bad precedent which, at another time, could be used by [other] dominated units to attack an editorial policy they approved of."[79]

Electronic Eavesdropping

Hoover stepped up surveillance, including newspaper surveillance, in early 1943 as the war continued in Europe and Japan. He described surveillance of the guild "one of the most delicate and one of the most important investigations the field is called upon to conduct."[80] Reports flowed in from field offices across the country, from Los Angeles to Sioux Falls, South Dakota, to Jackson, Mississippi, to Baltimore. Although agents collected a large cache of names and other information, not every journalist became suspect. The FBI continued to concentrate on officers and candidates for guild offices who were supported by the guild's secret Communist faction. An informant at the *El Paso Times* named a reporter "who was born in Russia and graduated from the Missouri School of Journalism"; the FBI redacted the names of both the informant and reporter before releasing the report sixty years later.[81] West Coast agents identified "a number of strong Communists" in the Los Angeles Guild. "At times it appears that a Communist faction of about 35 members practically controlled the organization and directed its policy and activity," a report said.[82]

In the mid-1940s Hoover increasingly came under pressure from Roosevelt administration officials who did not share his level of apprehension about Communists. With the United States and the Soviet Union fighting as allies, Attorney General Francis Biddle bluntly informed Hoover that there was no statutory authorization or other justification for keeping his Custodial Detention Index of citizens. "The Department fills its proper functions by investigating the activities of persons who may have violated the law," Biddle said.[83] However, Hoover was convinced that unauthorized surveillance was crucial to national security and evaded the directive by changing the designation of the Custodial Detention Index to "Security Index" and continued to monitor the Guild and other organizations that were considered Communist dominated.[84]

A 1944 report revealed an FBI plan to bug the Milwaukee convention hall where the guild was holding its annual convention. However, an agency official in Washington, D.C., rejected the idea because "the Bureau could not be in the position of having any such coverage on a group connected with the press."[85] Even so, agents tried to bug the hotel room of New York Guild president John McManus but found that the "use of a contact microphone proved unsatisfactory." The report noted that "continued observation throughout the evening disclosed that Mr. McManus occupied the room merely for sleeping purposes."[86] It gave no indication that the plan to bug the room had been cleared by the attorney general, which would have been required to satisfy legal constraints.[87] The FBI may also have been gathering photographs of guild members. Reports during 1943 and 1944 from St. Louis and Albany, where journalists had established among the earliest and most active guild units say that agents shipped film to Washington, D.C., for processing, but the reports do not describe any photographs or how the FBI obtained them. Extensive censorship makes it impossible to determine what the bureau learned.[88]

The FBI continued its surveillance of radicals throughout the war, although, like most of organized labor, guild members observed a no-strike pledge. Some field office reports stretched to more than one hundred pages, listing names and background information on hundreds of journalists who were suspected of being Communists and Communist sympathizers. One report from Los Angeles in October 1944 warned that "the newsboys are preparing for an intensive organizing campaign."[89] It listed eighty Los Angeles journalists, including William Oliver, Urcel Daniel, and Charles Judson of the *Los Angeles Daily News,* who were later called to testify before HUAC. Another report named Janet Scott, a reporter at the *(Albany, N.Y.) Knickerbocker News,* as "a prominent Communist functionary."[90] The document estimated that one hundred Communists belonged to the New York Newspaper Guild, including McManus a writer who used the byline "I. Kauffman" at the *Brooklyn Eagle,* where there was an active but secret Communist cell.[91]

A report from Milwaukee pointed to ten journalists at Wisconsin newspapers. "Seven of the ten have been identified, and another, tentatively identified, as members of the American Newspaper Guild," it said.[92] Agents noted that the New York Guild operated a small journalism school. "Several of the instructors are followers of the Communist line," the report said, meaning that the instructors openly expressed leftist views. They included Dr. Philip Foner, a labor historian on the faculty at the Jefferson School of Social Sciences, a school established by leftists to provide jobs to city-employed professors, many of whom had been fired after being called to testify before the state legislature's Rapp-Condert Committee's 1941 investigation of Communists in higher education.[93] Throughout the 1940s field reports reflected Hoover's insistence on discretion. "This is not an investigation of the American Newspaper Guild, but rather an investigation of Communist Infiltration of the American Newspaper Guild," said a report from Buffalo in late 1944.[94] Another directive, the one from Detroit, said, "It should be noted that all individuals contacted . . . were advised that the Bureau has no interest in employer-employee relationships or in any phase of legitimate union activities."[95]

Meanwhile Allied troops fighting the war in Europe were poised to begin their final advances against the Germans in early 1945. In Asia fighting raged in the Philippines and Burma. Tensions among the Allies were already rising when Roosevelt and Churchill met with Stalin at Yalta in February 1945 to map a vision for postwar Europe. They agreed to promote free elections, democratic governments, and constitutional safeguards. Two months later Roosevelt died at Warm Springs, Georgia, and Vice President Harry S Truman assumed the presidency. On May 7 Germany surrendered, marking the end of fighting in Europe. At 7 P.M. in

Washington on August 14, 1945, days after the United States dropped atomic bombs on Hiroshima and Nagasaki, Truman told White House reporters that World War II had ended.[96]

But the end of hostilities did little to ease the crisis atmosphere at the FBI. Hoover resisted pressure to downsize the FBI's domestic intelligence activities by promoting the notion that the United States was at risk from enemies on the inside. He fought to continue surveillance activities, including surveillance of the Newspaper Guild. FBI agents continued to collect the names of people who might be detained during a national emergency, including journalists, although the agency had no statutory authority to do so, especially in peacetime.[97]

CHAPTER THREE

Prelude to an Investigation

T HE GRAND ALLIANCE of the United States, the Soviet Union, and Great Britain that won World War II began to unravel in late 1945 as the Soviets began to take an aggressive stance against their neighbors. An early sign of trouble came when Stalin reneged on agreements to withdraw troops from Iran.[1] More trouble was brewing in Bulgaria and Czechoslovakia. The dangers of postwar espionage were brought home for Americans when the FBI raided the editorial offices of the scholarly journal *Amerasia* in June 1945 and found sensitive State Department documents; agents arrested six individuals and, later, several government employees. Republicans and conservative Democrats accused the Truman administration of failing to grasp the severity of the postwar Communist threat.

Criticism escalated four months later when Canadian officials cracked a Soviet spy ring that had stolen secret information about the atomic bomb, lending additional credence to fears of foreign espionage in North America.[2] In March 1946 former British prime minister Winston Churchill attracted front-page attention by warning that an "iron curtain" had descended on postwar Europe. "Behind that line lie all the capitals of the ancient states of Central and Eastern Europe," he said. His remarks would later be seen as marking the beginning of the Cold War.[3]

Also that March Hoover recommended that the Justice Department "determine what legislation is available or should be sought" to enable the federal government to detain "members of the Communist Party and any others" who "might be dangerous" if diplomatic relations with the Soviet

Union deteriorated further. He did not divulge to Attorney General Tom Clark that the FBI had been assembling its Security Index, under one name or another, for nearly twenty years.[4] Reports on the Newspaper Guild continued to flow into the FBI's Washington, D.C., headquarters. They carefully noted which members supported the Communist wing of the guild. A memorandum in November 1946 informed the Office of Naval Intelligence that thirty-two elected officials and staff members of the national guild and eighty-three members and officers of the New York Guild were Communists or alleged Communists, fellow travelers, or Communist supporters, whom Hoover considered as dangerous to national security as party members.[5] Throughout the war the Newspaper Guild, like most of organized labor, observed a no-strike pledge after Hitler invaded the Soviet Union, a seemingly patriotic posture promoted by the Communist Party. After the war the guild called a rash of strikes, including one at Hearst's *Los Angeles Herald-Express* that forced the paper to suspend publication for two months in 1946 before Hearst agreed to higher wages and provisions for arbitration.[6] The guild also targeted the *Wichita Eagle* after management refused to negotiate. In Springfield, Massachusetts, owners shut four newspapers rather than recognize the guild as a bargaining agent. The most significant clash came at the *Camden (N.J.) Courier-Post* and the *Philadelphia Record*, where nearly six hundred guild members walked out, forcing both papers to suspend publication. The conflict placed the guild in a difficult situation because the publisher of both papers was J. David Stern, an early supporter of the guild's who had signed the first newspaper contract in 1934. By 1947 Stern was insisting that he could no longer afford the guild's demands and ultimately liquidated his newspapers rather than concede, leaving hundreds of workers without jobs.[7] Guild officials absolved themselves of blame for the debacle, claiming the contract dispute was a smokescreen for a publisher who had "long contemplated" selling the properties.[8]

The following month the House Committee on Education and Labor opened hearings on postwar labor problems, including newspaper strikes, and turned to the FBI for ammunition. "Manly Shepard left the attached list of names of newspaper people who he states are members of the Newspaper Guild with the request that they be brought to your attention," Hoover told an assistant. Shepard worked on the staff of Fred Hartley, the New Jersey Republican who chaired the committee. "He [Shepard] states that the House Labor Committee is considering legislation to curb these people and Congressman Hartley is most interested in securing any information you can furnish him which we might already have on any of these people."[9] Hartley was one of many postwar conservatives intent on rolling back powers granted to organized labor under the New Deal, and he later became an author of the antiunion Taft-Hartley Act.

Donald M. Ladd, assistant director of the FBI's Domestic Intelligence Division, responded to the request with information about twenty-nine individuals in New York City, Los Angeles, St. Louis, Boston, Indianapolis, Rochester, Washington, D.C., and Birmingham, Alabama. "Blind memoranda relating to each of the individuals concerning whom derogatory information was found are attached hereto," he wrote.[10] Blind memoranda were standard FBI procedure for passing surveillance information to friendly outsiders in a manner that shielded the agency from being identified as the source because the FBI lacked authority to divulge information outside the executive branch. The documents contained no identifying letterhead and no signatures that would connect them with the FBI.[11]

Hoover had cooperated with the Dies Committee intermittently during the 1930s, but the relationship broke down when he grew fearful that the free-wheeling committee would embarrass the FBI by exposing its surveillance activities.[12] By the late 1940s he had reconsidered his position after recognizing the public relations value in leaking information to individuals who shared his anti-Communist perspective. Hoover thereupon designated a clerk to provide trustworthy committees with virtually unlimited access to the contents of FBI files. The list of acceptable recipients included the House Committee on Education and Labor and, later, the Senate Internal Security Subcommittee and the Senate subcommittee chaired by Sen. Joseph McCarthy.[13]

Hartley's hearings initially focused on the surge in labor unrest that followed World War II, especially in industries tied to national defense. "Nation-wide strikes and industrial disorder not only brought us to the brink of a productive standstill, but actually threatened the health, safety, and security of all of its people," he told the opening session. The committee's attention soon turned to ties between industrial unions and the Communist Party. In February 1947 Hartley focused on Communist involvement in the guild strikes at the *Philadelphia Record* and the *Camden Courier-Post*. Early witnesses soft-peddled Communist influence in the guild, but the following month guild president Milton Murray appeared before the committee and dropped a bombshell. "There are Communists in the American Newspaper Guild," he told the committee. "I can be certain that in our New York local, the executive vice president Jack Ryan, is a Communist . . . and in our Los Angeles local, the executive secretary, William Brodie, is a Communist."[14] Murray's comments echoed statements made a day earlier by Louis Budenz, a former member of the Central Committee of the Communist Party U.S.A. who had become an FBI informer. He said that Communists controlled the guild.[15] Richard M. Nixon, the California Republican who was a member of both the Committee on Education and Labor, and HUAC, latched onto Murray's allegations.[16]

> NIXON: You mean then that apart from the activities that Communists might indulge in on their own politically . . . they exert an influence in the guild which you feel is detrimental in the guild organization itself?"
>
> MURRAY: Where they exert influence, I believe it is detrimental; yes.
>
> NIXON: For that reason you believe that it is important that the guild not allow Communists to attain positions of power in the local organizations or in the nation organization?
>
> MURRAY: That is correct, sir, and we oppose them on every ground and every level.[17]

The public airing of the guild's internal conflict sent shockwaves throughout the membership and generated front-page news. "Guild Here Red-Run Says National Head," read a headline in the *New York Times*.[18] New York Guild president John McManus accused Murray of trying "to promote his own political ambitions within the Guild" and "matching lie and libel with the enemies of labor against members and branches of his own union."[19] Jack Ryan also denied the allegations, saying, "The present inquiry is an inquiry for the purpose of creating an atmosphere of political terror and I don't intend to be a party to it."[20] William Brodie described Murray's testimony as "the last gasp of a union politician."[21] The backlash consumed Murray the following summer when the guild met in Sioux City, Iowa, and the initiatives he introduced went down to resounding defeat. Faced with certain defeat for another term as guild president, he withdrew his candidacy. Ironically, the issue that had swept him into office in 1941— the membership's desire to purge Communists from guild leadership— swept him out six years later, a reflection of postwar sentiment inside the guild and across the nation.

In the meantime pressure intensified on leftist labor unions as the Republican-controlled Congress overrode a presidential veto and enacted the Taft-Hartley bill in June 1947. President Truman had objected to the measure, describing it as an attack against the workingman.[22] It shifted the balance that had been won by labor under the New Deal by banning the "closed shop," a step that newspaper publishers applauded. More important, it required labor leaders to sign affidavits attesting that they were not members of the Communist Party, Communist sympathizers, or members or supporters of groups believing in or teaching the overthrow of the government by force, violence, or other illegal methods. Failure to sign would leave their unions ineligible to use the services of the National Labor Relations Board in complaints against unfair labor practices.[23] In essence, the new law made it nearly impossible for Communists to conceal themselves in leadership positions in labor unions.[24]

Predictably, Taft-Hartley became a contentious issue throughout organized labor. Many non-Communist labor leaders condemned it as an attack on free speech and vowed to ignore it. At the CIO, President Philip Murray and Secretary-Treasurer James Carey announced that they had no intention of signing affidavits and would ignore the federally mandated deadline. Carey called on union members to defy the law "in the good old American tradition of the patriots who dumped the tea into the harbor of Boston."[25] The law carried far-reaching implications for the Newspaper Guild. "As far as the American Newspaper Guild is concerned, the measure would strip it down to a meaningless press club or 'society' unless new methods and techniques can be found so that the Guild may continue to gain legitimate ends for its members," guild officials said in the days before the measure was adopted. "The bill would hold Guild members to impossible standards of meekness in the face of provocation, and then hold the Guild liable for damages when the members rebel."[26]

The uproar aggravated factionalism across the labor spectrum, making Communists targets of open hostility. Conservative anti-Communists began to demand resignations from suspected Communists in leadership positions. In mid-July Philip Murray, who had tolerated Communists in the CIO, fired the organization's Communist publicity director, marking the opening salvo in a purge of Communists from the CIO bureaucracy.[27] United Auto Workers President Walter Reuther fired dozens of Communist staff members following the union's convention in November 1947 and then focused on the locals. There were earlier purges at the National Maritime Union, the Transport Workers Union, and the Minnesota Industrial Union Council.[28] Other unions stood steadfast until the CIO began expelling unions that refused to purge themselves. By 1950 eleven Left-led unions had been cast aside.[29]

The Newspaper Guild's international executive board agreed "reluctantly and with great repugnance" in November 1947 to comply with the Taft-Hartley requirements.[30] The affidavits were a nonissue for officials of the national guild but placed considerable pressure on the elected officials of the New York local, which had been plagued by rumors of Communist influence since the guild's inception. As the elections at the New York Guild approached in late 1947, internal conflicts broke into the open. Campaign flyers announced that it was time to "Clean Communist Influence Out of Our Guild." In essence, the postwar political climate enabled conservatives to advance their first successful slate of candidates since the late 1930s. Jack Ryan, the executive vice president identified by Milton Murray as a Communist, faced the strongest opposition. A fateful moment came during a campaign question-and-answer session in mid-December. "Are you now or have you ever been a member of the Communist party?" a member asked Ryan. "The fact is that if I answer the question in any form that it has been put here, I would be contributing to a witch hunt in our industry," Ryan responded.[31] The issue dogged him throughout the campaign, and he never stated flatly whether the allegations were true or false.

Conservative support rallied behind George R. Holmes, a former vaudeville actor who had joined the *New York Daily News* as a caption writer, to challenge McManus. "We've got to make the guild an out and out trade union and concentrate on wages, hours and working conditions," Holmes explained. "It is my own personal business what I think on China or Russia or Spain, but now it has nothing whatever to do with the guild."[32] When the votes were counted, the membership had swept the entire administration out of office in the heaviest voter turnout in the history of the New York Guild.[33] "The election is over," Holmes and the other newly elected officers told supporters. "There is no time now for crowing by one side or for recrimination by the other. . . . We can no longer count on a sympathetic law to make our work easier for us. Instead, the vicious Taft-Hartley Act lends its support to those who would destroy our union and the standards it has won. And inflation is daily cutting our paychecks."[34]

Targeting Hollywood

As labor wrestled with Taft-Hartley requirements, HUAC focused on Hollywood, a subject the committee had flirted with intermittently since J. B. Matthews had questioned the political leanings of Hollywood personalities before the Dies Committee in 1940.[35] The Dies Committee had held only occasional public hearings before its chairman announced in 1944 that he would not seek reelection. The Democratic Party in Texas had fallen under the control of unionized oil workers, who characterized the congressman a "demagogue," and Dies recognized that his days in Washington were numbered.[36]

As Cold War tensions escalated in the late 1940s and HUAC became a permanent committee, the newly constituted membership intensified the anti-Communist campaign to include investigations of school teachers and Hollywood.[37] Hoover testified in March 1947 that the committee rendered "a distinct service when it publicly reveals the diabolic machinations of sinister figures engaged in un-American activities." Seven months later the committee began its most celebrated investigation since its inception by focusing public attention on suspected Communist influence in the film industry, particularly within the Screen Writers Guild, which, like the Newspaper Guild, had sprung from Roosevelt's New Deal.

When the Screen Writers Guild formed in 1933, Hollywood was only beginning to become politicized. By 1935, as struggles with the studios began in earnest, the Communist-sponsored Popular Front was well under way on the East Coast and had begun to capture the public imagination on the West Coast, particularly in Los Angeles, where the workforce was comprised of blue-collar workers, white-collar professionals, and artists who tilted toward leftist ideology. When they were not at their typewriters and the negotiating tables, leftists in the Screen Writers Guild secretly lent their support to progressive causes that would later be labeled as Communist fronts.[38]

In early 1944 members of the conservative Motion Picture Alliance, an anti-Communist organization formed by Walt Disney and others, expressed concern to Sen. Robert Rice Reynolds, a North Carolina Democrat who was an outspoken ally of the FBI's. "The motion-picture industrialists of Hollywood have been coddling Communists and cooperating with so-called intellectual superiors they have helped import from Europe and Asia," said the letter signed by "A Group of Your Friends in Hollywood."[39] The message soon caught the attention of HUAC's West Coast investigator, William Wheeler, who reinstituted an investigation the committee began in the late 1930s but placed on hold.

In early 1947 J. Parnell Thomas, a New Jersey Republican who was the newly installed HUAC chairman, arrived in Hollywood with two committee investigators. The entourage met in closed-door sessions with studio representatives and officials from the various unions, including actors, screenwriters, and blue-collar workers. Armed with information from FBI files and from the Los Angles Police Department's "Red Squad," Thomas compiled a list of individuals to be summoned to hearings in Washington, D.C.[40] He told the *New York Times* and other newspapers that "90 percent of Communist infiltration" was confined to the screenwriters.[41] Committee investigators remained in Hollywood after Thomas returned to Washington and continued to warn Hollywood luminaries that anyone who refused to cooperate would face "dire consequences."[42] Thomas was convinced that Hollywood had become a hotbed of communism, a claim he promptly inserted into the *Congressional Record*. "Scores of screen writers who are Communists have infiltrated into the various studios and it has been through this medium that most of the Communist propaganda has been injected into the movies," he said.[43] By October the elements were in place for a full-blown investigation that had been in the offing for more than a decade. HUAC would furnish the stage, daily newspapers would supply the public spotlight, and a cast of Hollywood producers, actors, and writers would supply the drama. What was not known at the time was that the Hollywood investigation would set the precedent for inquiries into the Newspaper Guild in the 1950s and would play a role in determining which journalists would be called before the committee and what they would be asked.

The Hollywood hearings began in Washington, D.C., on October 20, 1947, with nearly four hundred spectators packing the hearing room, along with seventy-five reporters, thirty newspaper photographers, and six newsreel cameras. Chairman Thomas sat atop two telephone books and a red silk cushion to ensure that the photographers could get good pictures of him.[44] The first week brought a parade of friendly witnesses who pointed accusing fingers at various segments of the movie industry. A week later the committee called another handpicked group consisting of eight screenwriters, a producer, and a director who would be invited to defend themselves. The group of ten met beforehand; its members agreed not to cooperate with the committee and to challenge its authority to question them.[45] John Howard Lawson had been a successful playwright during the 1920s and began writing screenplays as the talkies began to invigorate the film industry in the 1930s. Seated at the witness table, he remained reticent, refusing to discuss his political ties, his activism, or his influence upon Hollywood writers.[46]

"Are you a member of the Screen Writers Guild?" asked Robert Stripling, the committee investigator who spearheaded the Hollywood investigation.

"The raising of any question here in regard to membership, political beliefs, or affiliation," Lawson began to say as Thomas tried to cut him off.

"It is a matter of public record that I am a member of the Screen Writers Guild," Lawson continued.

"Mr. Lawson, are you now, or have you ever been, a member of the Communist party of the United States?" asked Stripling.

"In framing my answer to that question I must emphasize the points that I have raised before," Lawson responded. "The question of communism is in no way related to this inquiry, which is an attempt to get control of the screen and to invade the basic rights of American citizens in all fields."[47]

Lawson and Stripling continued to spar until Thomas began pounding his gavel and ordered Lawson to leave the witness stand. But Lawson continued speaking, so Thomas summoned a security detail to lead him from the witness table, triggering an eruption of cheers and boos from spectators. The raucous exchange was repeated with the remaining nine, each brushing aside questions and challenging the committee's authority. Security police literally pried several witnesses from the witness table after Thomas ordered them to step aside and they refused.[48]

In late November the major film studios, fearing public protest, demonstrated their patriotism by placing a ban on hiring Communists and announcing their decision to "discharge or suspend without compensation" the ten witnesses, whom HUAC had cited for contempt. In effect, the industry established a blacklist that threatened to end the film-writing careers or force the ten to write under a pseudonym. A front-page account in the *New York Times* described it as "unprecedented in American industrial fields" and noted the studios' vows not to be "swayed by hysteria or intimidation."[49] The concern of the studio bosses, which was a concern for their bottom line, was not unfounded. Four years later, after the Supreme Court refused to hear the appeals of the "Hollywood Ten" and the group was jailed, HUAC resumed its film industry investigation, which was underscored by protesters who picketed several Hollywood theaters with signs reading: "This picture written by a Communist. Do not patronize."[50]

The decision to cite the defiant witnesses for contempt was one taken by the House of Representatives, not just HUAC, and the House did so by a wide margin. "The Constitution was never intended to cloak or shield those who would destroy it," argued Thomas.[51] Never before had an uncooperative witness been sent to jail. The ten waged an intense legal battle until the Supreme Court refused to hear their appeals. The episode set important precedents that would influence the prosecution of many other witnesses, including journalists called to testify nearly a decade later.

Trouble in the Newsroom

The Hollywood hearings generated tremendous front-page coverage across the nation, and HUAC members were surprised to find critical editorials in several major newspapers. "We do not believe the Committee is conducting a fair investigation," said the *Times,* even before the decision to cite the Hollywood Ten for contempt. "We think the course on which it is embarked threatens to lead to greater dangers than those with which it is presently concerned."[52] Moreover, a *Times* survey of public response in Chicago and five other cities found outright disapproval of the committee's grandstanding, with most Americans of the opinion that it had generated little more than "noise and heat."[53]

As the appeals of the Hollywood Ten wound through the courts, HUAC suspended its Hollywood investigation and turned to Russian espionage within the federal government.[54] Louis Budenz, the former editor of the *Daily Worker* who had defected from the Communist Party in 1945, set the stage for Elizabeth Bentley, a Vassar-educated secretary, to describe Soviet infiltration of the federal government. Dubbed the "Blond Spy Queen" by newspapers, she described a Soviet espionage ring with links inside the federal government and, in so doing, helped transform domestic Communists from raucous radicals to traitors in the eyes of the public.[55] Whitaker Chambers, an editor at *Time* magazine who was a former party member, provided additional dramatic evidence, pointing an accusing finger at Alger Hiss, a ranking State Department official who was later convicted of perjury. The hearings put a sinister edge on the Hollywood extravaganza and made domestic communism appear more threatening and the dangers more real.

The *Washington Evening Star* did not wait for a call from HUAC before Editor Ben McKelway confronted twenty-nine-year old Thomas Buchanan in a private meeting in May 1948.[56] Buchanan had joined the *Star* in 1939 as a $15-a-week copyboy. After serving as a captain in the army during World War II, he became a reporter on the newspaper's medical beat. McKelway called him aside to ask whether Buchanan belonged to the Communist Party. To McKelway's surprise the reporter readily admitted his membership. McKelway responded by assuring Buchanan that he had been a fine reporter and then fired him. "In good conscience we couldn't have assigned him to get information from government and other sources without telling them he was a communist," McKelway told the Associated Press.[57]

Buchanan later said he based his response to McKelway on a 1946 radio address in which guild president Milton Murray had urged Communists "to stand up and identify themselves." Buchanan assumed the guild would "go to the mat for their rights as union members."[58] What prompted the *Star* to confront him is unclear; however, both HUAC and the FBI maintained close contacts with important newspapers, including the *Star*.[59] Moreover, several HUAC staff members were former FBI agents and had been privileged to see bureau files.[60] McKelway may have felt he had no choice but to confront Buchanan. "His chief concern was that I might be called before some congressional investigating committee or similar group about my activities as a Communist—thus bringing 'discredit' on the paper, as one of its employes [*sic*]," Buchanan later wrote.[61]

The firing shifted debate within the Newspaper Guild from a question of Communists in leadership positions to the right of a newspaper to fire a reporter based solely on party membership. Buchanan appealed to the Washington (D.C.) Newspaper Guild for help, painting his firing as a breach of the guild's contract with the *Star*.[62] The executive board of the Washington Guild debated his request for two months and then turned him down. "The board is of the opinion that this severance cannot successfully be resisted as a breach of the Star-WNG [Washington Newspaper Guild] contract," they said.[63] As Buchanan sat on the sidelines, the Washington Guild put his request to a referendum, and his argument was resoundingly rejected once more.[64] At the national guild, however, he found a somewhat more sympathetic reception during the guild's annual convention the following July. After lengthy debate the delegates voted to censure the Washington local and admonished all locals that "any such discharges should be resisted to the fullest,"[65] The Washington Guild, however, stood steadfast and again rejected Buchanan in an overwhelming vote. "There are many of us here who—like myself—never were witch hunters and are not now," commented Dillard Stokes, a guild member at the *Washington Post*. "But by the same token we do not mean to be double talked into covering up for witches."[66] Buchanan's experience suggested that newspapers, unchallenged by the guild, were free to rid themselves of any journalist with ties to the Communist Party, regardless of the employee's job performance, without facing legal repercussions from the badly splintered Newspaper Guild. His firing put all journalists on notice: If they got into trouble over the Communist issue, their colleagues would be hamstrung in helping them to keep their jobs.

CHAPTER FOUR

Reds in the Newsroom

T HE ANTI-COMMUNIST campaign intensified in the late 1940s as Cold War hostilities between the United States and the Soviet Union escalated. The Soviet blockade of Berlin in the spring of 1949 triggered a massive American airlift that lasted nearly a year before the Russians backed down. When Communist forces in China overran the nationalists, Chiang Kai-shek and his followers took refuge on the island of Formosa. Communists appeared even more determined to expand their power later that year when the Soviets detonated an atomic bomb, ending America's short-lived monopoly of atomic weapons.[1] It was against this backdrop that HUAC focused its attention on Soviet espionage in the United States. At the same time the Justice Department began to prosecute eleven top leaders of the Communist Party U.S.A. under the 1940 Smith Act, which made it a crime to teach or advocate the overthrow of the U.S. government. Two years later, on March 29, 1951, Julius and Ethel Rosenberg were convicted on espionage charges and later executed. These and other events seemed to confirm the Communist threat as they produced a steady stream of front-page headlines that kept the anti-Communist campaign in the public consciousness. Newspapers and magazines routinely promoted congressional hearings and government prosecutions and perpetuated the stereotype of the Red menace under the control of party officials in Moscow.[2]

Four months before the outbreak of the Korean War in June 1950, Sen. Joseph McCarthy of Wisconsin launched his anti-Communist campaign, setting the Republican strategy to reclaim congressional seats lost in Truman's surprise election in 1948. During the early 1950s McCarthy was the point man for the anti-Communist crusade, but he commanded even greater attention after the 1952 elections handed the Republicans the White House and both houses of Congress.

The politically charged atmosphere reignited the moral fervor of the 1920s and 1930s. Isolationists now pointed to postwar Communist aggression as proof that Roosevelt's policies had failed and that American lives had been misspent in World War II. They viewed Truman as equally misguided and regarded the United Nations, collective security, and internationalism as the wrong course at the wrong time.[3] When isolationism reemerged after the war, it returned as anticommunism and seeped into nearly every sector of popular culture: magazines, radio, television, motion pictures, and literature. The media handed Americans constant reminders of the dangers posed by Communists and celebrated the work of the FBI and others to contain it. The Warner Brothers film *I Was a Communist for the FBI,* for example, told of an undercover agent who spied on the Communist Party. It was nominated for an Oscar for best documentary in 1951. The popular television series *I Led Three Lives,* which also became a radio series, revolved around a government witness at the 1949 trials of party leaders.[4]

With the onset of the Cold War attention shifted from suspicious actions, to which Americans had been alert during the war years, to suspicious thoughts, as anti-Communists began to focus more intently upon unpopular beliefs and the individuals who held them.[5] HUAC, which developed the investigative methods and institutional apparatus that drove the anti-Communist campaign in the 1930s, stepped up its agenda, though many sessions revealed information that was already known to the FBI.[6] New members added after the 1948 elections included Harold H. Velde, an Illinois Republican and former FBI agent. Louis Russell, another former agent, became the committee's chief investigator, providing an even closer link between the committee and the massive FBI filing system.[7]

During 1949 and 1950 the committee conducted twenty-four investigations into domestic communism in a reasonably calm and unemotional atmosphere, compared with its 1947 Hollywood hearings.[8] After the Supreme Court refused to review the convictions of the Hollywood Ten in April 1951, the committee moved into high gear, holding thirty-four investigations between 1951 and 1952.[9] It reopened its Hollywood investigation with help from the Los Angeles Police Department's "Red Squad"; HUAC called more than one hundred witnesses during its forty-three days of hearings, and most proved to be more cooperative than their counterparts had been in 1947.[10] Meanwhile Congress overrode a presidential veto to enact the 1950 Internal Security Act (also called the McCarran Act), which made it illegal to "combine, conspire, or agree with any other person to perform any act which would substantially contribute to . . . [t]he entailment of a totalitarian dictatorship." Truman complained in his veto message that the act would "put the Government into the business of thought control."[11] Although the requirement that Communists and Communist-front organizations register with the attorney general never took effect, the measure did establish the Senate Internal Security Subcommittee (later known also as the Eastland committee) to compete with HUAC for the limelight.

Following a Republican landslide in 1952, McCarthy became the chairman of the Senate Committee on Government Operations and appointed himself to lead its Subcommittee on Investigations, a position that granted him an important platform, as well as congressional subpoena power and the power to bring contempt charges, that he could use to investigate suspected Communists.[12] By early 1953 three separate committees were focused exclusively on the threat of domestic communism, frequently investigating the same topic and relying on testimony from ex-Communists who were more than willing to point an accusing finger at former comrades. Targets ran the gamut, from labor unions to youth organizations, minority groups, atomic scientists, schoolteachers, and university professors. A steady stream of press coverage consistently portrayed committee members and friendly witnesses as heroes while characterizing uncooperative witnesses as villains. Newspapers rarely examined what the committees' penchant for exposing Communists had to do with writing legislation.[13]

The Newspaper Guild managed to stay above the fray, having purged Communists from its leadership both nationally and within the large New York local. Demonstrating its own brand of Americanism, the guild adopted a 1949 resolution declaring a "deep conviction that the fight against the proved communist conspiracy at home must continue."[14] The most pressing problem confronting the guild was the postwar job cuts that newspapers made because of increasing operating costs and a newsprint shortage. The merger of the *Sun* and the *Times* in Chicago left more than one hundred jobless in 1948.[15] The closing of the *St. Louis Star-Times* three years later cost more than five hundred jobs. A walkout at the *New York World-Telegram,* the flagship newspaper of the conservative Scripps-Howard chain, forced that newspaper to shut down for two-and-a-half months, marking the guild's first walkout at a major New York newspaper since its 1937 strike against the *Brooklyn Eagle.*[16] Despite the unrest in some newsrooms,

Truman reached out to the guild at its annual convention in July 1950, praising it for setting higher professional standards. His appearance marked the first presidential appearance at a guild gathering.[17]

A thirty-three-page FBI report the same week included dozens of names, among them that of the journalist I. F. Stone, who was listed as "Washington correspondent—Communist."[18] Stone, a columnist for the liberal *New York Compass* and a frequent McCarthy critic, was identified in the Venona transcripts in the 1990s as a target of Soviet Intelligence.[19] Defenders have argued that while he may have met with KGB sources, there is no proof that Stone became a Soviet spy.[20] In fact, a Soviet operative described a lunchtime meeting where Stone refused to let him pay the bill.[21]

The FBI continued to monitor guild members in 1950, but most agents found little need for concern. A report from Los Angeles said, "Communist party members no longer hold any positions in this organization."[22] New York agents noted that there was "no apparent or known Communist agitation or direction" during the *World-Telegram* strike.[23] Nevertheless, Rep. Richard Vail, an Illinois Republican, drew from the guild's Communist past to introduce legislation to strip the guild of crucial labor protections, despite its compliance with the non-Communist affidavits required by the Taft-Hartley Act.

Vail, a Chicago manufacturer, had been elected in 1946 with the support of the *Chicago Tribune*, a conservative newspaper with a long history of condemning liberals. He served on HUAC until he was defeated after a single term in the 1948 election that sent Truman to the White House and handed the Democrats a majority in both houses of Congress. Reelected during the 1950 Republican comeback, Vail attacked the Newspaper Guild soon after his return to Washington. "Clearly, an alliance of newsmen with any organization having a vital self interest in news content is contrary to public interest and a departure from traditional reportorial independence," he said, claiming that his goal was "to prevent the slanting of news in behalf of labor or in behalf of the position taken by labor on any subject."[24] The guild characterized the measure as union busting. "No evidence has ever been offered to prove that Guild members working in Guild shops have slanted the news either to fit their own opinions or the opinion of a majority of the members of the Guild," a guild official said. "The evidence is to the contrary."[25]

Vail struck again six months later when he introduced another measure, one that would have required newspapers to attach the acronym "ANG-CIO" to articles, editorials, columns, or commentaries written by guild members. He pointed to the Communist links of Heywood Broun and the more recent decision by the guild to support Thomas Buchanan, the reporter fired by the *Washington Star*, even though the guild had subsequently refused to back Buchanan. "It is reliably reported that the New York, Detroit, and Los Angeles guilds have been Communist controlled and they are still Communist infiltrated," Vail claimed.[26] By the fall of 1951 both bills were languishing and Vail lost his bid for reelection.

In 1951 the Senate Internal Security Subcommittee initially focused on Truman's China policy and then held hearings to examine many of the same individuals and organizations that had appeared before HUAC, including youth organizations, a variety of labor unions, and personnel attached to embassies.[27] It was at this point that HUAC reopened its investigation of the movie industry.[28] HUAC also began looking into Communist activities within the West Coast defense industry and in professional organizations.[29] Los Angeles police furnished the committee's West Coast investigator, William Wheeler, with detailed information obtained by undercover agents who had infiltrated the Los Angeles branch of the Communist Party during the 1920s and 1930s.[30] The information included membership rolls listing members' names, along with their fictitious "party name," nationality, date they joined the party, and, in many cases, their employer.[31] The committee held closed-door sessions in Los Angeles in September 1951 and identified potential witnesses, primarily lawyers and doctors, to appear at an open session.[32]

The following January HUAC called Charles Daggett, a former editor at the *Seattle Star*, who explained how he began attending party meetings during the late 1930s when the guild called its strike against the *Seattle Post-Intelligencer*. Daggett said he became a party member soon after moving to Los Angeles in 1945. He said the arrangements were made through Ring Lardner Jr., a screenwriter who was one of the Hollywood Ten. Daggett said he dropped out of the party after only ten weeks, and he gave the committee the names of six guild members, including that of Charles Judson, a journalist who also belonged to a Los Angeles cell of the party. The next week Judson testified that he had belonged to the party for approximately one year in 1937 while working as the city editor of the *Los Angeles Daily News*. Reading from a small red notebook, he gave the committee the names of twenty Communists who belonged to "Unit 140," a party cell that was specifically aimed at newspaper workers. He described cell members as "very active" but cautioned that they represented "a very small percentage of the Newspaper Guild."[33]

Judson's testimony echoed what HUAC had heard two months earlier from Harvey Matusow, an ex-Communist who was quickly building a career as a government witness. During an investigation of the Communist infiltration of youth organizations, Matusow described Communist attempts to infiltrate American society and cited the Newspaper Guild as an example. "Now, they don't control the American Newspaper Guild," he said. "It is just that there are Communists in that union who are working to try and vote out of power or get out of power by any means they can the present anti-Communist administration." He named Harry Kelber, a Newspaper Guild member who wrote for a small trade newspaper, describing him as a leader of the Communist Party group within the guild.[34] Matusow would become a central figure in the campaign against Communists in the press.

Targeting the Los Angeles Guild

HUAC returned to Los Angeles in May 1952 and among the witnesses called to testify was Alice Bennett, an ex-Communist, who described her experience in the party from 1936 to 1942. She named forty individuals, many of them from the newspaper industry. Though Bennett did not belong to the guild herself, she was married to Charles Judson and maintained that her marriage placed her in a position to observe Communist influence in the Los Angeles Guild. "They tried to influence the decisions of the guild," she said of Communists. "They were intensely interested in the guild policy in many issues."[35] The committee also questioned one of the people she named, Tom O'Connor, formerly a reporter at the *Los Angeles Evening News*. Later in his career he worked as a reporter in the early 1940s at the liberal New York newspaper *PM*, where he became city editor. In 1948 he joined the *New York Daily Compass*, another liberal newspaper, where he became the managing editor.

The committee was most interested in the period when O'Connor had served as president of the Los Angeles Newspaper Guild in the late 1930s while working at the *Evening News*. On the witness stand he repeatedly invoked the Fifth Amendment. "For my family's sake, as well as my own, I am unwilling to risk my liberty," he said. "I object to the question asked and to this whole inquiry because I am a working newspaperman and because an inquiry into the past or present beliefs, politics, associations, or opinions of a newspaper writer [is] a clear interference with and limitation of the free functioning of the press."[36]

Velde, who had become HUAC's chairman, quickly returned the rhetorical fire. "I can only draw one inference from the manner in which you have testified, and that is that you have in the past been a member of the Communist party, and not only that, but you continue to be a member," he said. "In a position of managing editor of a large newspaper, I think you are extremely dangerous to this country."[37]

During the rest of May and through June the committee continued to hold hearings into Communist infiltration of Hollywood with another set of hearings in Washington, D.C. In June it also held hearings on Communist infiltration of the federal government. In July HUAC resumed the investigation it had begun in May into Communist activities in professional groups in the Los Angeles area. The principal witness was Urcel Daniel, a former *Los Angeles Examiner* reporter who later became the guild's research director. She told the committee she had joined the party and the Newspaper Guild in 1937. "When the guild started organizing in Los Angeles I became acquainted with some Communist Party members and it seemed to me that they were the hardest-working members of unions," she said. "They seemed to be the only ones who were doing anything to improve the conditions of people who were suffering from the depression and who were in an underprivileged position." Daniel said she dropped out of the party in the early 1940s because she had become disillusioned. "I had come to distrust their motives so that I wanted to eliminate them from positions of leadership . . . to make them ineffective and inactive," she said. Before leaving the witness table, she handed the committee nineteen names.[38]

The most recognizable effect of the hearings came in July 1952 when the liberal *Los Angeles Daily News* fired Darr Smith and Vern Partlow after they were named by witnesses. "It has been held in court that it is libelous to call a man a Communist," the newspaper said. "We feel that it is equally damaging for a newspaper to employ men who have been identified as Party members."[39] Neither was called to testify at an open session, but the *Daily News* considered mere mention of their names sufficient justification to fire them.

Although the Newspaper Guild had come to deplore everything the Communist Party represented, guild members agreed to support Smith and Partlow before an arbitration board because members regarded their firing as a contract violation. After hearing arguments from the guild and the newspaper, the arbitrators ruled 3–2 against the guild. "A newspaper is peculiarly susceptible to criticisms that flow from the supporting public, advertisers, subscribers and readers," the arbitrators said.[40] "A great newspaper like the Daily News . . . must be ever on guard to protect itself against adverse criticism or attack which threatens to diminish its circulation and thus to weaken its financial basis and its chances of economic survival." The arbitrators also pointed to the Korean War, now in its second year, to justify their findings. "We are at war with Communism," they said. "Our boys are giving their lives on the battlefields of Korea in defense of our freedom and American ideals and democratic institutions."[41] The newspaper trade publication *Editor and Publisher* published the arbitrators' decision in its entirety, signaling to publishers that Red hunting was justified on economic grounds.

In the spring of 1953 HUAC subpoenaed William Oliver, a drama critic at Hearst's *Los Angeles Evening Herald-Express* and a former president of the Los Angeles Guild. FBI reports on Oliver went back to the early 1940s when an informant described him as a guild member who "followed the Communist party line."[42] Given the anti-Communist culture of Hearst's newspapers, the subpoena alone placed Oliver in a particularly difficult position. He told the committee:

> I regard this questioning into my writing and into the act and fact of my writing as an invasion of freedom of the press. I do say that if a subpena [*sic*] server can peer over my shoulder while I am sitting down editing copy, then tomorrow he can peer over the shoulder of the editor and the next day he can peer over the shoulder of the publisher sitting in his office and bring him to account before some such committee to account for what he prints, and who he sends the paper to.[43]

Faced with almost certain firing, Oliver submitted his resignation. His defection gave the guild ample excuse to distance itself from a tainted member. "Officers of this Guild have no knowledge of any cell of the communist party now existing in the Los Angeles Newspaper Guild," the guild said. "The entire American Newspaper Guild organization is in full accord with the Congress of Industrial Organizations' stand against communist-dominated unions."[44]

Newspaper publishers, like the studio heads in 1947, feared pressure from outside interest groups that were part of an informal anti-Communist network that had grown significantly since the war. One loosely organized group threatened a boycott of *Collier's* in March 1953 after the magazine carried a firsthand account by Los Angeles housewife Dorothy Frank, who had fought anti-Communists' efforts to censor materials used in city schools.[45] Protesters called the magazine "pro-Communist" and demanded that it oust its associate editor, Bucklin Moon, whom HUAC had accused of having "a long record of Red-front affiliations." Although Moon had played no role in the decision to publish Frank's article, and denied any association with the Communist Party, the magazine fired him. "We are all distressed that this could happen on a magazine that once had a reputation for independent judgment," said Moon. "The magazine has, in bowing so spiritlessly to pressure, publicly 'admitted' its 'guilt' and injured the reputation of a man who has been given no chance to prove his innocence."[46]

Harry Martin, the president of the Newspaper Guild, recognized his organization's untenable position of wanting to defend embattled members without triggering a firestorm of criticism from anti-Communists. At the guild's 1953 convention he forcefully criticized "name-calling by investigators into subversive activity in the press, the libraries and the churches," but he avoided singling out HUAC. "At a time when the world is looking to the United States for leadership as never before, we stand before it, weakened by witch hunts, frightened by the professional fomenters of phobias that are foul and obscene in the extreme," he said.[47]

Beyond Los Angeles

HUAC generated additional publicity during 1952 and 1953 by holding "remote" sessions in Boston, San Francisco, Detroit, and Albany, New York. Although the sessions concentrated primarily on labor and education, the Newspaper Guild was intermittently cited as an example of a labor organization that had been infiltrated by Communists. In Detroit the committee called *Detroit News* cartoonist Joseph Bernstein to testify; he had been named as a Communist by an undercover FBI agent. Bernstein's name also appeared in a 1946 FBI report that identified him as a party member or sympathizer.[48] Seated at the witness stand before HUAC six years later, Bernstein repeatedly invoked the Fifth Amendment except when a committee member asked about his willingness to go into combat. "If you were called to serve today in Korea with many other young men of this country to combat communism, would you comply with the law and serve your country in time of war against Communist forces?" asked Charles E. Potter, a Michigan Republican. "I would," Bernstein replied.[49] Despite his pledge of loyalty to country, he was fired the next day after twenty-three years with the *Detroit News*.[50] Bernstein, like Moon at *Collier's,* had few ways to protest his dismissal because his position was not covered by a guild contract, making him ineligible for arbitration.

The *Detroit Times* fired copy editor Elliott Maraniss even before he was called to testify.[51] An FBI informant told the committee that Maraniss wrote under a pseudonym for a newspaper published by the Michigan Communist Party.[52] In a brief appearance before the committee several days after he was fired, Maraniss brushed aside many of the committee's questions. "I believe that [the First Amendment] is an unassailable guaranty of freedom of speech and freedom of expression for a newspaperman, and the right to indulge in any political activity without fear of penalization," he said. Although the Detroit Guild initially agreed to support him, it backed down after he invoked the Fifth Amendment.[53] Maraniss suspected that the reversal had been instigated by the Association of Catholic Trade Unionists (ACTU). The organization had become a powerful force inside the labor movement during the 1940s, seeking to wrest control of left-wing unions from Communist domination, particularly among auto workers, who were allied with the CIO.[54] In the 1940s the president of the Detroit chapter of the ACTU was also president of the Detroit Newspaper Guild and played a pivotal role in purging Communists from leadership in the national guild and the New York local.[55]

At hearings in Boston in April 1953, HUAC called Theodore Polumbaum, a television newswriter at United Press. An ex-Communist had named Polumbaum as a member of a "Red youth cell" at Yale in the mid-1940s. "I will not answer that question or any similar questions referring to my political affiliations and beliefs," he told the committee. "I will not be compelled to bear witness against myself or against any others and to turn informer before this committee and to cooperate in the apparent efforts of this committee to disparage and belittle the Bill of Rights."[56] After repeatedly refusing to respond, he brazenly challenged the committee's authority.

"If you have any information or evidence that I have engaged in any illegal conspiracy or any illegal activities, or committed any illegal act—you should take this to the proper authorities and you should have me prosecuted and give me a day in court under due process," he said.

"Well, that may follow," said Rep. Francis E. Walter, a Democrat from Pennsylvania.[57]

The wire service fired Polumbaum the next day, explaining that he had become "a serious liability."[58] Wire service executives pointed to a loyalty oath that Polumbaum had taken, denying he had held membership in any subversive organization. United Press maintained that his testimony "intentionally created a doubt as to his honesty," which the wire service saw as "incompatible with the best interests of journalism."[59] Recognizing the dangerous precedent that Polumbaum's firing represented, the Boston Guild agreed to support his appeal, which would take next two years.[60] When HUAC moved to Albany, New York, in July 1953, Janet Scott, a twenty-year veteran of the conservative *Knickerbocker News,* was a founding member of the Tri-City Newspaper Guild. In 1950 she had taken time off to run for Congress on the American Labor Party ticket but lost.[61] The FBI had been monitoring her activities since 1943 after receiving a letter that described her as "a definite 'red' and flaunts the fact."[62] An informant characterized her as "a red hot Communist" who worked in the labor movement and the civil rights movement. Her name was added to the FBI's "Security Index" of individuals who would be detained during a national emergency.[63] Her name did not become public until July 1947 when an electrical worker named her as a party member who worked as a newspaper reporter. Apparently, HUAC felt no urgency since it did not call her to testify until the Albany hearings nearly six years later.[64]

When she took the witness stand, Scott attempted to read a prepared statement, but she was cut short by the committee's chief investigator, Frank Tavenner. "My purpose in asking you these questions is to ascertain from you what knowledge you had, if any, regarding Communist activities within the Newspaper Guild," he said. Throughout the session Scott claimed a constitutional right to remain silent when asked about the party but acknowledged that she had played a "leading part" in establishing the Tri-Cities Newspaper Guild in the early 1930s.[65] The *Knickerbocker News* reported the story the next day and characterized her performance as "gross misconduct." Two days later it announced that she had been fired after twenty-seven years at the newspaper.[66] Scott, who had taken vacation time to attend the hearings, learned of the decision when she read the front page of the morning newspaper.[67] The Tri-City Guild voted unanimously to support her reinstatement the following December but reversed itself the next month when members became concerned that "the Guild would be classed with the communists."[68] Making matters worse, the carefully worded dismissal from the newspaper permitted state insurance officials to refuse to pay her unemployment benefits. "Communism is the antithesis of democracy," they ruled. "It is not an over-simplification to say that in this stage of national and international affairs, an acknowledged Communist is an enemy of this country and of its way of life. To claim to be a loyal American and a Communist is a lie, no more tenable than to claim to be a god-worshiping atheist."[69] Scott wrote in the *Nation* that what she found hard to believe was that "twenty-seven years of conscientious work were swept away in a surge of McCarthyism."[70]

Throughout 1952 and 1953 newspapers consistently fired journalists who were so much as mentioned publicly in the context of the Communist Party. One exception came in late 1953 when HUAC questioned James Benet, a copy editor at the *San Francisco Chronicle*. After an FBI informant named Benet as the head of a New York Communist club in 1936, Benet took the witness stand when he was called before HUAC and repeatedly invoked the Fifth Amendment. "I wish to protect myself in the American way against un-American activities, and by 'un-American activities' I mean, of course, the activities of this committee," Benet said. "I think that the committee is injuring every citizen, is an offense against the Constitution, and is, as President Truman called it recently—former President Truman—a cancer."[71] Despite his hostile response to committee questioning, the *Chronicle* took the unusual step of retaining him. "The *Chronicle*'s policy is that a member of the Communist party is not acceptable as a staff member," said executive editor Scott Newhall. "In the case of James Benet, the Chronicle has satisfied itself that he is not now, and has not been, a member of the Communist Party during his employment with the San Francisco Chronicle."[72] Through the balance of his career the subject never arose again, and he remained at the *Chronicle* until he retired in the 1980s. "I think a good many of the *Chronicle* people were pretty liberal," he later recalled. "There was one guy—a photographer—who was a devout Catholic—and a very odd guy—who chewed me out considerably."[73]

Targeting the Broadcasters

As pressure on newspapers intensified during the early 1950s, concern about the broadcast industry followed a different track. In June 1950 *Red Channels*, a small magazine published by American Business Consultants, appeared on newsstands. Three former FBI agents had launched the company in 1947 when they began publishing *Counterattack*, a newsletter that soon became a guide for blacklisting in the entertainment industry. *Red Channels* listed 151 entertainers with alleged Communist ties and said it based the list on names culled from a variety of sources. Among the names was that of Jean Muir, an actor who was fired by NBC when it abruptly canceled the fall premier of *The Aldrich Family*. Despite her denial of any involvement with Communists, General Foods considered her "a controversial personality" and feared that airing of *The Aldrich Family* might jeopardize sales of its many household products.[74] Harry M. Warner, president of Warner Studios, made it clear that his company would not tolerate any employee "who belongs to any Communist, Fascist or other un-American organization" and offered to buy a plane ticket for any employee who wanted to go to Russia.[75]

Red Channels named a half-dozen broadcast journalists among the entertainers who were thought to be Communists or Communist sympathizers, including Alexander Kendrick at the Mutual Radio Network; William L. Shirer, who had left CBS after the war to become a commentator at the Mutual Radio Network; and CBS correspondent Howard K. Smith, who later joined ABC.[76] Kendrick had worked in newspapers before becoming a broadcast correspondent at CBS and held elected offices in the Newspaper Guild. His name appeared in several FBI reports on the guild, including the "Official Red List" that Hoover had developed in November 1941.[77] A report three years later described him as "a known friend" of a Philadelphia writer for the Communist Party newspaper.[78] Shirer was convinced that he appeared in *Red Channels* because he had signed a petition against Hollywood blacklisting in the late 1940s. After Shirer's name surfaced, Mutual refused to renew his contract. Unemployable in the broadcast industry, Shirer wrote several books, including the voluminous *Rise and Fall of the Third Reich,* that arose from his experiences covering World War II, and he became a national sensation.[79]

Among the broadcast networks CBS may have attracted particular attention as a result of a strategy developed by company chairman William Paley in the late 1940s to overtake NBC.[80] He initiated the idea of producing programs that could be sold directly to advertisers, rather than rely on the traditional arrangement whereby advertising agencies tightly controlled the production and content of all network entertainment programs. With Paley's plan in place CBS began hiring its own cadre of writers, directors, producers, actors, and performers, many of whom brought a left-of-center political perspective, although few were actually connected to any organized political group.[81] "We unknowingly hired a lot of questionable people," remarked one executive.[82] Moreover, CBS had projected itself as the most liberal network during World War II, prompting some critics to later brand it "The Red Network."[83]

Smith continued at CBS during the early 1950s, covering postwar reconstruction from the London bureau. "I'm absolutely sure that Ed Murrow was the wall that kept anybody from approaching me," he said many years later.[84] Smith speculated that his "vociferous anti-Nazi student speeches" during his college years "had apparently caught up with me," but CBS never confronted him about it.[85] Instead, the network developed a loyalty oath for its employees, modeled after the one instituted by the Truman administration three years earlier; the impetus for CBS's loyalty oath apparently was Truman request to Congress for the authority to seize any radio or television station that might use its signals to guide planes or missiles to targets in the United States.[86] With the Korean War worsening and public hostility toward Communists deepening, Paley believed CBS "owed it to the public to assure people that its broadcasts were not being influenced by subversives."[87] ABC, the smallest of the three major networks, refused to look for Reds under its bed, even after the entertainer Gypsy Rose Lee, who hosted her own ABC television show, was named as a Communist by

Red Channels. After the network resisted demands that she be fired, it received a special Peabody Award in 1951 for "resisting organized pressure and its reaffirmation of basic American principles."[88] However, local stations in California, Pennsylvania, Michigan, and Ohio followed CBS's lead and asked hundreds of employees to sign oaths. Los Angeles station KFI, for example, fired an employee who claimed such an oath was an invasion of privacy and refused to sign.[89]

Meanwhile every departing employee at CBS became suspect. The only dismissal officially tied to the oath involved the network's firing of an "office girl" who refused to sign.[90] At a higher level of the company there was at least one exception. John K. M. McCaffery, moderator of *We Take Your Word,* refused to sign. "It is impossible for a Catholic to be a Communist," he said in a letter to network brass. Rather than press the issue, the network decided his statement was sufficient.[91]

NBC maintained a loyalty test it had adopted for new employees in the mid-1940s, but the CBS oath applied to more than its new employees.[92] Critics attacked the company's willingness to breach its employees' civil liberties. "Radio and television must recognize that no solution to the loyalty question ever will be achieved by subscribing to the tactics of the pressure groups," wrote Jack Gould, the *New York Times* television columnist. "It is time that there was an end to the conspiracy of silence which has put the industry in the position of condoning the totalitarian methods which its leaders have properly deplored."[93] John Crosby, who had a syndicated column in the *New York Herald Tribune,* that the broadcasting industry had always been more afflicted than other media with people who held unorthodox views. "Today the timidity has reached an all-time high," he said. "No one in broadcasting[,] from the network heads to the elevator operators[,] will defend these taboos; all scrupulously observe them."[94]

Former CBS executive producer Tony Kraber acknowledged during a 1955 HUAC hearing that he had been asked to resign in 1951 after the network learned he might be called to testify. He was among eight individuals named by film director Elia Kazan before HUAC in January 1952 when the Hollywood hearings continued.[95] When Kraber was asked in 1955 about Communist activities, he invoked the Fifth Amendment.[96] Another concern for CBS was the Federal Communications Commission (FCC), which began to deny broadcast licenses to station owners who were suspected Communists.[97] The list published in *Red Channels,* along with pressure from special interest groups and the FCC, left little need for congressional hearings to keep tabs on the broadcast industry, allowing the committees to concentrate on mainstream newspapers.

CHAPTER FIVE

The Specter of McCarthy

T HROUGHOUT THE 1950s federal prosecutors, state investigative agencies, immigration officials, and members of Congress relied on a variety of sources to fuel the anti-Communist campaign. Among these were ex-Communists who testified against party members before courts of law, loyalty boards, and investigative committees. Their testimony provided justification for Justice Department prosecutions of party leaders in the late 1940s and early 1950s and the questioning of witnesses before a string of congressional investigative committees. Although the chief target was domestic Communists, the investigators viewed anyone who was close to the party as equally dangerous. Allegations against the Newspaper Guild cropped up periodically before the House Un-American Activities Committee but also before Sen. Joseph McCarthy's investigative subcommittee and the Senate Internal Security Subcommittee (SISS).[1]

Newspapers came into the spotlight in October 1952 when Harvey Matusow appeared before SISS (which two years later became known as the Eastland committee) and cited the Newspaper Guild as an example of Communist domination of CIO unions. An ex-Communist, he had joined the growing legion of professional witnesses used by the government for their expertise. "In 1950, I attended Communist Party meetings, caucuses, in the Newspaper Guild in New York," he said, although it was unclear why he had attended the caucuses since he was not a journalist. "It has a large membership and is not a Communist-dominated union but in New York City today there are approximately 500 dues-paying Communists working in the newspaper industry."[2] He didn't stop there, also telling the commit-tee: "The *New York Times* has well over 100 dues-paying members." Time, Inc., has 76 Communist Party members, working in editorial and research, and just a few months ago the communist caucus regained control of that unit of the Newspaper Guild." Peppered with specific numbers for which he offered no hard proof, his testimony evoked McCarthy's 1950 Wheeling, West Virginia, speech in which he claimed to have "a list of 205 . . . mem-bers of the Communist Party" working at the State Department.[3] With the exception of J. B. Matthews's brief reference to Communists at the *New York Times* in the late 1930s, no other witness had so publicly targeted a mainstream publication.

Two weeks later Matusow embellished on his comments before an American Legion Post in Great Falls, Montana. "The Sunday section of the *New York Times* alone has 126 dues-paying Communists," he said. "On the editorial and research staffs of *Time* and *Life* magazines are 76 hard-core Reds; the New York bureau of the Associated Press has 25."[4] Both the *Times* and *Time* magazine were among the publications McCarthy regarded as left-wing.[5] In late 1951 *Time* had featured the senator in an unflattering cover story titled "Demagogue McCarthy."[6] Like FBI Director J. Edgar Hoover, McCarthy had a well-understood penchant for retaliating against anyone in the press who dared to criticize him. But the senator seldom went after major publications until 1952, when Matusow became his media hit man.

A native of New York, Matusow had joined the party in 1947 after serv-ing in the army during World War II. Although he knew little about com-munism, he had grown to respect two Communists in his infantry division in Europe and enjoyed the company of several French Communists he met during the war.[7] The party assigned him mundane tasks of selling subscrip-tions to the Sunday edition of the *Daily Worker,* the Communist Party newspaper, and to working in the party bookstore. He began to run into trouble with party officials after he took a job with a Harlem collection agency and moved in with an African American divorcee. He watched in 1949 as the government prosecuted top party officials under the Smith Act. A year later he read newspaper accounts of McCarthy's celebrated West Virginia speech and began to grow increasingly fearful that he too might be arrested and convicted under the Smith Act.

In March 1950 the twenty-three-year-old offered to become an under-cover FBI informant.[8] In return, he wanted the government to extend his disability payments from the Veterans Administration for injuries he had suffered during the war and to reimburse him for his expenses.[9] The FBI initially ignored his inquiry but later relented and offered him $25 a week to supply information on college students allied with the party and photographs of party members at strikes and demonstrations.[10] Party officials grew suspicious in late November 1950 and accused him of stealing money. The *Daily Worker* said in early 1951 that Matusow was considered "an enemy agent" and the party expelled him.[11]

Matusow made his debut as a professional witness the following year at a closed hearing before HUAC. In conjunction with his appearance the *New York Journal American* carried a front-page story, "Secret FBI Man Reveals: 3,500 Students Recruited Here for Red Fifth-Column," with Matusow's byline.[12] He later admitted that he invented the large number to enhance his credibility, but his ruse was not clear in the early 1950s when he became part of a stable of witnesses assembled by the Justice Department to provide "friendly" testimony at investigative hearings, deportation hearings, and political trials. Although the government refused to acknowledge the program publicly, the *New York Times* revealed in 1955 that the Justice Department maintained eighty-five witnesses on its payrolls between mid-1952 and mid-1954.[13] The primary value of these witnesses was to provide the legal basis for prosecutions of party officials under the Smith Act and for the deportation of immigrants who belonged to the party. As events later showed, the arrangement provided ample incentive for these witnesses to embellish the truth and manufacture testimony to enhance their credibility and extend their appeal to prosecutors and the press.[14]

During the early 1950s Matusow became one of the government's most energetic witnesses; in 1952 he testified at the trial of fifteen secondary Communist leaders and claimed that party officials urged youths working at Midwest industrial plants to sabotage industries in the event of war with the Soviet Union. The court found thirteen of the fifteen guilty and sentenced them to jail.[15]

Milking the Red Menace

Riding the adulation he received as a government witness, Matusow walked into McCarthy's Capitol Hill offices in the fall of 1952 and volunteered to campaign for his reelection. With the senator recuperating from surgery and unable to campaign personally, the campaign staff welcomed Matusow's offer and dispatched him to speaking engagements in Wisconsin. During a rally for Republican governor Walter J. Kohler, Matusow told supporters in Madison that forty Reds working at leading New York newspapers had engaged in a "smear campaign" against McCarthy but provided no details and no names, claiming the senator "makes no accusations or says anything about anybody unless there is documentation to back it up."[16]

Impressed by Matusow's ability to garner headlines, McCarthy took a personal interest in the young man. Journalists had become familiar with the senator's disdain for reporters who questioned his methods, motives, or accomplishments and his habit of quickly turning the tables. After Phil Potter wrote several unflattering articles for the *Baltimore Sun,* he discovered that investigators from McCarthy's office were combing Baltimore with questions about Potter's past. Potter claimed McCarthy threatened to subpoena him on three or four occasions.[17] McCarthy also threatened Marvin Arrowsmith at the Associated Press after the wire service ran several unflattering stories. "I know you've got six kids, Marv, and I don't want to kick about your work, so I hope there is no further reason to do so," McCarthy told him. When Arrowsmith continued to write negative stories, the senator contacted hundreds of newspapers, complaining about the AP's coverage.[18]

McCarthy's favorite tactic was to compare critical newspapers to the *Daily Worker.* In his home state of Wisconsin he described the *Capital Times* in 1949 as "a Red mouthpiece for the Communist Party in Wisconsin" after the newspaper ran an unflattering profile. He waged an attack by sending letters to four hundred editors at daily and weekly newspapers across the state.[19] After the unflattering cover story in *Time* McCarthy demanded that publisher Henry Luce, an ardent Republican, correct statements that "deliberately misrepresented" McCarthy. When Luce refused, McCarthy flew into a tirade. "I am preparing material on *Time* to furnish to all of your advertisers so that they may be fully aware of the type of publication they are supporting," McCarthy told him.[20] Leery of McCarthy's vindictiveness, Luce advised his staff to carefully avoid any suggestion that the senator was dangerous.[21]

In the weeks leading to election day 1952, Matusow touted Republican candidates in Utah, Washington State, and Montana, emphasizing Communist infiltration into American life and including references to the *New York Times.*[22] He later acknowledged that he had derived his estimate of forty Reds at New York newspapers from talking with party members who belonged to the Newspaper Guild. He also acknowledged that he had discussed with McCarthy his decision to voice the allegation when the two met during a Labor Day campaign rally in Milwaukee.[23] "Once the 'facts' were in the record McCarthy knew that he could accuse the *Times* and *Time* of being pro-Communist, and we would both make headlines," Matusow wrote in the affidavit he gave to the *New York Times.*[24]

The accusations caught little interest among the press until January 1953, when Walter Winchell, the New York gossip columnist, referred to them in his syndicated column. "The testimony of Harvey Matusow (an undercoverman for the gov't) before a Senate investigating group: . . . in New York today [claims] there are approximately 500 dues-paying Communists working in the newspaper industry. The *New York Times* has well over 100 . . . and *Time* magazine has 76 Communist Party members working in editorial and research . . . Confirming What I Said For Years!" wrote Winchell in his inimitable, gossipy style.[25] Columnists Joseph and Stewart Alsop repeated Matusow's claims in their influential political column a few days later but questioned how he could use the figure "126 dues-paying Communists" when the entire staff of the Sunday *Times* numbered eighty-seven, including two part-time copyboys.[26]

Watching from the *Times*'s offices, publisher Arthur Hays Sulzberger speculated that Matusow had obtained his information from the FBI.[27] That February Sulzberger dispatched representatives to FBI headquarters, where Hoover briskly informed them that he was not at liberty to divulge the contents of bureau files but suggested that bureau records held nothing that would substantiate Matusow's claims. He did not tell them that the FBI had secretly gathered information on at least fifty-two individuals who either worked at the *Times* or were former employees.[28]

At Hoover's suggestion the *Times* attempted to contact Matusow by sending a registered letter to his home in Dayton, Ohio. By May Sulzberger had become concerned that the accusation might trigger a congressional investigation. "We do not tolerate on our news staff any Communist or other person whose mind is closed by the Iron Curtain," he said in a statement drafted for use in case the situation got out of hand.[29] When no subpoenas arrived, Sulzberger tucked the document away for another day. As Matusow continued to appear at grand jury inquiries and deportation hearings in Texas and New York, the FBI began to press him to substantiate his public allegations. He eventually gave thirty-three names, all belonging to employees of the *Daily Worker* and the leftist publications *National Guardian* and *Morning Freiheit* but none from the *Times* or *Time* magazine.[30] The FBI considered *Morning Freiheit* to be "either owned or supported by the Communist Party."[31]

McCarthy and the *New York Post*

In April 1953 McCarthy subpoenaed *New York Post* editor James Wechsler. It was no secret that Wechsler had belonged to the Young Communist

League in the early 1930s while attending Columbia University, but he had dropped out in 1937 following a visit to Russia. During the late 1940s he became an outspoken anti-Communist, helped establish Americans for Democratic Action, an anti-Communist liberal organization, and worked to oust Communists from leadership positions in the Newspaper Guild.[32] McCarthy called Wechsler to a closed hearing, ostensibly to ask about books written by Wechsler that were housed at libraries at U.S. embassies. The State Department prohibited books and other materials by "known Communists" in the government's overseas libraries.[33]

After a string of preliminary questions about his books, McCarthy asked Wechsler about the internal affairs of the *Post,* which had published a seventeen-part series two years earlier headlined "Smear, Inc.: Joe McCarthy's One-Man Mob." The series characterized McCarthy's anti-Communist campaign as "the most fabulous hoax of the century."[34] The newspaper later received a Newspaper Guild award for "best job of reporting and writing," but the series did not please the senator.[35] The exchange continued:

> McCARTHY: Mr. Wechsler, do you have any other people who are members of the Young Communist League, who were or are members of the Young Communist League, working for you on your newspaper?
> WECHSLER: I believe that it is a citizen's responsibility to testify before a Senate committee whether he likes the committee or not.
> McCARTHY: I know you do not like this committee.
> WECHSLER: I want to say that I think you are now exploring a subject which the American Society of Newspaper Editors might want to consider at some length. I answer the question solely because I recognize your capacity for misinterpretation of a failure to answer. . . . To my knowledge there are no communists on the staff of the *New York Post* at this time.[36]

McCarthy then asked a barrage of questions about stories in his newspaper. "Have you been making attacks upon J. Edgar Hoover in the editorial columns of your paper?" McCarthy asked. Wechsler confirmed that the *Post* had carried a couple of editorials criticizing the FBI.

"Have you always been very critical of the heads of the Un-American Activities Committee?" McCarthy asked. Wechsler confirmed that he had not spoken highly of J. Parnell Thomas, the HUAC chairman who was later for sent to prison padding his office payroll and accepting kickbacks.[37]

McCarthy demanded a list of party members as a crude test of Wechsler's break from the Communist Party and his loyalty to the United States. The senator told Wechsler:

You say you have severed your connection, I am not going to, at this time, try to pass on [addressing] whether that is true or not. If you or I were a member of the Communist Party and we wanted to advance the communist cause, perhaps the most effective way of doing that would be to claim that we deserted the Party and, if we got control of the paper, use that paper to attack and smear anybody who actually was fighting communism. Now, without saying whether you have done it, you would agree that would be a good tactic would you not?[38]

"I regard this inquiry as a clear invasion of what used to be considered the newspaper's right to act and function independently," Wechsler said. "I am hopeful that there will be voices raised by newspapers throughout the country in protest against this inquiry."[39]

A few days later Wechsler called on McCarthy to release a hearing transcript. McCarthy responded that under Senate procedures a transcript would not be released until his hearings were complete. "Will you therefore please immediately furnish the list of people known to you to be active in the communist movement while you were an officer in the Young Communist League?" McCarthy insisted.[40] He explained to reporters that he had called Wechsler "not as a newspaperman but as an author" and a one-time member of the Young Communist League, and then accused Wechsler of having four people on his staff who were former members of the Communist Party or followers of the Communist line.[41]

Wechsler returned to the hearing room with a list, only to hear McCarthy renege on the agreement:

Mr. Wechsler, the only remaining evidence we had requested was the list of those whom you either knew to be members of the Communist Party or the Young Communist League. I got the impression from your wire that you felt that that was a condition precedent to making the record public. That is not the case. I took the matter up with the committee and they voted unanimously to give me permission to make the record public at the earliest possible moment. So the order is that you give us those names and it has nothing to do with making the record public.[42]

Wechsler recognized that if he withheld the names, he would be seen as a Communist sympathizer. If he provided them, he would be seen as a stoolie. During a brief recess he telephoned *New York Post* publisher Dorothy Schiff, who advised him that the decision was "between you and your God."[43] When he returned to the hearing room, he surrendered sixty names, using the list as an opportunity for an avowed anti-Communist to beat the senator at his own game if he could demonstrate that it was possible to be both anti-Communist and anti-McCarthy. McCarthy handed Wechsler's list to two assistants, committee counsel Roy Cohn and *Journal American* reporter Howard Rushmore, who worked with the committee as a consultant. The *New York Journal American* and the *New York Post* were fierce competitors.[44]

"As far as I can see, there may be a few names I do not recognize here, but most of them have been exposed as having been active in the Communist Party over a long period of time," McCarthy intoned after a few minutes. "Did you feel, Mr. Wechsler, that it is your status as a newspaperman which gives you some special immunity or do you feel . . . we have the same right to call newsmen as we have lawyers and doctors?"

"I ask no special immunity," Wechsler responded. "I say only that I believe I am here because I am a newspaperman and because of what I have done as a newspaperman."

"I ask you that because you have been shouting that this is interfering with freedom of the press," McCarthy continued. "It puts me in mind of so many people screaming that their right to scream has been denied. I have not found that your right to scream has been denied you at all. I have not found that your right to distort and twist the news has been interfered with since you have been here."[45] He was resorting to his stock-in-trade innuendo, even as he was trying to get away with reneging on the deal. McCarthy tried to keep the confrontation secret, but Wechsler proved equally stubborn in his insistence that the transcripts be made public, and he found allies among the reporters covering the story. Under pressure from the reporters McCarthy finally acquiesced and released the transcripts.

For the Record

After reviewing the exchange between McCarthy and Wechsler, a variety of large and small newspapers found themselves divided on the issue of freedom of the press. "The real question is whether or not Mr. McCarthy was using his undoubted right of investigation as a cover for an attempt to harass and intimidate Mr. Wechsler as an editor who has bitterly and uncompromisingly opposed Mr. McCarthy," said the *New York Times*.[46] Conservative newspapers, like the *Washington Star,* for example, called Wechsler's defensiveness absurd. Although the *Star* characterized McCarthy's behavior as "discreditable," it argued that editors were "supposed to be hardy enough to stand up under that sort of thing, and if they cannot do it they ought not to be editors."[47] Arthur Krock echoed the *Star* a few days later in his influential *Times* column, saying there was nothing in the transcripts that sounded like intimidation. "If McCarthy has not frightened The New York Post into surrendering any part of its guaranteed freedom, the guarantee had not been infringed," he said.[48]

The American Society of Newspaper Editors (ASNE) hastily assembled an eleven-member committee headed by J. Russell Wiggins, managing editor of the *Washington Post,* to review the transcripts. Though ASNE President Basil Walters granted Wechsler's request, he had reservations about the editor's claims "Regardless of any personal views, it seems to me freedom of information or freedom of the press may not be involved," Walters said in a memorandum to the organization's members. "If anybody wants to investigate a newspaper on the same basis that other businesses and individuals are investigated, it seems to me a newspaper should welcome the opportunity to let the public have all the facts."[49] Matusow testified before McCarthy's committee two weeks later and repeated his accusations against the press. "I was a member of the American Newspaper Guild while in the Communist Party," he said. "It is an anti-Communist union, but there are Communists in it." McCarthy directed Matusow to prepare a list of Communists he had known at various news organizations, including newspapers, radio, and television. Matusow later admitted that he had told McCarthy what he thought the senator wanted to hear.[50]

The ASNE committee studied the transcripts for three weeks and was unable to reach a consensus. It said:

> The disagreement ranges from the opinion that Senator Joseph McCarthy, as committee chairman, infringed freedom of the press with his question of the Post (an opinion held by the chairman of the committee), to the contrary viewpoint that the senator's inquiries did no damage to this freedom. In between are committee members who were disturbed by the tenor of the investigation, but do not feel that this single interchange constituted a clear and present danger to freedom of the press justifying a specific challenge.... Since the committee is not in agreement on this crucial issue, it is the responsibility of every editor to read the transcript and decide for himself, and, if he likes, to try to convince the public his view is the correct one.[51]

The final report fell short of the resounding condemnation Wechsler had envisioned, but a minority of Wiggins and three other members provided his vindication. "A press put to the frequent necessity of explaining its news and editorial policies to a United States Senator armed with the full powers of the government of the United States, is not a free press—whether the Senator be a good or a bad Senator," the four wrote.[52]

McCarthy countered their rebuke with his own interpretation of the minority report. "When you dig out a crooked lawyer other lawyers do not say you are impairing the freedom of the legal profession," he said. "When you dig out a dishonest banker other bankers don't plead injury. It seems rather ridiculous to me that there are claims of infringement of freedom of the press whenever you attempt to dig out crooks or Communists in that profession."[53] He then aimed his anger at Wiggins and the *Washington Post*, claiming Wiggins had "prostituted and endangered" freedom of the press. McCarthy was incensed by the *Post*'s characterization of his hearings as a pretext to conduct an "intense interrogation" about editorials that were critical of him. "The question, of course, is not whether Mr. Wechsler actually was intimidated, but whether he was answerable to an arm of the Government for his editorial comments," the *Post* had said.[54]

The chilling effect was apparent at the Newspaper Guild's 1953 convention when the president of the Boston local addressed the growing number of journalists who had been called before investigative committees. He described the guild as "caught in a squeeze between the sinister communistic left and the vicious, reactionary right."[55] In a later address Louis M. Lyons, curator of Harvard's Nieman Foundation, told guild members that he found it disturbing that few newspapers had defended Wechsler and offered a stern warning. He told his colleagues: "They are short-sighted . . . those editors who took the attitude: This isn't serious. It didn't touch us. Do not send [*sic*] for whom the bell tolls. It tolls for you."[56]

At the same time HUAC subpoenaed Cedric Belfrage, a British expatriot who had cofounded the left-wing American magazine the *Guardian*. It was not a socialist publication, but the magazine did discuss socialism sympathetically, which was enough to earn it a place on HUAC's list of subversive organizations.[57] Belfrage had moved to the United States in 1926 and became a resident alien. His name came to the attention of the FBI in 1945 when Elizabeth Bentley, the Communist Party defector who helped operate a Russian spy network during World War II, identified Belfrage as a journalist who had met with Soviet operatives on several occasions. She also said he had worked with British Intelligence during the war and claimed that he had turned over documents from that agency to a Russian spy ring.[58] The Venona cables, transcripts of deciphered cables between Moscow and the party officials in the United States during the 1940s that were released by the federal government in 1995, indicate that Belfrage indeed worked with the New York office of Soviet Intelligence.[59]

After repeatedly invoking the Fifth Amendment before HUAC in May 1953, Belfrage was called before McCarthy's committee a week later and he again balked. "It is quite obvious that any answer I might give to a question would be used to crucify me," Belfrage told McCarthy's committee.[60] After the hearing federal immigration officials arrested Belfrage and detained him on Ellis Island as a "dangerous alien" until he was released pending the outcome of his appeals. When he was named by an informant who testified before HUAC in 1954, immigration officials arrested Belfrage a second time. Faced with almost certain deportation, he left the United States the following year.[61]

Matusow's Downfall

Harvey Matusow continued to testify in court cases, before government loyalty boards, and at public hearings where he leveled a string of accusations at the Boy Scouts, USO, United Nations, Voice of America, and the Farmers Union. In October 1953 he made a dramatic call to the *Times* newsroom.

"I can give you a story that you will find very interesting," he said.

"Is this about changing your testimony about the *Times*?" asked Frank Adams, the city editor.

"You've hit the nail on the head," Matusow replied, saying he would not discuss it over the telephone.[62] The next day *Times* officials contacted him and arranged a meeting with the head of the newspaper's Los Angeles bureau, who was directed to bring back a signed statement spelling out specific Communists whom Matusow knew at the newspaper.

At a hotel in Reno, Nevada, Matusow admitted that he could name only two suspected Communists at the *Times,* a woman in the advertising department and a copyboy.[63] When asked how he had arrived at the figure of 126, Matusow said he had made an estimate based on his impressions as a guild member. After negotiating satisfactory wording Matusow signed a document stating that he could name no more than six Communists working at the *Times.* The *Times* kept silent publicly, hoping the episode would soon be forgotten. At the same time the newspaper forwarded a copy of Matusow's affidavit to Hoover at the FBI and urged him to share it with columnist Walter Winchell. Hoover recoiled, telling the *Times* he could "never, under any circumstances, attempt to influence any columnist or writer."[64] In fact, Hoover had grown concerned that Matusow had become reckless and warned the Justice Department against using Matusow in the witness program.[65]

Meanwhile the newspaper learned that McCarthy would soon name its Washington bureau chief, James "Scotty" Reston, as a Communist. A native

of Scotland, Reston had joined the *Times* in 1939 as Sulzberger's adminis-
trative assistant and then made a name for himself when he became a
reporter based in London during the German blitz of World War II. By the
1950s he was regarded as one of the newspaper's crown jewels.[66] Why he
would be targeted by McCarthy was unclear, except that he had written a
1952 article that relied on telegraph messages that he had exchanged with
Joseph Stalin.[67] When McCarthy delivered the attack that Reston had been
anticipating, he was as shocked as anyone to find that the senator had targeted Clayton Knowles, the paper's political correspondent, although
McCarthy did not refer to him by name. "[T]he reporter they have covering
me used to be a member of the Young Communist League!" McCarthy
claimed.[68] Reston was even more surprised when Knowles confirmed that
the accusation was true, explaining that he had joined the Communist
Party during the guild's bitter labor dispute with the *Long Island Press* in
the summer of 1934.[69] Knowles said he became disillusioned after eighteen
months and dropped out of the party, nine years before joining the *Times*.[70]
"I could see that control of the Guild was the Party's primary objective,"
he told Reston.[71]

Sulzberger received a call the following day from New York Municipal
Judge Robert Morris, former counsel to the Senate Internal Security Subcommittee, who urged the publisher to encourage his reporter to put his
story on the record. Morris described the subcommittee as "anxious to . . .
help those who are truly reformed, and they are convinced that this man
is okay." Sulzberger brushed the suggestion aside, advising Morris that the
situation "could not be lightly resolved."[72] Morris then contacted Knowles,
telling him that if he agreed to testify, Morris would introduce him to a
member of Congress who needed a publicity director.[73] Knowles next
received a call from the committee's director of research, Benjamin Mandel, who had been active in the anti-Communist campaign for many years
before joining the subcommittee staff. Mandel advised Knowles that if he
"told all" to the subcommittee, its new chairman, James Eastland, might
call the *Times* and suggest that he be returned to his former job. Knowles
again declined but recognized that he would have to talk to the FBI if he
had any hope of remaining at the *Times*. After giving the FBI a statement
describing his past association with the Communist Party, Knowles told
Sulzberger, "I gave the FBI every name, date and place I could recall. I have
assured the FBI that I will be available in any capacity I am wanted."[74]

The Communist issue had been dormant within the Newspaper Guild
since its leadership purge in 1941. It began to take on new life in the early
1950s as Matusow and HUAC fostered public anxiety. In 1954 the guild

voted to bar Communist members, rescinding a twenty-year-old policy that permitted "any person gainfully employed by an editorial department of a daily or weekly newspaper published in the United States" to belong.[75] Heywood Broun had prevailed upon the founders to adopt criteria that were as broad as possible in order to favor leftists, but by the mid-1950s they had become undesirable.[76] The new criteria, similar to rules already in place at a number of labor unions and professional groups, prohibited membership to anyone who participated in "a conspiracy whose policies and activities and ultimate purpose is to subvert and overthrow the constitutional systems of the United States and Canada." Guild president Joseph Collis described it as a monumental shift.[77] The newspaper industry trade magazine *Editor and Publisher* characterized it as a "long-overdue and welcome appreciation of the threat of the Communist conspiracy—an expression of faith in American principles to which the vast majority of Guildsmen have freely given their allegiance."[78] Even as it adopted the ban, the guild vowed "to resist by every means possible any discharge or discipline" aimed at any member who refused to sign a loyalty oath or who invoked the Fifth Amendment in testimony before an investigative committee.[79] "This protects the guild from infiltration tactics and at the same time protects our civil liberties," commented Henry Santiestevan of the Los Angeles Guild.[80]

Requiem for McCarthy

In the spring of 1954 a series of events threw McCarthy's political fortunes into a steep decline, making it difficult for him to carry his campaign against the press any further. A March 9 CBS documentary by Edward R. Murrow and producer Fred Friendly used film clips of the senator to portray as a reckless, self-promoting politician.[81] When in April McCarthy launched hearings on Communist infiltration of the army, the televised proceedings revealed him as a blustering bully. The following December the Senate voted 67–22 to censure McCarthy on the basis that he had acted improperly on the behalf of an aide who had been drafted into the army. During the debate in the Senate, New York Democrat Herbert Lehman, one of McCarthy's most outspoken critics, referred to McCarthy's vindictiveness toward the press:

> [Sen. McCarthy] has made wholesale and unconscionable attacks upon the press, charging publications such as *Time* magazine, *Commonweal,* the *Saturday Evening Post,* the *New York Post,* and the *Milwaukee Journal* with

following the Communist line. . . . He has sought to smear such outstanding journalists as the Alsop brothers, Edward R. Murrow, James Wechsler, and Drew Pearson with implications of being Communist sympathizers. . . . He has used his position as a Member of the Senate, and as chairman of one of our committees, to ride roughshod over the Government service, over two administrations of different political complexion, and finally, over the Senate itself.[82]

McCarthy later told several reporters that his career as a Red baiter had been a mistake, a startling turnabout that left journalists unsure whether his admission was sincere or he was desperate to climb back into the headlines.[83] Harvey Matusow also fell into a steep downward spiral in the spring of 1954 after starring in the anti-Communist crusade. After his marriage to the ex-wife of a Republican member of Congress ended in divorce after only four months, Matusow sank into a deep depression.[84] In April 1954 he contacted Methodist Bishop G. Bromley Oxnam, whom Matusow had met during the 1952 campaign, and confided that many of his accusations had been lies, including accusations against party leaders who had been convicted in 1952 under the Smith Act.[85] Matusow made his last appearance as a professional witness six weeks later.[86]

The *Washington Star* learned of his turnabout and reported that Matusow "wished someone to undo 'all the lies I have told about many people.'"[87] The disclosure triggered alarms at the FBI and at HUAC, which summoned him back to the witness table, and he resumed his informer role by denying Oxnam's allegation: "If he was correctly reported by the newspapers, the bishop is a dishonest man."[88] Matusow also tried to renege on the affidavit he had given to the *Times*. "I read where this statement was purported to be a 'retraction,' but the statement was not," he said. "The statement I gave them was that I did not personally know of the names of every member of the Communist Party, and when I gave a few speeches somewhere . . . I stated the correct figure to the best of my knowledge."[89]

The following October Matusow relocated to Utah, where he was baptized a Mormon, claiming he had been influenced by his journalist friend Jack Anderson, the nationally known newspaper columnist who was Mormon, and Arthur Watkins, the Utah senator who was also an active Mormon.[90] Matusow said he had grown fearful that the FBI might try to kill him to keep him quiet.[91] He later filed an affidavit with the federal district court in New York describing his testimony against party leaders as a lie. "My manner of presentation and my theme was encouraged by Senator

Joseph McCarthy and in fact was at the behest of McCarthy and made during the heat of a political campaign," he told the court.[92]

In February 1955 Matusow announced at a raucous New York news conference that a left-wing publisher would publish *False Witness,* a book in which he would "right some of the wrongs."[93] Now it was the Senate Internal Security Subcommittee's turn to subpoena Matusow back to the witness chair. Eastland, an anti-Communist Mississippi Democrat who had become chairman the year before, confronted Matusow with a list of 244 individuals he had named. "I believe . . . that some aspect of my testimony regarding each of these individuals, to the best of my recollection now, is false," Matusow responded.[94] The committee tried to salvage its own credibility by characterizing Matusow as part of a Communist campaign "to discredit Government witnesses . . . and thus to immobilize the prosecution and investigation of the Communist conspiracy." It maintained that the only time he had lied was when he claimed he had been lying. "Publication of 'False Witness' was a shameless attempt to mislead United States courts, the United States Congress, and the people of the entire world, and thus to give aid and comfort to the Communist conspiracy against human freedom," it said.[95] A committee report nine months later claimed Matusow's book was "conceived, financed, and published by a conspiracy of Communist lawyers, labor leaders, and publishers who decided that he was to become an 'author.'"[96]

Throughout the late 1940s and into the 1950s investigative committees had done little more than taunt the press, observed former *Milwaukee Journal* reporter Edwin Bayley.[97] There had been no full-blown investigation of Communists in the press, but the saber rattling by the investigative committees had left a discernable chill. *New York Times* editorial page editor John Oakes noted that McCarthyism "has had a profound effect on all of us—on our writing, our speaking and even thinking."[98] New York newspaperman James Aronson noted that subtle self-censorship affected everyone in the newspaper business.[99] What no one realized in late 1954 was that the pressures applied to the press marked only the beginning of the trouble that lay ahead.

CHAPTER SIX

Dark Clouds over the Newsroom

B Y 1955 THE RIVALRY among congressional investigative committees had grown so intense that they agreed to avoid overlapping
investigations. The House Un-American Activities Committee
focused on labor issues at hearings held in Seattle, Milwaukee, San Diego,
and Fort Wayne, Indiana. The Senate Internal Security Subcommittee
turned its attention toward the press.[1] An FBI memorandum in November
1955 showed that the previous January, Ralph Roach, the FBI's White
House liaison, had told Alan Belmont, the agency's assistant director, that
Julien G. "Jay" Sourwine, the subcommittee's counsel, had requested "a list
of individuals" who were "reportedly connected with the New York Times."[2]
Although the document bears a stamp that says "Do Not File," the document apparently slipped through Hoover's cleverly devised and elaborate
screening procedure, which was designed to hide potentially embarrassing
information, such as court order or congressional subpoena, from the public.[3] The memo also noted that the FBI had furnished Sourwine with "brief
succinct resumes of information in Bureau files" about eight individuals,
including five who had been subpoenaed to testify in public. The names
that Sourwine received were only a small part of the FBI's arsenal. An earlier report from the New York field office to FBI headquarters listed seventy
suspected employees at the *New York Times*.[4]

At the same time rumors of an investigation of the press began to cir-
culate through city newsrooms. Fearing the possibility of being called
before a committee, Charles Kraft, a writer in the *Times*'s radio-television

department, walked into the office of Jack Gould, a well-known writer who acted as head of the newspaper's radio-television department, and volunteered that he had belonged to the party between 1936 and 1939. Moreover, Kraft said, he had helped organize a Communist cell at the *Times* in 1932. Kraft said that the idea for a cell came from a mechanic who tended to the Associated Press teletype machines at the *Times*, the *Herald Tribune*, and the *World-Telegram*. According to Kraft, the leader of the *Times* group was a discontented copyboy who was attracted to the Communist Party's campaign for higher wages. Kraft described the cell as a "haphazard operation" with no indication that it was supported by any party masterminds.[5]

It was hardly a secret that Communists worked at the *Times* in the 1930s. By 1936 party members were a familiar sight at the newspaper's doors, where they would hand out circulars signed "Communist party Nucleus at The New York Times."[6] Eugene Lyons, a leading anti-Communist writer, wrote an exposé of the party in 1941 in which he noted that Communists published "shop papers" at the *Times* and *Time* magazine that "made life miserable not only for the bosses . . . but for anti-Stalinist radicals on the staff."[7] Although the papers were openly distributed, the journalists who edited them carefully concealed their identities by using pseudonyms. Cells had also formed at the *Brooklyn Eagle, Long Island Press,* and *Herald Tribune,* where members worked for the right of journalists to unionize and for better wages. Given the large number of immigrants who had settled in New York City after the turn of the century, it was not surprising that Communists were active in nearly every substantial enterprise in the city. In the mid-1930s New York served as the intellectual and political center of the American Communist movement.[8]

Kraft told his superiors that the most prominent members of the *Times* cell were political reporter James Kieran and copy editor James Glaser. Kieran had been an organizer of the guild unit at the *Times* and had worked closely with the national guild's founder, Heywood Broun. After joining the *Times* in 1923, Kieran had worked on the night rewrite desk before becoming a political reporter and transferring to the Albany bureau to cover then-governor Franklin D. Roosevelt. During the 1932 presidential campaign Kieran coined the phrase "brain trust" to describe Roosevelt's informal cabinet of professional advisers. Kieran left the newspaper in 1937 to become press secretary to New York mayor Fiorello La Guardia and died in January 1952.[9]

Glaser joined the *Times* in 1929 and, at the same time, secretly wrote for the Communist newspaper, *the Daily Worker,* under a pseudonym.[10] He left the *Times* in 1934 to work full time as the *Worker*'s managing editor.

By then his party membership was hardly a secret, except perhaps at the *Times*. In announcing its new managing editor the *Worker* carried a headline that read "James Casey (Glaser) Editor on the Times Resigns to Join Daily Worker Staff."[11] Kraft said members were under strict orders from the Central Committee of the Communist Party not to slant news stories in any way to fit their political beliefs. "No one was to do this under any circumstances, as it would invite the risk of exposure and might jeopardize the whole Communist movement," Kraft said.[12]

The best estimate of the number of Communists working at the *Times* during the 1930s and 1940s was fewer than fifty in the news-editorial department. The number declined in the early 1940s as membership in the Communist Party U.S.A. dropped off. *Times* reporter Will Lissner suggested in an internal memo that relatively few Communists were working in the press because "newspapermen, printers and pressmen were more sophisticated on these matters than the general public."[13] His report put the number working at the *Times* in the early 1950s at fewer than thirty, none of whom worked in the news, Sunday, or editorial page departments where they could influence the newspaper's content.[14]

Kraft repeatedly assured the *Times* that he had had no contact with the party since the late 1930s. "I realize what a fool I have been to have ever engaged in this political adventure and I hope you will understand this and accept my explanation as sincere," he told managing editor Turner Catledge.[15] "Go ahead with your work with assurance that the past is past, and together you and we cast our sights to the future," Catledge responded.[16] Kraft was never called to testify, at least not at any public sessions and probably not at any secret, closed hearings.

Spotlight on the Press

In late June 1955 Sourwine informed reporters covering Capitol Hill that the subcommittee would hold hearings on "espionage work," and he distributed a list of potential witnesses that included CBS correspondent Winston Burdett.[17] The announcement was the first indication that Congress would move beyond sporadic questioning of journalists and would place the entire newspaper industry under an anti-Communist microscope, as McCarthy had threatened earlier.

When Sourwine made his announcement, the Newspaper Guild was set to begin its annual convention in Albany, where it had been scheduled to amend its constitution to ban Communist members.[18] During the spring, however, guild officials began to reconsider the ban after the American

Civil Liberties Union urged the union to abandon the idea. Although the ACLU had adopted a similar ban in 1940, its officials advised the guild that a discriminatory restriction such as the one being considered by the guild membership violated ACLU policy and was a bad idea.[19] Part of the ACLU's rationale was that the government's onslaught against the Communist Party had taken its toll. By the mid-1950s the Communist Party U.S.A. was without a leader and without direction, and membership had shrunk from a high of 100,000 to about twenty thousand. However, the party's atrophy did not slow down the efforts by anti-Communists to annihilate it; they continued to warn of the Communist threat to national security.[20]

Eastland, chair of the Senate Internal Security Subcommittee and one of the Senate's most ferocious anti-Communists, began the hearings with an ominous warning:

> Today we shall have an opportunity to hear an ex-Communist disclose a phase of the Communist conspiracy which has not been told before. The subcommittee is fully appreciative of the agonizing inner struggle experienced by one who has once become entangled in the toils of the Red octopus and who finally decides to free himself from its grasp. It is fully aware of the mud guns of vilification which will be directed against him by the communists and their allies. Therefore, we are deeply grateful to this witness, and welcome his courageous effort to roll up the Iron Curtain protecting the communist conspiracy in the highly important area of his competence.[21]

The committee's star witness was Burdett, who was well known to millions of radio listeners from his World War II broadcasts and whose testimony therefore was certain to be front-page news. He had more recently reported on international affairs from the United Nations for both CBS Radio and the CBS Television Network. He had distinguished himself as a member of the elite team of war correspondents assembled by Edward R. Murrow. Burdett had covered the Nazi campaign along the Balkans and through eastern Europe, northern Africa, and, later, Iran. Now he was a government informant who could link the Communist Party to the Newspaper Guild, and his testimony triggered the long-anticipated Senate investigation of Communists in the press.

The path that led Burdett to the witness chair began in 1934 after he graduated summa cum laude from Harvard at nineteen and joined the *Brooklyn Daily Eagle*. "One of his great passions at Harvard was acting, the stage and theater," Richard Burdett later recalled of his father. "His first assignments at the *Eagle* were to write film and theater reviews."[22] Winston

Burdett worked for a short time with Alvah Bessie, who left the newspaper in 1934 to pursue a career as a Hollywood screenwriter and later became a member of the Hollywood Ten, refusing to answer questions before HUAC in 1947 and serving time in jail.[23]

In September 1937 the guild became embroiled in a bitter dispute with *Eagle* publisher Preston Goodfellow. After Goodfellow rejected the guild's demand for higher pay for advertising employees, more than three hundred workers walked out, including many from the editorial department, marking the first guild strike against a large New York daily. Cynical observers saw it as a tactic to pressure the *Times,* which had been loath to negotiate with the guild.[24] Burdett played a central role in the *Eagle* strike by coordinating the picket line. As the newspaper continued to publish, the guild stepped up its pressure by calling on local retailers to cancel their advertisements.[25] Those who refused soon found a "Yell Squad" at their doorstep forcefully denouncing the *Eagle* and scaring off customers, a strategy that later became illegal under the Taft-Hartley Act. Newspaper executives suspected the strike and the agitation of its advertisers were Communist inspired. After fifteen weeks the two sides settled after state labor officials negotiated a settlement that called on the newspaper to limit work hours and reinstate strikers who had been fired, but the agreement went no further.[26]

Burdett moved from the culture desk to the news department after the strike, until editors complained that he was too painstaking and slow to handle news. He then went to the "Trends" section, a Sunday feature that recapped the week's news. There he became fascinated with events far from the peaceful atmosphere of Brooklyn. In Europe, Nazi Germany was making threatening gestures toward its neighbors, particularly the Soviet Union. The Soviets tried but failed to negotiate territorial rights with Finnish authorities to establish a protective buffer, and Russian troops prepared to invade.[27]

With little prospect of advancing at the *Eagle,* Burdett grew increasingly restless and worked out an arrangement with his editors that would allow him to report on escalating tensions in Scandinavia, where German troops would soon clash with the Russians. The plan gave the *Eagle* an opportunity to compete with New York's larger, more profitable newspapers, which maintained European news bureaus. The newspaper agreed to provide modest payment and to support his passport application as a war correspondent, which would permit him to travel in some of the most dangerous locales in Europe.[28] The Passport Office questioned his status as a freelance reporter, but its examiners eventually dropped their objections and permitted the twenty-six-year-old to sail for Bergen, Norway, in February 1940.[29]

Burdett wrote his first story aboard ship, describing a dangerous encounter between British forces and a German freighter in the North Sea. By the time he arrived in Norway, world attention was focused on the Soviet forces that were advancing on Finland's southeastern quadrant. After a brief stop in Oslo he traveled to some of the fiercest fighting, a trip that required him to slog along dirt roads in arctic temperatures unimaginable in Brooklyn. His adventure was cut short after only two weeks when the Soviets announced that Finland had signed a treaty to surrender sixteen thousand square miles to Moscow on a long-term basis. Nearly twenty-five thousand Finns had died or were missing, and as many as 200,000 Russian soldiers had been killed.[30]

As he continued to report, now from Stockholm, Burdett received an unexpected opportunity to join Transradio Press, the pioneering broadcast organization modeled after the wire services for newspapers. The service provided voice reports to American broadcasters that could not afford to send their own reporter.[31] Burdett reported from Norway as German troops invaded, ostensibly to protect Norwegian neutrality. He described how the British tried but failed to deliver reinforcements to the Norwegian resistance. He wrote:

> Storlien, Swedish-Norwegian Border (by Telephone to Stockholm), April 25—The British and French forces and their Norwegian allies appear today to be in desperate straits in central Norway. The whole Allied attempt to drive a salient through the Swedish border seems in danger of failure. The next hours may tell whether or not the Allied forces will be retreating and new contingents have to start a drive along the western coast.[32]

His April 1940 account described having to travel in an "ancient American automobile" along one of the last roads not yet cut by German forces.[33] In a graphic and engaging manner he described hitching a ride with a Norwegian army officer when they suddenly heard the drone of German fighter planes in the distance. He wrote: "As Major Hvosleff and I drove along the highway overhead we heard the drone of motors. Quickly, we stopped the car, jumped out and threw ourselves face down in the snowbanks at the side of the road, wondering if those low-flying planes would drop their cargoes of death."[34]

After the German invasion Nazi troops ordered Burdett and other Western journalists to pack their bags. Back in Stockholm, he learned of CBS's decision to replace Betty Wason, who had been fired because network brass felt she sounded "too young and feminine" for war reporting.[35] CBS arranged for Burdett to begin broadcasting from a hotel telephone connected to London, where the network had jury-rigged shortwave transmitters to send the reports back to the United States.[36] Like Edward R. Murrow's reports from London, Burdett's accounts became more dramatic as the war progressed.

When Nazi troops caught up with Burdett in Oslo, they ordered him to leave the country along with journalists from neutral countries, preferring that the world depend on the German-operated DNB news agency for news about the war. Burdett was assigned to Romania, Bulgaria, Turkey, Yugoslavia, and Italy between July 1940 and V-E Day in May 1945, with occasional assignments in Iran and northern Africa. From a listening post in Yugoslavia he reported on riots in northern Italy in January 1941 until the Nazis ordered him to leave.[37] An account by the Associated Press said he was "barred from use of the telephone for seven days and use of the radio indefinitely."[38] From another listening post, this time in Turkey, he confirmed the Nazi attack on the Soviet Union in June 1941, Burdett's first major scoop of the war.[39]

While reporting from Belgrade in 1940, he married Lea Schiavi, an Italian journalist, ardent antifascist, and a suspected Communist whose writings for left-wing journals got her into trouble with government officials.[40] Two years later Schiavi accepted a photography assignment in northern Iran for the New York newspaper *PM* while Burdett traveled to a story in New Delhi. A few days later he learned that she had been killed when border police opened fire on the automobile she had hired for the assignment. Her death attracted wide attention in the U.S. press, although details remained sketchy.[41]

Burdett took several months off to mourn and then resumed his reporting duties, traveling to northern Africa as General Dwight D. Eisenhower took control of Allied troops. On December 16, 1942, Burdett told CBS listeners: "British advance troops are headed down a three-lane highway which Mussolini built from Tripoli and they have been making good time, despite blown-up bridges and mines galore. . . . Where they are tonight I cannot say. I can't report either where Rommel is keeping the African corps, although it is known that Italian troops led the retreat. Our zero-one forces were among the last to pull out."[42]

When V-E Day arrived, he positioned himself in Rome as Allied troops liberated the city.[43] He told radio audiences: "The people of this ancient and still splendid capital have seldom celebrated such a riotous holiday as they did today. The whole city was in the streets, overflowing the great public squares, jamming the long boulevards, laughing, shouting, crying, singing. No one thought to ask how far the Germans had retreated beyond this city. Everyone acted as if the war were over—for the moment. This was indeed a Roman holiday."[44]

Burdett and others who covered the war survived enormous risks. Dozens of correspondents were killed by enemy ambush, helicopter crashes, and jeep collisions. By March 1943 twenty-three journalists had died, including twelve Americans. Three correspondents were missing, sixty wounded or injured, and nineteen were being held by German forces.[45] After the war Burdett returned to the United States and worked at the CBS radio affiliate in Washington, D.C., until CBS sent him back to Europe in 1948. From the network's Rome bureau he covered Central Europe and the Vatican, building upon his reputation as a talented and intense reporter who had captivated radio audiences during the war.[46] Sig Mickelson, the first head of television news at CBS, described Burdett as one of the network's most respected correspondents.[47] Correspondent Marvin Kalb said, "He had a gift for explaining complicated issues in elegant language."[48] Richard C. Hottelet, a colleague on the Murrow team, remembered Burdett as "a very good reporter who spoke beautifully."[49] Walter Cronkite said, "He knew his territory better than anybody I've ever been associated with."[50] But others privately described Burdett as an aloof and mysterious man who projected an unidentifiable sense that he might be hiding something.[51]

Coming Clean

At his desk in Rome Burdett received a routine envelope from CBS in the spring of 1951. Inside he found an anti-Communist affidavit that, two months earlier, CBS had distributed to all its employees, asking them to sign. The document posed a particularly troubling dilemma for Burdett, who faced the prospect of having to reveal a past he wished to forget. After mulling for several days, he began to complete the questionnaire and acknowledged to CBS for the first time that he had been a member of the Communist Party during the late 1930s while he worked at the *Eagle*. The document landed like a bombshell at network headquarters in New York. Distressed executives ordered him back to the United States to discuss it. Burdett gave every assurance that his break from the party in the 1940s had been complete and final.[52] Several colleagues, including Charles Collingwood, Eric Sevareid, and Edward R. Murrow, who had become a CBS vice president, rallied to Burdett's defense. Murrow convinced the network to retain Burdett, provided Burdett was willing to made a full disclosure to the FBI.[53]

Five months later, on August 31, 1951, Burdett sent a letter to J. Edgar Hoover and attached a copy of the affidavit. "I feel it my duty and my inclination to send you the two documents which I have enclosed," he said. "I shall, of course, be ready to answer any questions you may have regarding the circumstances, if that is required."[54] The disclosure did not come as a complete surprise because Burdett's name had come up during the FBI's 1945 interrogation of Elizabeth Bentley, the Communist defector who had helped operate a Russian spy network during World War II. The FBI noted that Bentley recalled during interviews in the late 1940s that she had received a cable from Burdett signaling that he was in Stockholm, but she could provide only sketchy details.[55] Burdett's name also turned up in 1942 report at the Office of Naval Intelligence—which had been collecting all sorts of information since the Pearl Harbor debacle a year earlier—when an informant described him as "a supporter of the Communist leadership of the New York Newspaper Guild." The source described him as "either a Party member or a close sympathizer." In 1946 an investigation of a Soviet espionage ring in Canada turned up Burdett's name, along with his parents' address, in a notebook belonging to a Russian agent who had eluded Canadian authorities in 1945. While Burdett was working in Rome, the FBI never questioned him.[56]

With Burdett's signed affidavit in hand, Hoover initiated a preliminary investigation, assigning agents to watch Burdett's mail, canvass informants for additional information, check his bank records, review his passport records, examine his voting records, and monitor his newscasts on CBS.[57] Hoover directed the New York field office to interview Burdett "exhaustively," which led to a series of meetings in which Burdett repeated the assertions he had made to CBS, that he had joined the Communist Party in the summer of 1937 while he worked at the *Eagle*. As he had told CBS, he said he became disillusioned in January 1940 and dropped out of the party before he left for Europe. As a sign of his break from the party, he gave the FBI the names of twelve former colleagues at the *Eagle* who were also party members; the list included the names of some of his closest friends. The FBI assured Burdett that he would not be identified as the source. One agent described him as "extremely cooperative at all times."[58]

A Change of Tune

In October 1951, almost one month after his initial FBI interview, Burdett informed the agency that some of his previous statements were false. He said he had dropped out of the party in February 1940, not before leaving the country, as he stated earlier. He also gave a more detailed account of his enlistment in the party's ranks and named Nat Einhorn, the head of the New York Newspaper Guild, as his initial contact. He said Einhorn had introduced him to another guild member, Joe North, editor of the Communist journal *New Masses,* and to a mysterious third man who met with Burdett at a series of street-corner meetings and later provided money for his steamship ticket to Europe. He said the man instructed him to contact a New York woman (he could not recall Elizabeth Bentley's name) after he reached Stockholm.[59] The man also asked for a photograph, a biographical sketch, and his Communist Party membership card, a standard KGB practice for screening potential recruits.[60]

Records of the Communist International, which are housed in the Soviet archives in Moscow, confirm long-held suspicions that Soviet Intelligence relied on the Communist Party U.S.A. to recruit of hundreds of Americans into Soviet espionage during the late 1930s and early 1940s. (The Communist International, also called Comintern, was the Moscow-based organization that coordinated Communist parties worldwide from 1939 through 1943.) The documents, opened to Western researchers in the early 1990s, reveal that Russian intelligence targeted journalists to gather information that lay beyond the reach of the average person.[61] The documents also support Bentley's claims in 1945 that the party maintained "lookouts" to identify individuals suitable for espionage work—including Joe North, whom she described as a primary recruiter at the guild.[62]

The archives also make it clear that the party enlisted Americans to carry out clandestine activities in Europe during the war.[63] Comintern records show that Moscow officials were particularly interested in journalists. "We ask you to select two comrades with good bourgeois references as salesmen or journalists of a solid bourgeois newspaper who will be able to live in Europe and to move from one country to the other," read a September 13, 1939, cable from "Brother," the code name used by George Dimitrov, then head of the Comintern, to party leaders in the United States. "They have to go to Stockholm and wait there for our instructions. When arriving in Stockholm they have to send to me a post card indicating only their hotel. This comrade you have to choose from the best—that they will be able to assure our communication."[64] The cable echoed the account that Burdett gave the FBI, suggesting that he had been targeted for recruitment in the late 1930s. A second target may have been Peter Rhodes, a reporter who covered World War II for United Press, although the second reporter's identity is not clear. The FBI observed meetings between Rhodes and Soviet agents in 1941, but he denied any involvement with Soviet intelligence during an FBI interview six years later.[65]

Burdett was far more forthcoming than Rhodes, agreeing to provide detailed descriptions of his espionage activities. He said he met with a man who came to his Stockholm hotel room in 1940 and identified himself as "Miller." Miller instructed Burdett to travel to Finland to monitor public morale as the Russians attacked. At a later meeting, Burdett said, Miller told him to travel to Moscow, where he would be contacted by intelligence officials. He would then travel to Romania for another clandestine rendezvous. But Burdett said that when he attempted to contact the Russian consulate, as he had been instructed, he received no response before CBS sent him to Yugoslavia. After he arrived in Belgrade, he said, he was directed to a tram stop to locate his contact, who would be carrying one glove. At the rendezvous site a man fitting that description called to Burdett by name and, after a brief conversation, instructed him to introduce himself to several officials at the Yugoslavian Ministry and report back a week later, Burdett said. The reporter said he never carried out the assignment and later admitted he had bungled it by going to the wrong address.[66]

Although Burdett's affidavit says he dropped out of the party in 1940, he told the FBI that he met with a Soviet operative in Belgrade a year later and informed his contact that he no longer wanted to conduct espionage activities. He said he repeated his decision to a second contact in Ankara. He assured the FBI he had had no further contact with the party or any party members since March 1941 and insisted that neither CBS nor the *Eagle* had been aware that he was also working for the Soviets.[67] Between September 1951 and July 1953 the FBI conducted seven interviews with Burdett. During one session he referred to party membership as a logical extension of his interest in the Newspaper Guild. "Active participation in the guild's activities at the Brooklyn Daily Eagle and membership in the CP were synonymous," he said. He also gave additional details of his wife's death in 1942. "It has always been a mystery to me as to why my wife was killed, inasmuch as robbery was apparently not the motive involved and no other person in her party of five was injured," he told the FBI. "I first suspected that pro-Fascist Italians in Iran had been responsible for her death, due to the fact that she had been an outspoken and active anti-Fascist." He claimed the Russian military had her assassinated after she stumbled upon a secret Russian training base.[68]

FBI records give no indication that the government made any attempt to substantiate Burdett's account or his innocuous assessment of his espionage work. However, the FBI considered charging him with espionage and contacted lawyers at the Justice Department for an opinion. After studying the transcript, government lawyers determined that it was unclear whether Burdett had violated any federal law since his activities were conducted on foreign soil and there was no evidence that he had spied against the United States. Given the ambiguity of the circumstances, the FBI closed the case.[69]

More to the Story

The FBI's interest in Burdett might have ended in late 1953 except for an assignment that he received from CBS to cover a story in Paris. When he submitted an application to renew his passport, a passport examiner at the State Department stumbled onto his disclosures to the FBI. Secretary of State Dean Acheson had vowed a year earlier to deny a passport to any person "whose activities, either at home or abroad, promote the interests of a foreign country or political faction . . . to the detriment of the United States or of friendly foreign countries."[70] One of the most dramatic examples involved singer-actor Paul Robeson, who had commented in 1949 that if the United States went to war with the Soviet Union, American blacks would not be obligated to fight. By revoking his passport, the government prevented him from performing at a mine workers' convention in Canada.[71] Playwright Arthur Miller faced similar problems in 1953 when the Passport Office prevented him from attending the Brussels premier of *The Crucible* and later blocked his planned honeymoon with Marilyn Monroe in London. Miller had no Communist past to deny, but he had made the mistake of lending his name to a host of progressive causes during the 1930s, which made him suspect in the McCarthy era.[72] In Burdett's case passport officials were concerned that the journalist had not sufficiently purged himself because he had kept his party activities secret until 1951, when he contacted the FBI.[73]

Essentially grounded while the government held his travel documents in limbo, Burdett met with State Department representatives in June 1954 for two-and-a-half hours. The officials informed him that his story sounded "incomplete" and asked him to reiterate his story in a sworn statement.[74] "I think that a careful investigation should be made of the banking activities of Mr. Burdett and his father prior to and during his stay abroad with a view to ascertaining whether he told us the truth," an examiner wrote in a summary report. "I also think that his connection with [name deleted] and the Transradio Press and the Columbia Broadcasting in 1940, 1941, and 1942 should be investigated." The examiner questioned whether CBS and the *Eagle* had kept Burdett on their payrolls "to cover for his espionage activities."[75]

Burdett submitted a sworn affidavit two weeks later, hoping to resolve the deadlock. "The fact is that working and residing abroad, far from the American scene, I did not fully appreciate how the question presented itself in my own country," he said. "I came to this appreciation much more rapidly once I had returned home. I came to see my personal situation in the light of the larger political situation, and consequently to see my personal duty to face the facts and to report them to the proper authorities."[76] Rather than allay the government's concerns, however, the document raised more suspicions. "There seems to be a discrepancy in the date of Burdett's final break with the Communists," observed an official at the FBI. "A review of the Bureau files and Burdett's signed statement reflects that the Bureau has not been advised heretofore of Burdett's contact with a female Soviet official in Turkey in February or March, 1942."[77]

Burdett contacted the FBI again in March 1955 and requested another meeting to "correct and amplify" his previous statements.[78] In another interview he told the FBI he was "personally embarrassed" and "professionally ashamed" that he had not fully disclosed his involvement in Communist and Soviet matters. He admitted for the first time that his celebrated career as a foreign correspondent had begun at the behest of party members, who not only suggested that he report on the war but furnished his steamship ticket.[79] The FBI questioned him at four more sessions, culminating in a signed statement in which he described various contacts with Soviet agents between 1940 and 1942, including two in New York City and six abroad. He said that in 1942, while working for CBS News, he furnished reports to Soviet intelligence for five months until he announced to Soviet agents that he was quitting. "When I consider what I now think and feel about the Communist Party and all its works, and then remember that I was a Communist Party member and as deeply involved as I was in Communist Party affairs, I still find it hard to suppress a certain shudder and feeling of guilt and shame," he said.[80]

Although he had come clean with the FBI, Burdett had not given a complete account to CBS.[81] When the network began to reduce his broadcast appearances in early 1955, he feared he would soon be fired. In fact, CBS had decided to fire him until an executive who knew none of the specifics derailed the plan when he questioned the logic of firing one of the most effective correspondents on the network's roster.[82] Finding himself cornered by the conflicting accounts he had given the FBI, Burdett turned to Morris Ernst, a long-time anti-Communist activist and New York attorney who served as CBS's general counsel. Ernst had spearheaded a drive in the 1930s to oust former Communists from the rolls of the ACLU. He also served as a government informant and maintained a close personal relationship with J. Edgar Hoover.[83] Moreover, Ernst had been a close personal friend of Heywood Broun's during the 1930s and had served as an unpaid legal counsel to the newly formed Newspaper Guild but withdrew when he concluded that Communists had taken control.[84]

When Ernst met with Burdett in 1955, he expressed his concern that his firm's association with CBS might pose a conflict of interest and referred the reporter to New York Municipal Judge Robert Morris, the ardent anti-Communist who had served as counsel to the Senate Internal Security Subcommittee and counseled Clayton Knowles a year earlier.[85] Burdett's contact with Morris linked him with a thriving anti-Communist network that had worked behind the scenes for many years to cripple the Communist Party, helping to transform domestic communism into a dominant political issue.

Morris urged Burdett to clear himself of suspicion by testifying before the Eastland committee and arranged for a subpoena for him to address the committee at a closed session in October 1954. When CBS learned of the plan, network lawyers quickly had the subpoena quashed. Morris warned network officials on Burdett's behalf that they would find themselves in an untenable position if they fired a man who was attempting to come clean before a congressional subcommittee.[86] "Individuals who come forward and make a full disclosure should not be penalized," Morris argued. An FBI memorandum indicates that this information came from Daniel O'Shea, the CBS vice president of security whom the network had hired in 1950 to implement and oversee its loyalty questionnaire.[87]

Faced with a passport entanglement that threatened to end his illustrious career as a foreign correspondent, Burdett informed CBS that he wanted to testify publicly as a sign of his break with the past and his loyalty to the United States. Top executives warned that any public airing that embarrassed the network would result in his dismissal. CBS may have been particularly sensitive to possible repercussions following Edward R. Murrow's tough criticisms of Sen. Joseph McCarthy during a segment of "See It Now" a few months earlier. Murrow's strong denunciation of the senator trod dangerously close to CBS Chairman William Paley's proscription against editorializing and produced tension between the two men that ultimately prompted Murrow to leave the network.[88] Wary that Burdett's predicament might fuel additional criticism that the network was soft on communism, Daniel O'Shea, a CBS vice president, suggested that Burdett consider disclosing his story in a magazine article or a book, where it might attract less public attention.[89]

The FBI, however, welcomed an opportunity for Burdett to put his story on the record, even if it took place behind closed doors. "Burdett still is contemplating appearing before the Senate Internal Security Committee and making a full and complete disclosure in a public hearing," Louis B. Nichols, an assistant FBI director, told Hoover's assistant, Clyde Tolson. Nichols recognized that the ramifications extended beyond CBS and would place considerable pressure on the Newspaper Guild. "[Name deleted] feels this will do a great deal of good and bolster Elizabeth Bentley's spy role in the newspaper guild and put the Indian sign on some of the current big shots at the guild," he wrote.[90] Putting an Indian sign on someone was tantamount to putting a hex or curse on the person through some form of witchcraft.[91]

The following week Burdett testified at a closed session of the committee, essentially repeating the story he had told the FBI incrementally between 1951 and 1954. "Burdett makes a very effective witness," wrote Nichols. "I think the Domestic Intelligence Division should promptly review our files on the individuals named as the Internal Security Subcommittee is going to call all of them in Executive Session with the hopes that they can develop sufficient information on those who deny Communist Party activities to lay the foundation for perjury cases."[92] Four months later arrangements were in place for Burdett to tell his story again, this time in a setting where it would gain maximum public exposure.[93] The remaining questions were whether it would resolve his passport problem and whether CBS would support him.

CHAPTER SEVEN

The Investigation

WINSTON BURDETT sat confidently before the Senate Internal Security Subcommittee in late June 1955 as a battery of photographers and reporters scrambled into position to snap pictures and listen to his testimony. The cavernous chamber had been the setting for many of Joseph McCarthy's most spectacular sessions, including the army investigation a year earlier that had precipitated the downfall of the man who had come to personify anticommunism. Unlike many people called to testify before McCarthy's and the other Red-hunting committees, Burdett exuded confidence and composure. *Time* described the CBS correspondent as looking "poised, precise, prissy."[1]

Among the spectators sat a dozen men and women who had testified a day earlier at a closed session. They had been called back to be scrutinized in public. The questioning would be led by committee counsel Julien "Jay" Sourwine, a former newspaperman from Reno who became a legislative aide to Sen. Pat McCarran when the Nevada Democrat became chairman of the powerful Senate Judiciary Committee in 1943.[2] The questioning began:

SOURWINE: Were you ever a member of the Communist Party, USA?"
BURDETT: I was. I joined the Communist Party in August of 1937.
SOURWINE: Who recruited you into the Communist Party?
BURDETT: I can't attribute my recruitment to any one individual. There were various persons in the unit of the party at the Brooklyn Eagle whom I knew to be Communists, and whom I knew well as friends and as colleagues.[3]

The first third of Burdett's testimony concerned his work at the *Eagle* and his decision to join the party. Sourwine soon shifted attention to more sensational aspects of Burdett's story.

"Did you ever engage in espionage?" Sourwine asked.

"I did, sir," Burdett replied as he began to spell out his wartime activities in eastern Europe, painting himself as a journalist who was posing as a spy rather than a spy who was posing as a journalist, which the committee did not challenge.[4] As he had to the FBI, he described himself as a bumbling, fumbling operative who satisfied his Soviet handlers with information that was widely available, and he expressed bewilderment that several of his rendezvous with Soviet agents suddenly fell through. He described instances when Soviet contacts failed to respond to his messages and appointments he had missed, including a rendezvous in Belgrade. "It was the second experience of things going up in the air mysteriously and for unexplained reasons," he said.[5]

Burdett's goal was not so much to expose Soviet espionage or betray former colleagues, although he would do both, as to exonerate himself and salvage his broadcasting career. He was prepared to provide much of what the committee wanted to hear, including the names of friends and newsroom colleagues from his early days in journalism:

> I have wished to come before this committee because I felt it my duty to do so in order to discharge what I feel to be a very definite obligation. I was not a casual member. I was a very devoted member. I was young; I was enthusiastic; and I was very earnest. . . . I did not join because of any profound conviction of the truth of Marxist theories; I did not join because of any advance indoctrination. The indoctrination, such as it was, came afterward. I joined, I think, primarily because I was emotionally impelled to identify myself with a larger movement outside myself, a larger cause which I then believed to be a good one.[6]

Burdett demonstrated his patriotism by describing the darkness of communism and described himself misguided:

> The party presents itself as a party interested in democratic and progressive causes. But it is an instrument for the furtherance of the interests of a single power and a totalitarian power. . . . I began to see, when I went abroad, that things did not happen all according to the book which I had learned by rote, back in New York City, and that the Communist Party did not function as an independent Communist Party, and that the Communist Party did function as a tool of a cynical power which used it cynically.[7]

He also described his wife's murder in 1942. "I thought at the time that it must be Italian Fascists," he said, adding that he later learned that she had been assassinated "at the instigation of the Russians."[8]

Committee members asked few questions as Burdett articulated his story in crisp, clear detail that sounded as if he were broadcasting to the world. Toward the end of his appearance he returned to a discussion of his work at the *Eagle* before he went to Finland. He handed the committee twenty-three names. Fourteen belonged to people he had known as members of the party cell at the *Eagle* and nine to people he knew from party meetings in New York City, including several who held leadership posts in the Newspaper Guild.[9] Although the names were known to the FBI, it was Burdett who now made their names public.

"I want to thank you for your testimony and the very fine service you have rendered to your country," said Eastland, who described Burdett's testimony as "a real service" to the nation. "I believe he should be commended for it and encouraged in every way possible. I know that he has some tough times ahead of him, and I earnestly hope that [CBS] will stand by him."[10] The chairman's endorsement took the pressure off CBS. The network issued a statement, saying, "It is our judgment that Mr. Burdett's break with communism was complete and final thirteen years ago and that he has been a loyal and honest citizen ever since." The statement said the network had no intention of firing him.[11]

Burdett had barely left the hearing room before the committee began calling six witnesses whose names were on his list. Those six people learned for the first time in the hearing room that it was Burdett who had named them. All but one invoked the Fifth Amendment and refused to answer questions. Alvah Bessie, the former journalist-turned-screenwriter who had relied on the First Amendment when he was hauled before HUAC in 1947 and later served a jail term, invoked the Fifth Amendment when the Eastland committee questioned him about his earlier career at the *Eagle*.[12] As witnesses brushed aside questions, Sourwine became increasingly agitated. Murray Young, a former *Eagle* reporter, told the committee he had not been a party member in the past decade but would go no further. When he invoked the Fifth Amendment after being asked about a string of names, Sourwine became exasperated.

"Do you know a man named Julius Rollindorfindorfer?" he asked.

Young sat stone faced.

"To the best of my knowledge and belief of counsel there is no such person," Sourwine continued. "It seems to me that the witness was mechanically claiming the [F]ifth [A]mendment without any exercise of judgment and I think we demonstrated that."[13] The tactic was one of several that questioners relied on to force witnesses into compliance or face the possibility of prosecution.

Questions about the Newspaper Guild began to dominate as the hearings progressed. Monroe Stern, former president of the New York Guild, was the only witness willing to answer questions openly.

> SOURWINE: Was the guild Communist-dominated at that time to your knowledge?
>
> STERN: I would not say dominated. I had a feeling that there was a Communist influence, but so far as I recall the activities of these individuals you have named, it was all, so far as appeared on the surface, it was all toward a strengthening of democratic procedures in the guild, getting more and more people in, or getting more and more people to meetings to participate in discussions.
>
> SOURWINE: Did you, sir, make any arrangement, agreement or arrive at any understanding with the Communist faction in the guild with respect to their support of your candidacy for office in the guild?
>
> STERN: No, sir, none that I recall.[14]

News coverage predictably focused on Burdett. "CBS Newsman Says He Was a Soviet Spy," the *New York Herald Tribune* reported. "Wife Murdered after He Quit," said Hearst's *New York Daily Mirror*. "I Spied for Reds: CBS Aid [*sic*]," bannered the conservative *Chicago Tribune*. Transcripts of the testimony accompanied the news accounts in the more moderate *Washington Post, New York Times,* and *New York Herald Tribune*. Conservative columnists predictably praised Burdett's candor. David Lawrence, the publisher of *U.S. News and World Report* and a syndicated newspaper columnist, said, "A true American has performed a great service to the crusade against Communism."[15]

Times publisher Arthur Hays Sulzberger was jubilant when he learned that the committee had not implicated his newspaper. "I found very pleasant reading in The Times this morning in the listing of some good old Guild names which have come into the Washington spotlight," he said. "I couldn't have believed it."[16] The animosity between Sulzberger and the guild was no secret. Although the newspaper had supported the unionization of printers years earlier, unionized editorial workers raised serious concerns that they would "undermine impartiality on which the paper's reputation was based."[17] Sulzberger steadfastly refused to recognize the guild during the 1930s as it organized other city newspapers.

Meanwhile guild officials reacted to the hearings defensively, pointing out that Communist leadership had been purged from both the national guild and the New York Newspaper Guild. "That was nearly fifteen years ago, and a year before Burdett himself—by his own admission—broke with the Communist Party," it said.[18] The New York Guild checked membership rolls and told reporters that "none of the individuals named as employees of The Brooklyn Eagle have worked for that paper in a number of years and consequently had no voice in Guild affairs in the unit or local."[19]

The Hearings: Day Two

The second day brought six more witnesses from Burdett's list and focused even more intently on the guild. Five people invoked the Fifth Amendment and refused to answer questions linking the guild to the Communist Party. Charles Grutzner, a reporter at the *Eagle* who had joined the *New York Times* in 1934, was the only one who spoke openly by admitting that he had belonged to the party for three years before he dropped out in 1940. He had been warned by *Times* officials that he would jeopardize his job if he refused to respond openly.[20] "I hope you will understand that my membership in the party was not the dedicated, emotional sort of thing that Mr. Burdett testified about yesterday," he said. "I could take my communism and I could leave it, and I left it when I was fed up with it."[21]

"Did you know that General Craigie recommended that you be removed from the Korean theater for giving classified information to the enemy?" asked Eastland, referring to dispatches Grutzner had filed from the Korean War zone. The senator was attempting to use Grutzner to show Communist influence on newspaper content. The ploy brought a strong rejoinder from James Wechsler, the *New York Post* editor who had been grilled by Senator McCarthy two years earlier. "Are newspapermen now to be put on notice that they may one day be called to account before Congressional committees for honestly reporting the sins as well as the triumphs of U.S. soldiers?" Wechsler wrote.[22] But Grutzner maintained that each of his articles was cleared through proper channels at the Defense Department and that none of his stories contained classified information.[23] The Pentagon later supported his account, to the embarrassment of Eastland. "It would appear that The Times did nothing to violate security," the senator told reporters the next day.[24]

In the meantime the guild learned that more hearings were scheduled and complained to Eastland that the hearings were leaving "the totally false impression" that the guild was riddled with Communists. "Attempts being made by the press to tie today's policies to those prior to 1941 are malicious and do great damage," said a guild statement. The union offered to provide a witness to "clear the record."[25] Eastland welcomed the prospect of hearing from a representative of the guild but denied that the committee was investigating the union. "We are investigating communism," he said, echoing J. Edgar Hoover's admonition to his agents during the 1940s. "The subcommittee has made no charges against nor cast any slurs upon the American Newspaper Guild," Eastland added. Guild officials quickly backed down. "It is evident what false impressions remain, and there should be none, are certainly not attributable to your committee," they said. "Your telegram . . . makes it entirely unnecessary for us to make use of your generous offer to permit us to testify."[26]

Trouble Ahead

When the hearings resumed in mid-July, David Gordon, a reporter at the *Eagle* who later joined the *New York Daily News,* captured the greatest attention.

"While you were on the Brooklyn Eagle were you a member of the Communist Party?" Sourwine asked.

"I am not a Communist and have not been in any way for the past twelve years," Gordon told the committee. He refused to confirm that he was responsible for a Communist Party "shop paper" at the *Eagle.*

> SOURWINE: Were you a member of the New York Newspaper Guild?"
> GORDON: Yes, sir.
> SOURWINE: Did you hold office in that Guild?
> GORDON: No, sir.
> SOURWINE: Were you a Communist while you were a member of the New York Newspaper Guild?
> GORDON: I decline to answer on the ground that it may tend to incriminate me.[27]

The committee later heard from Melvin Barnet, a former *Eagle* reporter who had become a copy editor at the *Times* in 1953. Copy editors may have held greater concern for the committee than reporters because they are the last editors to read a story before the presses start to run. Because of their positions copy editors held even greater power over the content of newspapers than the bylined writers. Barnet learned from radio news reports that Burdett had named him as a Communist. The two had been friends since the early 1930s when they attended Harvard and shared a small apartment. Burdett had served as best man at Barnet's 1938 wedding.[28] The FBI had known of Barnet since the 1940s when it obtained subscription lists for the *National Guardian,* a newspaper the bureau considered "a virtual official propaganda arm of Soviet Russia."[29] The bureau then placed Barnet on its "Detention Index" of individuals who could be detained in the event of a national emergency.[30]

After hearing the news reports Barnet met with editors in a small conference room just off the *Times*'s newsroom. He explained that he was not a Communist and had not been a party member while he worked at the *Times.* Newspaper executives informed him that his response would not satisfy the publisher and might jeopardize his job.[31] "My lawyer told me that my only choices were the Fifth Amendment or go to jail," he later said.[32]

When he was called to testify in July 1955, no one knew how he would respond. "Were you a member of the Communist unit on the Brooklyn Eagle?" Sourwine asked.

"Since February or March of 1942, sir, I have not been a Communist," said Barnet. "As to the time prior to that, I assert my privilege under the Fifth Amendment."[33] In an interview many years later Barnet said that when he was asked that question, uppermost in his mind was that Sulzberger was on record as saying the *Times* didn't fire people.[34] In a 1953 speech Sulzberger had endorsed a qualified "political amnesty" for "persons who had joined Communist fronts but had clearly dissociated themselves before the Berlin Airlift in 1948." Sulzberger also said that while he "would not knowingly employ anyone who is presently a Communist on the news or editorial staff," he would not permit a witch hunt in the *Times* newsroom. "I must take the risks of determining this soundness in my own organization and be prepared to take the consequences of any false evaluation that I may make," said Sulzberger.[35] But now the *Times* was in a difficult position. It recognized that one of its newsroom employees had refused to cooperate with a congressional investigative committee, and no one could predict how the public might respond.

As Barnet continued to invoke the Fifth Amendment, Sourwine tried to outwit him. "Do you know Leonard Boudin?" he asked, referring to the well-known civil liberties attorney who had accompanied Barnet to the hearing. Boudin quickly leaped into the exchange, although lawyers were cautioned against becoming actively involved in congressional hearings, unlike court cases.

"I am asking you to tell counsel not to behave that way," Boudin told Eastland.[36] Sourwine then turned to Barnet's relationship with the *Times*, implying that the newspaper coddled known Communists on its news staff.

> SOURWINE: Were you told that if you took the Fifth Amendment here you would be discharged?
> BARNET: I was not so told.[37]

At the end of the hearing a *Times* official directed Barnet to the newspaper's Washington office, where a message was waiting for him.[38] When he arrived, a secretary handed him a letter from Sulzberger that advised Barnet that his "course of conduct" was unacceptable. The *Times* had lost confidence in him, Sulzberger explained. "Accordingly, this will serve as notice of termination of your employment," he wrote.[39] The next day the *Daily News* followed Sulzberger's example and fired David Gordon. "Your conduct as a witness . . . together with other disclosures and circumstances regarding alleged Communist activities, has destroyed your usefulness to 'The News,'" said the executive editor.[40]

Meanwhile the hearings continued as the committee called Ira Freeman, a veteran reporter who had joined the *Times* in 1928 and became a charter member of the Newspaper Guild when it was founded five years later. Freeman said he was recruited into the newspaper unit of the Communist Party in 1937 by Milton Kaufman, the executive secretary of the New York Newspaper Guild, and an unidentified second man. "They talked earnestly with us about joining the Communist Party which, they said, was by far the leading influence in the New York Newspaper guild," he said. "I was a charter member in the guild and willing to get any help I could. That was my primary consideration in considering party membership."[41] Freeman expressed surprise to find only one other person from the *Times* at his first meeting. "There was certainly no one at that meeting from the editorial department except myself," he said, telling the committee that only about a dozen people had joined the unit, including spouses and friends, out of a total workforce of about five thousand employees. After finding the party's demands intolerable, he said he dropped out after attending a half-dozen meetings. "The whole thing seemed to me to be inept and futile," he said. "Far from helping me in the organization of the guild, actually, it hampered me."[42]

Crisis for the Newspaper Guild

After Freeman's appearance, attention shifted back to Melvin Barnet as he pressed his colleagues for help in taking his firing to arbitration. Sulzberger grew increasingly concerned that an adverse decision would force the *Times* to reinstate Barnet. "What happens if the judgment is against us and if the arbitrator says that Barnet must be returned and WE REFUSE TO RE-EMPLOY HIM?" he asked the *Times's* attorney.[43] Sulzberger seemingly had little to worry about because the *Times* grievance committee refused to support Barnet, arguing that he had misused the Fifth Amendment to avoid incriminating others, not to protect himself. "The Grievance Committee believes that every loyal American should cooperate with authorized Government agencies investigating Communism and . . . that Barnet's use of the Fifth Amendment showed an indifference to the best welfare of the country," it said.[44]

Another setback came when the New York Guild put the question to a citywide referendum of the membership and the result was overwhelming against him.[45] The rejections from the guild were particularly demoralizing for a man who since the 1930s had considered organized labor the salvation of working people. He had been a loyal guild member for twenty-one years, since 1936 when he joined the *Eagle* at a meager $15 a week. He had served his country during World War II and received the American Service Medal, Asiatic-Pacific Service Medal, Good Conduct Medal, and the World War II Victory Medal.[46]

Desperate to have his case heard, he distributed a two-page, single-spaced letter to the more than one thousand guild members at the *Times*. "No valid charge can be made against me of lack of candor with The Times," he said. "It was simply my assertion of Constitutional privilege that cost me my job."[47] Recognizing the dangerous precedent that Barnet's firing created, the executive committee of the New York Guild voted to over-rule the referendum, choosing to interpret it as a "non-binding recommendation."[48] But complications arose in March 1956 when a New York court reversed the reinstatement of Theodore Polumbaum, the reporter who had been fired by United Press after he answered questions before HUAC in 1953.[49] Although the decision seemingly helped Barnet, it only complicated his predicament after a New York court ruled that his dismissal was subject to arbitration. The *Times* objected to the ruling because the *Times* unit of the guild had rejected Barnet's arbitration request, only to be overruled by the guild. The *Times* then sued the guild, triggering a cat-and-mouse skirmish between the union and the powerful newspaper.

After a series of backroom meetings the two sides agreed in February 1957 to an arrangement whereby the *Times* would drop its suit against the guild provided the guild dropped its support of Barnet, David Gordon, and William Price. The agreement served other journalists with notice that the guild could do little to help them if they refused to cooperate with an investigative committee.[50]

More Trouble for the *Times*

As the legal battle over Barnet played out, the *Times* was rife with rumors that the Eastland committee would call more journalists to testify. An anonymous letter in October 1955 questioned the patriotism of one of the newspaper's brightest stars. "You are about to step into a hole," it said. "Up to 1948 Joan Linda Rannells was a leader in a Communist Party cell on the campus of Cornell University at Ithaca, New York. At least three official agencies of government know this."[51] Rannells was married to *Times* reporter Anthony Lewis, who had won a Pulitzer Prize in 1954 for his stories in the *Washington Daily News* that exposed the injustices of the federal loyalty oath. Lewis suspected the letter came from McCarthy aide Roy Cohn, who had been a close friend when they were classmates at New York's Horace Mann School for Boys.[52]

James Reston, chief of the Washington bureau, quickly jumped to Lewis's defense. "This is an old story here, and it is true," he told Turner Catledge, the managing editor. "It was known when he originally joined the Sunday Department, and, as a matter of fact, he brought it up himself with me when I talked to him about joining the Washington Bureau over a decade ago."[53] The *Times* never questioned Lewis about his patriotism; however, Sulzberger considered questioning the loyalty of applicants for positions in "sensitive" positions in the newsroom, but the newspaper stopped short of instituting a formal questionnaire like the one adopted in 1950 by CBS.[54] Meanwhile, uncertainty hung over the newsroom until early November, when a Senate clerk arrived with a stack of subpoenas.[55] FBI files show that a week earlier Sourwine had contacted the FBI for "brief summaries" about more than twenty individuals believed to be connected with the *Times*. According to the records, Louis Nichols, the assistant director of the FBI, provided several "succinct resumes" that described *Times* employees' activities in the Newspaper Guild and the Communist Party.[56]

Times officials politely escorted the clerk throughout the building as he delivered the subpoenas to staffers whose names appeared on the envelopes, sending a chill across the entire newsroom. "Members of the staff were more concerned about how The Times management would support its own staff," recalled *Times* reporter Herbert Mitgang.[57] In one case the clerk discovered that there was no "Willard Shelton" at the *Times*. "Well, do you have anybody named Shelton?" he asked, prompting someone to mention the name of Robert Shelton. *Times* officials watched in amazement as the clerk scratched through *Willard* and wrote in *Robert*.[58] Another surprise came when the entourage arrived at the foreign desk with a subpoena for Jack Shafer and found him editing a dispatch from the paper's Moscow bureau.[59]

"There were two professional patriots on the staff [including one] who was said to report regularly to the FBI," Alden Whitman said many years later. "I assume there was a carry over from the Herald-Tribune, where I was indeed active on the union grievance committee. And it was very well known in the Guild that I sat in the left bench."[60] Whitman, then a copy editor, explained to the newspaper's lawyers that there may have been "some activities in his past that would excite the curiosity of the committee if they knew about them."[61] Seymour Peck, an editor in the Sunday section, thought he had escaped notice when the committee failed to call him during the summer. "I remember I had been terribly outspoken one day at lunch with a man on the Times about how terrible I thought the Eastland committee was," he said later. "After I got the subpoena, I thought: well, he must have gone to the FBI."[62]

Times attorney Louis Loeb met with each subpoenaed person privately, in sessions that have been described as emotional and "sometimes painful."[63] Whitman acknowledged that he had belonged to the party from 1935 until 1949. Music critic Robert Shelton explained that he had joined while he was a student at Northwestern University, when he worked in the presidential campaign of Henry Wallace, who was accused of being soft on communism; Shelton's history was in the FBI files, but the *Times* did not insist that he disclose the information publicly.[64] Herbert French concluded that he had been listed as Red after a guild election in the late 1940s when the Communist faction supported his candidacy for office.[65] Jack Shafer said he had joined the party in 1940 but dropped out a year later, then reactivated his membership in 1946. He said he dropped out again in 1949 before joining the *Times*.[66] The paper's executives found Shafer's indecisiveness disturbing. When he said that he would invoke the Fifth Amendment, the *Times* fired him.[67] The newspaper took similar action against Nathan Aleskovsky, an assistant editor of the *Book Review* since 1949.[68] Book reviews were a sensitive topic among anti-Communists, who saw them as an accessible platform that radicals and former radicals could use to espouse their views. The FBI considered the *Times* book review section to be "the most heavily infiltrated department" at the newspaper.[69] The situation for Aleskovsky became especially complicated when news executives reviewed his work and determined that he had "let his politics influence his selections of reviewers for books on politics and economics."[70] After he informed the *Times* that he would stand on his constitutional rights before the committee, he gave them what he called a "forced resignation."[71]

Ten of the sixteen argued that they had never belonged to the Communist Party or any other subversive organization. Six acknowledged that they had belonged at some period in their lives.[72] When it became clear that a large number of *Times* employees would be called to the witness table, Sulzberger drafted a statement that could be used if additional employees turned to the Fifth Amendment. It said:

> By this action, in our judgment, he failed to meet the obligations which we feel every member of our news or editorial staff must assume. It is a citizen's right to invoke it when he believes it to be to his interest to do so. What must also be taken into account is the duty of the newspaper imposed on it by the First Amendment. That guarantee of a free press carries with it implicitly the conception of responsibility. Such responsibility demands frankness on the part of the newspaper as well as from all those who are employed in its sensitive departments. A community which assures freedom to its press is entitled to a frank press. In the present instance, frankness was not forthcoming.[73]

John Oakes, a member of the *Times* editorial board and a nephew of Adolph Ochs's, pointed out that the newspaper's personnel policy on the Fifth Amendment contradicted its editorial position. "I still don't see how we can take a position automatically firing Fifth Amendment people and at the same time remain consistent with our own editorial view as expressed as recently as this spring," he said.[74] Similarly, Catledge argued that "a *Times* employee, like any other American citizen, should be free to exercise any constitutional right, including the Fifth Amendment protection against self-incrimination."[75]

The Eastland committee distributed subpoenas in November 1955 to thirty-eight journalists, requiring them to testify at closed hearings to be held in New York and Washington. But the sessions were suddenly postponed when Sourwine realized that the third week of November was Freedom of the Press Week.[76] Publicly, he attributed the postponement to the illness of Senator Eastland, who had contracted influenza.[77] When the hearings were rescheduled for mid-December, syndicated columnist Drew Pearson reported that the session had "all the earmarkings of a McCarthy witch-hunt." He speculated that the investigation was "chiefly aimed at the original members of the Newspaper Guild."[78] The *New York Post* took what may have been the strongest position of any newspaper. "We have never believed that newspapermen can claim any special immunity from the laws of the land," it said. "Surely no one would suggest that a Communist espionage agent should be spared prosecution if he carried a press card. But a line must be drawn when a Congressional inquiry appears primarily designed to harass and discredit a newspaper which has been a consistent critic of the methods and spirit of that committee."[79]

I. F. Stone, a radical from the 1930s who became one of the most dissident voices in American journalism, accused the *Times* of "knuckling under" by urging its employees to cooperate with the committee. "The most effective way to abridge freedom of the press would be to do to newspapers what has already been done by the congressional witch hunters to other businesses and professions," he wrote in his newsletter. "The lists seem to have been compiled in no small part from persons who were active in the Guild, though all kinds of other odd choices have been included, among them several printers."[80] In a daring display of showmanship and gall, Stone took the Eastland committee to court, arguing that its subscription to his newsletter was tantamount to a misappropriation of public money for surveillance of the press. The suit was ultimately dismissed on the ground that the court could not interfere with the legislative functions of Congress.[81]

Meanwhile an anonymous letter circulating among New York newspapers warned that publishers might resort to a blacklist. "We are faced with it as subpoenaed witnesses who also intend to resist the committee's inquiry into our political beliefs, personal lives and associations," the letter said. "We also feel that you may agree with us that such blacklisting is the committee's attempt to control the hiring policies of the publishers and acts, in effect, as a 'prior restraint' on the publishers and a form of censorship that demands political conformity of newsmen and therefore newspapers."[82]

CHAPTER EIGHT

Deeper Trouble

JOURNALISTS WHO WERE CALLED to testify at the Senate Internal Security Subcommittee's closed hearings in December 1955 waited anxiously throughout the Christmas holiday wondering if they would be called to testify in public. On January 3 Drew Pearson confirmed their worst fears with a brief item in his "Washington Merry-Go-Round" column. He reported that the Eastland committee had scheduled another series of public hearings to begin the next day and would focus most of its attention on the *New York Times*. Pearson also noted that most members of the committee did not know about the probe. "This is a situation which would not have occurred even in the heyday of McCarthyism," wrote Pearson. "Senator McCarthy, with all his grandstanding and witch-hunting, would not have dared investigate the world's most respected newspaper without the consent of his own committee."[1] The point raised by Pearson may have seemed inconsequential, but it would later become a critical issue as journalists faced prosecution for having refused to cooperate.

With the bulk of the witnesses coming from the *Times* newsroom—both current and former employees—publisher Arthur Hays Sulzberger and other executives began to suspect that the goal was to embarrass the *Times*. Lester Markel, the Sunday editor, speculated that the inquiry was triggered by the newspaper's unfavorable review of *Seeds of Treason*, a 1950 book by Ralph de Toledano of *Newsweek* and Victor Lasky of the *New York World-Telegram and Sun*, on the perjury conviction of Alger Hiss after his 1948 clash with Rep. Richard Nixon before HUAC.[2] Other editors saw Senator

Eastland's hearings as retribution for the *Times*'s groundbreaking coverage of the fledgling civil rights movement. Sulzberger had hired a black reporter in 1945 as "an experiment" and later hired the first civil rights specialist on a major daily newspaper, George Streator.[3] More recently the newspaper had published an editorial supporting the Supreme Court's landmark decision in *Brown v. Board of Education* (1954) and had repeatedly denounced McCarthyism. The *Times*'s stance infuriated southern conservatives, including Eastland, a conservative Democrat from Mississippi.[4]

News of the new round of hearings prompted the American Civil Liberties Union (ACLU) to voice concern. The liberal organization had been uncharacteristically restrained during the height of the anti-Communist campaign in 1953 and 1954 but began to take a more assertive role in 1955. "We respectfully but vigorously urge that the subcommittee do everything possible to help preserve the principle of free association, by exercising special care in its quest not to invade constitutionally protected areas of private political beliefs," an official said. The organization cautioned newspaper publishers against dismissing employees who invoked the Fifth Amendment. "If newspaper men are dismissed by their papers solely for the invoking of a constitutional right, then newspapers have chipped away at the very structure of freedom which insures their existence."[5] Eastland did not take the criticism lightly and returned rhetorical fire, accusing the ACLU of engaging in "guilt by anticipation."[6] He maintained that it was "vitally important that newspapermen remain free to do their job without a hint of pressure of any kind," particularly "coercion or control by the Communist party," and he argued that newspapers had every right to fire employees who had "lost the confidence of the newspaper's readers, an overwhelming majority of his fellow workers, and his employers" by invoking the Fifth Amendment.[7]

The *Washington Post* editorial cartoonist Herblock took aim at Eastland. It was he who had coined the term *McCarthyism* to describe the blustery tactics that had become a political art for anti-Communists. As the Eastland hearings were about to resume, Herblock depicted the senator throwing bricks at the entrance to the Supreme Court as an aide held his daily schedule. The caption read: "Time for your Investigation of the Press, Senator."[8] It was a pointed jab at Eastland's recent attack on the press, neatly evoking at the same time Eastland's unhappiness with the *Brown* decision.[9]

When the hearings got underway at 10 A.M. on Wednesday, January 4, Eastland pounded his gavel to quiet the gallery of anxious spectators. "The hearings we are about to open stem from sessions . . . in which we heard the testimony of Mr. Winston Mansfield Burdett," he said. The witness list would soon show that none of the scheduled witnesses had been named by Burdett. *New York Times* foreign correspondent Harrison Salisbury later speculated that the names came from "raw unevaluated files of the FBI."[10] In fact, most of the names appeared in FBI files marked "Communist Infiltration into the New York Times." One noted that eighty-three current or former *Times* employees were under investigation or had been investigated in the past. Nine were in the FBI's "Security Index" of individuals to be taken into custody in the event of a national emergency.[11] Ironically, one of the journalists named was Allen Drury, the *Times* Washington reporter assigned to cover the hearings, although Drury did not know that the FBI considered him a suspect as he was never called to testify.[12]

The session began with seven witnesses, all of them linked directly or indirectly to the *Times*. The five who invoked the Fifth Amendment included a proofreader and an indexer who worked in the typographical department. Most attention focused on James Glaser, who worked at the *Times* as a copy editor from 1929 to 1934, and later at the *New York Post*, before becoming the managing editor of the Communist *Daily Worker*. He had cooperated with the committee at a closed hearing and resented that he was now called into an open session to be publicly exposed:

> The closed hearing held about 4 weeks ago convinced me that the sole benefit which could be derived from my presence here today would be to place me on exhibition, to make a sort of public spectacle out of me, because of the dreadful, terrible mistake which I made more than 21 years ago. I have suffered long and bitterly as a result of this terrible mistake. It has been to me a horrible nightmare. And I see no just reason why this committee, two decades later, should open up, rake up, old wounds, and cause me to suffer all over again.[13]

Asked about Communists in the Newspaper Guild, Glaser said he had known some but had not supported the slate of Communist candidates.[14] "For many years I have been active in the drive to rid the New York Newspaper Guild of Communist obstructionists," he said. "It is my firm conviction that what this country sorely needs is implementation of our traditional democratic ideals and a more sober respect by Government bodies for the civil rights of individuals, regardless of race, creed, or national origins. The fungus of communism would wither and die in such a land."[15]

Clayton Knowles, the *Times* reporter who had been targeted by McCarthy two years earlier, was next up. He too questioned why the committee had brought him into a public setting after he had acknowledged his party membership to the FBI, the *Times*, and the Eastland committee in private:

I believe very deeply, sir, that a man's political beliefs are his own, that he has a right to privacy in those matters. I want to state further that in trying to respect that right in others when you are presented with a list of names, the question of free choice no longer remains. I found myself in a very uncomfortable position trying to be a decent, law-abiding, cooperative citizen, because I was confronted with a list of names. . . . I tried to emphasize that I had nothing, nothing, gentlemen, to tell you that would reveal a conspiracy. . . . I joined the Communist party after a rather bitter strike on the Long Island Press. While this and other committee investigations have brought out the story of intrigue, subversion, and conspiracy, I knew of none such; that my activity and the activity of the people I here can testify about was little more . . . than an extension of our work in the founding days of the American Newspaper Guild.[16]

Thomas Hennings, a Democrat from Missouri, quickly rose to Knowles's defense. Hennings was thought to be a conservative and an ardent anti-Communist, but he had been an outspoken critic of the tactics used by McCarthy. "I have known you around here and in your capacity as a reporter for the New York Times and covering a good many hearings, some of which I have participated in myself," he told Knowles. "I have always had the impression that you were an exceedingly accurate, factual, able reporter."[17]

The committee confronted each of the witnesses with questions about the Newspaper Guild. The most intense were put to John McManus, a former head of the national guild and of the New York local. There was plenty in his background to raise suspicions—McManus had helped establish the leftist New York newspaper PM in 1937 and twice ran for governor in the 1950s as a candidate of the radical American Labor Party, an organization whose leadership had been dominated by Communists. A 1952 letterhead identified him as a member of the Committee to Serve Justice in the Rosenberg Case after the couple were charged with leaking atomic secrets to the Russians.[18] But committee counsel Sourwine wanted to know about McManus's support from Communist members of the guild.

SOURWINE: When you ran for president of the New York Newspaper Guild in 1947, did you receive Communist support?

McMANUS: I received the support of a considerable portion of the New York guild membership, and they were the only ones entitled to vote in this election. Whether or not they were Communists is a matter of their own determination, and not mine.

SOURWINE: Did you enter into any negotiations with persons in the guild known to be Communists?

McMANUS: My participation in the leadership of the New York guild
was a part of a whole middle-of-the-road attempt to bring together
warring factions . . . for the achievement of better wages and working
conditions. . . . We did bring together almost all sections of the guild
into one united group which did in the course of those years achieve
giant steps in gains in wages and work conditions. . . . We had no
time, nor did I devote any time or energy in trying to catalog or
otherwise separate . . . my colleagues in the membership of the
Newspaper Guild.[19]

The next morning, January 5, a *Washington Post* editorial warned that
the investigation was "moving in a dangerous direction." While conceding
that journalists possessed no special immunity from having to testify, it
argued that "when they are questioned, as newspapermen, about past
political vagaries which are suspected of having in some way influenced
the editorial policies of their newspapers, the inquiry intimately touches
the press as an institution."[20] Even stronger criticism came from the *New
York Times,* which had remained editorially silent since the investigation
began. Now, with so many witnesses from its newsroom, Sulzberger became
convinced that his paper had been singled out, and his editorial board
responded by accusing the committee of abusing its investigative powers
in order to intimidate the press generally and the *Times* in particular. Written by Charles Merz, the long-time editor of the *Times's* editorial page, the
piece drew from themes struck forty years earlier when a congressional
committee had subpoenaed *Times* editor Charles R. Miller about an editorial that criticized government ownership of merchant vessels.[21] After the
Eastland committee subpoenaed dozens of *Times* employees, the newspaper echoed what it had said in the past. It said:

The Times has been singled out for this attack precisely because of the vigor
of its opposition to many of the things for which Mr. Eastland, his colleague Mr. Jenner and the subcommittee's counsel stand—that is, because
we have condemned segregation in the Southern schools; because we have
challenged the high-handed and abusive methods employed by various
Congressional committees; because we have denounced McCarthyism and
all its works; because we have attacked the narrow and bigoted restrictions
of the McCarran Immigration Act; because we have criticized a "security
system" which conceals the accuser from his victim; because we have
insisted that the true spirit of American democracy demands a scrupulous
respect for the rights of even the lowliest individual and a high standard
of fair play.[22]

Years later Turner Catledge, the managing editor in the 1950s, called it one of Sulzberger's "finest hours."[23] Alden Whitman called it "a real act of courage."[24] The newspaper received nearly five hundred letters of support, including one from former first lady Eleanor Roosevelt, who wrote, "Thank heavens for courage."[25] Newspapers also rallied to the *Times*'s defense. "We don't think the Eastland subcommittee will get anywhere in attempting to lower public confidence of The New York Times," said the *Louisville Courier-Journal*. "The Times editorial . . . is wise, moderate, thoughtful, and rings with the power of truth and right," said the *Milwaukee Journal*.[26] Columnist Murray Kempton, who had belonged to the Communist Party in 1938 but had long since renounced his membership publicly and frequently wrote about his experience, wrote an amusing commentary in the *New York Post*. "Someday a Sunday edition of the *New York Times* is going to fall out of a truck and kill a pedestrian," he said. "And Jim Eastland of Mississippi will know just how the victim feels." The influential *New York Herald Tribune* columnist Walter Lippmann weighed in by describing the hearings as tantamount to congressional oversight of newspaper employment practices and questioned congressional power to censor newspaper employees by calling on them to testify about their pasts. *Editor and Publisher,* the trade magazine of the newspaper industry, objected to the investigation but not on First Amendment grounds, declaring: "If law violators take refuge on a newspaper staff they are not protected by the First Amendment any more than if they were working for a box factory."[27]

On the same morning that the *Times*'s editorial appeared, only Senator Eastland (Kempton called him "a reeky fat man with a cold cigar") and committee counsel Sourwine had arrived at the hearing room by 10 A.M. The session was delayed for three hours until four of the nine members finally took their seats. Kempton noted that one carefully seated himself at the end of the table "apart from the company of the damned."[28] The witness list included only one person from the *Times,* a printer who quickly invoked the Fifth Amendment. The committee then focused its attention on William Price, a police reporter who had begun his career as a copyboy at the *New York Daily News* in 1946 and later served as a navy pilot during the Korean War. When asked if his candidacy for a guild post in 1949 had been supported by Communists, he turned hostile:

I respectfully object to this question on the grounds that it is not within the power and the jurisdiction of this committee to inquire into my political beliefs, my religious beliefs, or any other personal or private affairs and any

associational activities. I further object on the ground that I am a private
citizen engaged in work in the newspaper field. I hold no office of public
honor or trust. I am not employed by any governmental department.[29]

Sourwine next confronted Price about a small airplane he had purchased
in Panama. Sourwine claimed the airplane was linked to a Communist
courier, which Price denied:

> Never any place in the world, any time in my life, have I ever been involved
> in such an activity as suggested here in any way whatsoever at anyone's
> direction, at the direction of any of the organizations as were mentioned in
> the closed hearings, or any such organizations; that anyone who ever flew
> with me was ever engaged in such an activity; that I had knowledge of such
> activity; or that I was ever approached to participate in such activity.[30]

The committee similarly approached Daniel Mahoney, a reporter for
twenty-two years at Hearst's *Daily Mirror.* Mahoney told the committee:

> To suggest that the Mirror might have printed Communist slanted stories
> is ridiculous. Not only am I not a member of the Communist Party, but
> never in my life have I performed a disloyal or subversive act of treason,
> sabotage, or espionage. I have broken no laws beyond the traffic violation.
> I have never advocated defiance [interrupted by Eastland] of the law of the
> Supreme Court of the United States [interrupted by Eastland] or any other
> court of the land.[31]

Sourwine pressed Mahoney about his guild activities, particularly his
candidacy for secretary-treasurer in 1949 on the Communist-supported
slate. Mahoney acknowledged his role in guild affairs but refused to name
members who were thought to be Communists.[32]

Following the session the *Daily News* told Price that his conduct had
destroyed his usefulness.[33] Similarly, the *Mirror* fired Mahoney. "Your course
of conduct has terminated your usefulness," his newspaper said.[34] The New
York Civil Liberties Union (NYCLU) and the New York Newspaper Guild
quickly defended the two. "We believe . . . that it is an unconstitutional invasion of the First Amendment guaranties [*sic*] of belief and expression for a
Congressional committee to interfere with these freedoms by investigating
newspaper men when there is not a showing of danger to our people or our
government from Communist influence in the press," said the NYCLU.[35]
The guild pledged to "evaluate" the firings but showed none of the indignation it had expressed after Barnet's firing five months earlier.

Trouble in the Ranks

On the third day, Friday, January 6, it was clear the *Times* editorial had stirred divisions among the committee members. Senator Hennings complained that the members had not seen a list of prospective witnesses: "The thing that I think perhaps this committee might want to give some attention to is whether [in] calling some witnesses . . . we can be sure that we do not do an injustice and cause undue embarrassment and humiliation to a man who has completely rehabilitated himself, if he has no new or additional information to give this committee." Eastland bristled and offered a lackluster response. "I don't think that the Senator from Missouri will say that it has ever been the chairman's position to try to humiliate or hurt anyone," he said. "We are attempting to conduct these hearings and elicit all the facts."[36] The exchange set the tone for what would be the committee's most dramatic day and became a turning point in the investigation.

Three witnesses, including Nathan Aleskovsky and Jack Shafer, both of whom had been fired by the *Times,* invoked the Fifth Amendment. Three others invoked the free speech guarantee in the First Amendment, one strategy that the Hollywood Ten had used to avoid having to name names and that had landed them in jail. Three other journalists from the *Times* would lay claim to the press protection clause of the First Amendment, rather than the free speech guarantee. Shelton, the copy editor whose name was written on his subpoena at the last minute, was the first on the hot seat.

> SOURWINE: Are you a member of the Communist Party?
> SHELTON: No one who knows me would doubt my loyalty to the Government of the United States; because I am a loyal American, I must, as a matter of principle, challenge questions into my political beliefs and associations as a violation of my rights under the [F]irst [A]mendment to the Constitution.
> SOURWINE: Do you, sir, consider membership in the Communist Party a matter of political belief?[37]

In a series of contentious exchanges Shelton attempted to answer the question as Sourwine and committee members continually interrupted him in an attempt to prevent him from presenting a monologue. But Shelton persevered, expressing his complaints about the hearing and enunciating his defense of the First Amendment rights of journalists:

> This subcommittee is nudging the end of my copy pencil, it is peeking over my shoulder as I work. This subcommittee is engendering the fear that

soon it will be looking into newsrooms all over the country. If, as a result
of my being called here, I am put under mental pressure to change one
word or one sentence in material that I edit, an abridgment of freedom of
the press will have taken place. . . . Your question acts as a form of "prior
restraint" on publishing, telling newspaper executives who should or who
should not work on their staffs. . . . It is my understanding that the [F]irst
[A]mendment is the door to America's freedom of conscience. It is just as
strong and secure a door as that on the house of the chairman in Dodds-
ville, Mississippi. It can be opened at will any time from within; it cannot
be forced open with the wedges of a subpoena, with threats of contempt
citation, or in any other form.[38]

Copy editor Alden Whitman forcefully echoed Shelton when he took
the stand. FBI files identified Whitman in 1941 as a Communist who had
participated in the American Committee for the Protection of Foreign
Born, a Popular Front organization during the 1930s.[39] A December 1953
report from an undercover informant identified Whitman as an influential
Communist.[40] He acknowledged to the Eastland committee that he had
joined the party in the late 1930s and worked for brief period at the Soviet
news agency TASS before joining the *New York Herald Tribune* in 1943. He
said he left the party in 1948, three years before joining the *Times*. When
asked to name party colleagues, he refused. "My private affairs, my beliefs,
my associations, are not, I believe, proper subjects for investigation by this
subcommittee," he said. Whitman questioned whether the hearings were
related to any legislative purpose, an argument that had dominated legal
challenges waged by embattled witnesses before other investigative committees. Sourwine was not swayed by Whitman's bold challenge.[41]

SOURWINE: Do you believe . . . that you as a private individual would
    have a right to associate yourself with a conspiracy to overthrow the
    Government of the United States by force and violence and to claim
    immunity from being investigated in that association?
WHITMAN: I have never been a member of a conspiracy to overthrow
    the Government by force of violence. I have freely admitted, sir, with-
    out taking the immunity provisions of the Fifth Amendment to the
    Constitution, my own membership in the Communist Party. . . .
    I have explained just now that I myself—and that is the only person
    I can speak for—have never to my knowledge taken part in any con-
    spiracy whatsoever.[42]

Seymour Peck, an editor on the *Times*'s Sunday magazine, became the
third to invoke the First Amendment but told the committee he had been a

party member from 1935 to 1949. He said he joined the Young Communist League at age seventeen and remained a member while he worked at the leftist New York newspaper *PM* and its successor, the *New York Star*, where he belonged to a Communist cell of about three or four members.[43] "When I secured my job on PM, after a rather unhappy career of a not very good job in a department store and not very successful home existence," Peck said, "I found quite a new life opening up to me, a fulfillment of my ambitions in the newspaper field, a fulfillment of my personal desires for success, for the respect of the community, and I have devoted myself to this career since 1942."[44]

When asked for names, Peck refused but made no claim to special immunity. "I believe that journalists, like all other citizens, owe an obligation to their Government to give information which may be required in aid of an authorized legislative inquiry," he said. "But the inquiries conducted by congressional committees must bear some reasonable relation to the lawmaking function of Congress," and he suggested that the hearings lay beyond the constitutional powers of Congress.[45]

> SOURWINE: Would you be willing to give the Federal Bureau of Investigation the names of persons you know to have been members of the Communist Party?
>
> PECK: I have no knowledge whatever of sabotage or espionage or any menace or threat to our institutions of Government. So I can't see what information I might have that would be of benefit to the Federal Bureau of Investigation.[46]

Following the session, Eastland and William E. Jenner of Indiana, the ranking Republican on the committee, told reporters that the investigation had disclosed "a significant effort" on the part of Communists to penetrate leading U.S. newspapers, but Eastland and Jenner acknowledged that the committee had been unable to cite a single instance where Communists had influenced editorial content. Eastland said:

> Some witnesses have been frank and have fully and freely given the committee information regarding this effort. They have performed a patriotic service for which we are grateful. Others have sought refuge in claiming privilege under the Fifth Amendment. Others have challenged almost as though by concerted design the jurisdiction of this committee, and have defied the committee's authority. We shall meet this challenge with the full weight of the law.[47]

He said the committee had information that a Communist cell continued to operate in New York City and promised that he was developing a new round of hearings.[48] "We feel confident that the American press will prove fully competent to deal with the problem in its own American way," said Jenner.[49]

Robert G. Spivack, writing in the *New York Post*, said the committee's greatest achievement was showing that the *Daily Worker* was "distinctively under Communist influence."[50] Spivack was the *New York Post*'s Washington bureau chief. In the *New Republic* Gerald W. Johnson, a celebrated North Carolina editorial writer who became a freelance writer and critic in the mid-1940s, castigated Eastland and his colleagues. "The only rational ground for objecting to the presence of Communists in the press, or in the pulpit, or in the movies, or anywhere else is the danger that they may propagate lying arguments in favor of Communism," he said. "But the Eastland committee has not yet presented in evidence one line from the Times that is definitely a Communist lie but which the newspaper presented as truth."[51]

Two weeks after the hearings ended, Sourwine resigned as counsel to return home to Nevada to run for the Senate seat once held by his former boss, Pat McCarran. Eastland replaced Sourwine with Robert Morris, who resigned his post as a New York municipal judge to resume the position he had held on the subcommittee under McCarran. It was unclear whether Sourwine's departure was voluntary or whether he had been ousted by Hennings and others who privately objected to his approach. In a profile of Sourwine *Times* bureau chief James Reston described him as the central strategist of the subcommittee's investigation of the press. According to Reston, Sourwine was the only person who had known about more than fifty subpoenas that the subcommittee had issued to members of the press. Eastland had told Reston that not even he was aware that the hearings had been scheduled. Sourwine insisted, however, that he did nothing without Eastland's approval. The contradiction would become an important factor a year later as the journalists fought prosecution.[52] In the meantime Sulzberger faced an important decision about the fate of the three uncooperative journalists from the *Times*. The issue was essentially the same as it had been six months earlier when he fired Melvin Barnet. The only difference was that Shelton, Whitman, and Peck had invoked the First Amendment rather than the Fifth. Sulzberger wrote a personal note to each; Whitman's said:

> As you are already aware, The Times would have preferred that you answer all such questions frankly. We believe that the grant of freedom of the press found in the First Amendment imposes a responsibility upon newsmen and that in consequence full frankness regarding yourself and your past

associations is called for by virtue of your position as a copyreader in the News Department. We have, however, carefully reviewed the facts with relation to your one-time membership in the Communist Party, and we are prepared to accept your statement that you have now severed all connections with it. This note, therefore, is to advise you that your association with The Times will continue.[53]

According to Catledge, Sulzberger was "coming to recognize that some men, as a matter of individual conscience, felt compelled not to cooperate with the Eastland subcommittee, and he saw that, however much he might disagree with them, he had no right to impose his beliefs on them."[54] In April 1956 the Eastland committee subpoenaed William Goldman, a night editor at Hearst's *New York Daily Mirror*. He told the committee that he was not a party member, but he went no further despite prodding by Robert Morris, the former counsel to the committee who had resigned his judgeship in order to replace Sourwine. Morris claimed the committee had obtained information from an unnamed witness who had named Goldman as a Communist.

MORRIS: There are no charges against you; you are simply being asked about your experiences, as a witness.
GOLDMAN: I must decline to answer that question . . . because I feel that the question is an invasion of my rights as a newspaperman under the [F]irst [A]mendment.
MORRIS: Mr. Chairman, may I have a ruling?
EASTLAND: That is overruled. You are ordered and directed to answer the question.
GOLDMAN: Well, under those circumstances, I must exercise my constitutional rights under the [F]ifth [A]mendment and decline to answer.[55]

Facing certain dismissal by the *Mirror*, Goldman submitted his resignation the next day. In essence, he removed the issue from the hands of the guild. He had been with the newspaper for fourteen years.[56]

A Press Divided

The confrontations left the newspaper industry deeply divided. Not surprisingly, conservative newspapers defended the committee. "The committee's questions did not indicate a purpose to impose standards of its own on newspapers but did serve to remind publishers that there is a standard expected of them by the vast majority of their readers," said the *Chicago Daily Tribune*.[57] Moderate and liberal newspapers that had long defended civil liberties viewed the committee's efforts as an encroachment on responsible journalism. The *Washington Post* went further:

> This is an approach to the press which opens up fascinating, though dangerous, possibilities. It might afford a justification for some other committees of the Senate to investigate selected newspapers in an effort to show such attempts as may be disclosed to influence or subvert them on the part, say, of the China lobby or the public utilities or the National Association of Manufacturers. It is perfectly possible that a reporter here or there has been a member of the Ku Klux Klan or has accepted a subsidy from some special interest group or is secretly working in behalf of a political Party or candidate. Perhaps such persons ought to be weeded out of newspaper staffs. But the responsibility for weeding them out belongs, in the American system, to publishers and editors, not to Congress.[58]

Though powerful voices addressed the complexities, most publishers remained ambivalent. The most telling incident occurred at a 1956 celebration of the contributions of Benjamin Franklin. Richard W. Slocum, president of the American Newspaper Publishers Association, complained of abuses of governmental power but did not include Eastland as an example. "A few publishers view any questioning of newspapermen by Congressional investigators on any civil rights subject as being per se attempted intimidation," he said. "This is a view I do not share, for the press is subject to proper inquiry. It is the manner and motive of the investigators that tell the story."[59] In the early 1930s the publishers had played a major role in defining freedom of the press by fighting a Minnesota gag law that had permitted government officials to suppress publications deemed malicious and scandalous. The irony was that in waging a battle against government intrusion in 1931, publishers had won a landmark Supreme Court decision that, by finding the Minnesota law unconstitutional, set an important precedent against prior restraint.[60] By the 1950s, as the Eastland hearings showed, publishers were more concerned about gaining access to government information than they were about government attempts to intimidate the press.

Newspaper editors proved to be as divided as the publishers were. A *New York Post* survey of nearly two hundred daily newspapers in the nation's largest cities found editorial writers evenly split. Thirty-five criticized the hearings, thirty-three viewed them as justified, and more than one hundred took no editorial stand, including the *New York Herald Tribune* and *World-Telegram and Sun,* two of New York's most vocal Republican papers.[61] Irving Dilliard, editorial director at the *St. Louis Post-Dispatch,* speculated that some editors were so intimidated that they felt safer not commenting.[62] At an editors' convention during the summer of 1956, Dilliard debated Vermont Royster of the *Wall Street Journal.* Dilliard argued that regardless of whether the *New York Times* had been intimidated, the First Amendment issues raised were paramount. Royster, on the other hand, argued that if the press had been intimidated, it was the fault of the newspaper's owner. Royster said:

> We do not have any Constitutional protection against intimidation. I insist that freedom of the press is the right to speak and to publish. It is not violated when we are questioned, when we are criticized, when we are pilloried, when we are exposed even to public ridicule, however difficult for us all those things may be. If we stop speaking for those reasons, then we have not been denied freedom; we have simply yielded it up and thrown it away.[63]

In the meantime the Eastland committee prepared contempt citations against Shelton, Peck, and Whitman at the *Times,* and William Price at the *Daily News.*[64] In September the Senate unanimously approved the citations and forwarded them to a grand jury for indictment. The *Times* reacted cautiously. "We'll ride along with you through the court of last appeal," *Times* attorney Louis Loeb told the three at his newspaper. "If you win somewhere along the line, fine."[65] In the meantime they would be relegated to parts of the paper where they would have no influence over news content. Shelton and Peck wrote entertainment features and reviews, whereas Whitman was reassigned to the obit desk. They understood that if they lost their battles in the courts, they would be fired. Price also understood the ramifications. He had already lost his job and perhaps his career.

CHAPTER NINE

Journalists and the
First Amendment

A FEDERAL GRAND JURY in Washington handed up indictments in the summer of 1956 against Alden Whitman, Seymour Peck, Robert Shelton, and William Price. Each was charged with one count of contempt of Congress for each question he had refused to answer: nineteen counts against Whitman, five against Peck, three against Shelton, and eight against Price.[1] If convicted, they faced a fine of as much as $1,000 and a jail term as long as a year—on each count. Each pleaded not guilty and posted a $1,000 bond. Under the mistaken impression that they could post bond with personal checks, Peck found himself whisked into a jail cell in a scene reminiscent of the Hollywood Ten. "They put me in the high security division, among the most dangerous characters, without any explanation as to why," he recalled. "I had a man above me who was awaiting execution." Peck's apprehensive family called I. F. Stone, who arranged for his bail.[2]

Many lawyers during the 1940s and 1950s shunned such cases for fear of being accused of helping former Communists escape prosecution, but a few were driven by a sense of social justice, no matter the professional risks.[3] Among them was the well-known Washington lawyer Thurman Arnold, who agreed to take Whitman's case. A lawyer in Franklin Roosevelt's Agriculture Department in the mid-1930s, Arnold later headed the Antitrust Division of the Justice Department. By the mid-1950s he had established himself as an effective defender of employees who ran into trouble before loyalty review boards.[4] The noted civil liberties lawyer

Joseph Rauh Jr. agreed to represent Shelton. Rauh was a founder of the fiercely anti-Communist Americans for Democratic Action in 1947, and he was outspoken critic McCarthy's method of punishing and stigmatizing law-abiding citizens.[5] William Price would be represented by Leonard Boudin, a New York civil liberties lawyer whose record of helping people in distress went back to the 1930s. In the early 1950s he had handled some of the most controversial political issues involving witnesses' rights.[6] New York lawyer Telford Taylor took on Seymour Peck. Taylor had built a illustrious career in private practice after serving as a principal prosecutor of Nazi war criminals at Nuremberg following World War II, and he became an outspoken critic of McCarthy during in the 1950s.[7]

Although the journalists managed to enlist an impressive roster of prominent lawyers, they faced potentially staggering legal costs. The New York Civil Liberties Union agreed to underwrite Whitman's because he faced the largest number of charges. The organization also agreed to help Shelton, because his subpoena raised particularly unusual civil liberties questions.[8] The journalists also issued an appeal to their colleagues through a letter published in the newspaper trade magazine *Editor and Publisher.* "The right to skewer a newspaperman for what he has thought in the past, what he thinks now, or what he may think in the future would surely be a big step in the direction of authoritarian journalism wherein the prime test of a newspaperman is his political conformity," it said.[9] They also asked the Newspaper Guild for help. "We feel that in our honest application of the Bill of Rights, combined with other ethical and legal reasons, our refusal to answer certain questions about communism was in the finest American democratic tradition," they said. "We feel that we responded honorably as newspapermen and trade union members who have a duty to resist abuse of Congressional power when face to face with it."[10] The New York Guild sent a terse letter telling them that the board had voted to "table and file" their request.[11] The national guild sent a similar response.[12] Whitman complained that the guild was ignoring important issues involving the First Amendment:

> Can a Congressional committee, on pain of contempt, force a newspaper man to disclose the names of fellow newspaper men (and Guild members) who, at some time in the past, may have shared what are now discredited political opinions? Since disclosures are followed by firings— among other consequences—it is clear that effective press freedom—the right of members of the press to practice their profession without political restrictions—is abridged.[13]

The guild brushed aside Whitman's admonitions and informed him that its lawyers had "found no freedom of the press issue involved in this case."[14]

By late 1956 prospects for the journalists looked bleak, given the history of the legal skirmishes regarding the power of Congress to punish uncooperative witnesses.[15] Congressional authority to conduct investigative hearings had stood virtually unchallenged until the late 1800s when the Supreme Court ruled that committees could not probe into purely "private affairs," which it ruled were within the domain of the judiciary.[16] No significant challenge to this safeguard arose until the late 1920s when the Court required the committees to state a proper legislative purpose for their inquiries. Even so, the restriction left Congress with wide latitude to investigate a broad range of issues, including the activities of the Communist Party and its members.[17]

Civil liberties became a serious concern after HUAC was created in 1938, but witnesses who did not wish to become informers found little protection from the courts in the political atmosphere created by the Cold War. Throughout the late 1940s and early 1950s, judicial reasoning at every level placed national security above individual civil liberties.[18] In the case of John Lawson, one of the Hollywood Ten, a federal appeals court held in 1949 that workers in the "opinion field" were particularly obliged to divulge their political affiliations because their work influenced millions of moviegoers, and the Supreme Court refused to review his conviction.[19]

After the Korean War judicial sentiment began to shift as liberal members of the Supreme Court began to assert witnesses' civil liberties in order to curb congressional witch hunts. Edward Rumely, a leftist publisher who had refused to divulge to an investigative committee the names of his customers, was convicted of contempt of Congress, but the Court overturned his conviction in 1953.[20] But the Court sidestepped the constitutional issue of whether the committee's questions had violated Rumely's First Amendment rights.[21] Instead, the Court based its decision on the technicality that the investigation was outside the committee's power. Nevertheless, Justices William O. Douglas and Hugo L. Black raised First Amendment concerns in a strong dissenting opinion. Douglas wrote:

If the present inquiry were sanctioned, the press would be subject to harassment that in practical effect might be as serious as censorship. . . . Congress has imposed no tax, established no board of censors, instituted no licensing system. But the potential restraint is equally severe. The finger of government leveled against the press is ominous. Once the government can demand of a publisher the names of the purchasers of his publications, the free press as we know it disappears. Then the specter of a government agent will look over the shoulder of everyone who reads. The purchase of a book or pamphlet today may result in a subpoena tomorrow. Fear of criticism goes with every person into the bookstall. The subtle, imponderable pressures of the orthodox lay hold. Some will fear to read what is unpopular, what the powers-that-be dislike. When the light of publicity may reach any student, any teacher, inquiry will be discouraged.[22]

When journalists were called to testify before the Eastland subcommittee in the mid-1950s, it was still unclear whether the courts would judge a witness's refusal to divulge the names of Communist Party members as a First Amendment issue because the Supreme Court had refused to hear the First Amendment appeal of the Hollywood Ten. And when cases are presented to the courts in terms of national security, such arguments have consistently outweighed civil liberties considerations under the "balancing" test used by the courts.

But the unanimous decision in *Rumely* determined that HUAC had overstepped its powers and marked the Court's first ruling on the procedures of congressional committees. Although *Rumely* failed to establish an absolute First Amendment defense, the decision signaled that the Court might extend the protection in a subsequent case. Three years later *Rumely* became the basis for a string of acquittals in cases in which witnesses had refused to answer questions before the McCarthy committee.[23]

The Prosecutions

Given the legal history, lawyers for the four journalists focused on the procedures used by the Eastland committee to subpoena and question witnesses. Convinced that a jury of federal workers who had been subjected to a government loyalty oath would be unsympathetic, Shelton's lawyer convinced him to waive his right to a jury trial. Joseph Rauh argued at Shelton's January 1957 trial that the Eastland committee had called his client by mistake. He claimed the committee had no evidence linking Shelton to the Communist Party.

Committee counsel Julien Sourwine took the witness stand, where he acknowledged that Shelton's subpoena was misaddressed, but he maintained that the committee had information linking Shelton with Communists working at the *Times*. Sourwine said the committee had received information about Shelton in a letter from a source identified as "Finbar" whose identity was known only to Robert Morris, while he was a New York judge and had became a central figure in convincing Winston Burdett to testify before the committee a year earlier. "Why didn't you interrogate the man who wrote that letter, instead of issuing a subpoena without checking on that?" Rauh asked Sourwine.

"Because we already had received enough information from him [Finbar] which checked out to indicate that his leads were good, and because Mr. Morris knew who he was and said that he was a reliable person who was attempting to assist the committee," said Sourwine. "It is confidential and it contains information outside of this case which is confidential to the committee." Sourwine added that the committee became convinced of Shelton's sympathy toward communism after he said he considered the Republican Party in the same political category as the Communist Party. "That position is only taken by a person friendly with or sympathetic to the communist cause," said Sourwine.[24] Although the evidence is scant, the secretive Finbar was probably New York attorney Morris Ernst. Not only had Ernst played a decisive role in the ACLU's purge of Communists from its board of directors in the late 1930s, he had been a confidant of Heywood Broun's during the formation of the Newspaper Guild. More important, Ernst had secretly supplied the FBI with internal ACLU documents.[25] And he had defended the FBI in a 1950 *Reader's Digest* article, saying the agency was "doing its work with a fervid insistence on respecting the rights and privileges of individuals."[26] Five years later he was instrumental in arranging for Winston Burdett's testimony before the Eastland committee.

Rauh directed a second prong of his strategy at the subcommittee's procedures for issuing subpoenas and questioned whether the chairman had actually signed each document as required by Senate rules. Both the Senate and the House of Representatives had adopted procedural rules for their committees and subcommittees that required that each committee "conform strictly to the [rules] establishing its investigatory power" when issuing subpoenas.[27] Rauh asked Sourwine about Eastland's habits in issuing committee subpoenas.

"Does he give them to you in blank and you type the names in?" Rauh asked.

"No, sir, he does not," Sourwine insisted. "A list of proposed witnesses in this instance, and this is the course followed in most instances, went up to the chairman's office. The chairman approved the list. . . . I don't know of an instance where the chairman has signed a subpoena in blank."[28]

The discussion was important because, if the subpoenas had been signed by anyone other than Eastland, they would have been invalid. Indeed, more than a year earlier the senator had said he knew nothing about the subpoenas and referred James Reston of the *New York Times* to Sourwine for an answer.[29] Confronted with Reston's account, Sourwine said he was at a loss to explain the discrepancy between the senator's recollection and his own. "I might say that I don't think Mr. Reston was at that time particularly friendly towards Senator Eastland," Sourwine said.[30]

Another element of Rauh's defense was to show that the committee had had no legislative purpose in calling the hearings. The Supreme Court had insisted that investigative committees could compel witnesses to testify only if the committee had shown a legislative purpose.[31] Rauh contended that the investigation had been conducted as a "reprisal" against the *New York Times*, although he did not speculate on what had triggered the reprisal. He pressed Sourwine for answers:

> RAUH: How did you decide whom to call in public session?
> SOURWINE: On the basis of who would be helpful in giving the committee information.
> RAUH: Isn't it a fact that the people you did not call in public session would not have reflected on the New York Times if they had been called?
> SOURWINE: Yes, I think that's a fair statement. Also, some had no information to help the committee.[32]

Rauh also asked whether the committee had made any effort to investigate any other New York newspaper. "No effort was made with respect to any newspaper," Sourwine said. But he added that he had become convinced of Shelton's sympathy toward communism. Not only had Shelton invoked the First Amendment, but he had testified that he considered the Republican Party in the same political category as the Communist Party, Sourwine said. "That position is only taken by a person friendly with or sympathetic to the communist cause," Sourwine averred from the stand.[33]

U.S. District Judge Ross Rizley, a former Republican congressman from Oklahoma, deliberated for four days before finding Shelton guilty. "If the same circumstances should arise tomorrow, I'm inclined to believe that you still would want to defy the Congress," he told Shelton. He also addressed Rauh's contention that the investigation was aimed at the *Times*. "The evidence shows that no one was contending that the New York Times was a communistic newspaper. If necessary, the court would hold the Times was not a communistic newspaper." He sentenced Shelton to six months in jail and a $500 fine.[34]

The conviction set a precedent for Shelton's colleagues. When William Price's trial began two months later, his attorney argued that the committee had not subpoenaed Price because of some activity under congressional examination but "to embarrass him economically and socially."[35] Sourwine testified that Price was called to testify because he had been a candidate for vice president of the New York Newspaper Guild on the "Rank and File" ticket backed by the guild's Communist faction. Sourwine also cited a 1941 statement by Price, as quoted in the *Daily Worker,* that defended the Communist Party.[36] Attorney Leonard Boudin argued that the investigation lay outside the powers of Congress, "blatantly in violation of the First Amendment prescription against governmental interference with a free press."[37] After deliberating for two days, U.S. District Judge Richmond B. Keech found Price guilty and sentenced him to three months in jail and a $500 fine.[38]

Peck opted for a jury trial. Moreover, his lawyers took the unusual step of calling Senator Eastland to testify, which triggered a minor constitutional crisis.[39] Democrats feared his appearance would set a dangerous precedent. Eastland ultimately "volunteered" to comply and took the witness stand to deny that the committee contemplated legislation that would infringe on freedom of the press. Under questioning by Whitman's attorney, Telford Taylor, Eastland claimed the investigation stemmed from information that the Russians were trying to recruit journalists as spies and pointed to Burdett's testimony as proof.

> EASTLAND: I could not imagine a more sensitive field and I wanted to know how far the recruiting had gone.
> TAYLOR: Isn't it a fact that a number of the witnesses were asked about the actual slanting and distortion of the press by Communists?
> EASTLAND: I don't recall.[40]

U.S. District Judge Luther Youngdahl expressed concern about the constitutionality of the hearing but agreed that the conviction of Hollywood screenwriter John Lawson, whose appeal the Supreme Court had refused to hear, set a compelling precedent.[41] The jury deliberated for half an hour before finding Peck guilty on all five counts.[42]

Attorneys for Alden Whitman struggled to find a new strategy. "I am quite convinced that attacks on these Committees are at the least a waste of time, and at the worst an actual handicap," Gerhard Van Arkel, Whitman's lead attorney, told his client.[43] And Van Arkel told the New York Civil Liberties Union: "The more I reflect on it, the more convinced I am that we can show, if Whitman takes the stand, that his activities and those of his associates were purely lawful political activities and thereof protected from scrutiny under the First Amendment."[44] Whitman agreed and began to craft an explanation for his refusal to answer questions before the committee. "I did not think in a political vacuum, and I did have two kinds of conscience in mind," he told Van Arkel. "One was the personal ethic of not informing and the other was the feeling that it was wrong to know how freedom had been won over the ages and not to do something about it when I had the chance."[45]

When Whitman took the stand in his own defense, he told the court he had never joined the Communist Party "with the idea of trying to overthrow the government," nor did he consider this to be the purpose of the party. He said he dropped out after World War II when it became clear that the Communist movement would not become the basis for a broader labor party. Asked about his refusal to name party members, he expressed his personal abhorrence of informers. "I knew the result would be terrible trouble on the heads of people whom I knew, like myself, were innocent," he said. "I am not anxious go to jail. But I'm even less anxious to become in my own eyes an ignominious person."[46] Despite Whitman's impassioned testimony, U.S. District Judge Edward M. Curran found him guilty on all nineteen counts. "The Congress of the United States has the power to investigate the history of the Communist Party," Curran ruled as he sidestepped the First Amendment issues. "If the committee of the Senate is denied the opportunity of ascertaining the present and past membership of the Communist Party, it might well be stymied in making the proper recommendations to the Congress of the United States." Clyde Doyle, a conservative California Democrat and member of HUAC, had the verdict reprinted in the *Congressional Record*.[47]

The convictions marked only the beginning of what would become a complex and tortuous legal battle that would span the next eight years. Each appeal would test the willingness of the courts to interpret the First Amendment in a manner that recognized protection of journalists' thoughts and beliefs. Each loss in the courts would test the journalists' resolve to confront government interference.

Meanwhile the questioning of journalists before investigative committees continued. Among the journalists subpoenaed by HUAC was William Goldman, an editor at Hearst's *New York Daily Mirror* whom an anonymous witness had named as a party member during a secret session. Goldman had worked at the *Newark Star-Ledger* and the *Long Island Daily Press* when the papers were targets of the Newspaper Guild, but he refused to answer questions related to the Communist Party. Recognizing that he had placed himself in an untenable position as a reporter at Hearst's *Mirror,* he submitted his resignation rather than be fired.[48]

Embattled journalists suffered another setback seven months later when a federal arbitrator refused to order the reinstatement of *Mirror* reporter Daniel Mahoney. "The Constitution does not guarantee to a person exercising the privilege against self-incrimination, his job, the respect of his neighbors, or an absence in the minds of his fellow workers and employer of a gnawing doubt as to his guiltlessness," said the arbitrator. "His refusal to answer pertinent questions about his relationship with the conspiracy called 'communist' must shatter his employer's confidence irreparably."[49] Mahoney had been with the newspaper for twenty-two years.

Turn of the Tide

As lawyers prepared appeals for the four journalists who had openly challenged the Eastland committee, a profound shift began to take hold in the courts and weaken the legal underpinnings of congressional witch hunts. One of the most important cases involved the 1954 conviction of John T. Watkins, a labor organizer who had been active in the Communist Party during the 1940s but never actually became a member. Watkins agreed to answer questions about individuals in the party before the 1940s, but he refused to identify any who had left the party since that time. A federal appeals court upheld his conviction in 1956. On June 17, 1957, a day that conservatives would come to regard as "Red Monday," the U.S. Supreme Court issued a series of decisions, including a stunning 6–1 ruling that overturned Watkins's conviction based on a technicality that required investigative committees to apprise witnesses of the pertinence of the questions they were asked.[50] The Court's views on civil liberties had shifted between 1953 and 1957, beginning with President Dwight D. Eisenhower's appointment of former California governor Earl Warren as chief justice. Although Eisenhower was elected on a conservative Republican platform, the man he appointed to succeed the late Fred Vinson turned out to be a social liberal.[51] This was particularly evident in the 1954 *Brown v. Board of Education* decision that struck down school segregation, as well as in the *Watkins* decision in 1957.[52] The Vinson Court had sidestepped the First Amendment implications of investigative committees, but the Warren Court recognized a need to balance the investigative role of Congress with the individual's right to privacy.

The *Watkins* decision triggered another storm of protests from conservatives, who were already incensed by the 1954 desegregation decision.[53] Morris, the former judge who had returned as counsel to the Senate Internal Security Subcommittee, accused the Court of attempting "to level most of the erected barriers against Soviet infiltration" and worked with committee staffers on a bill to limit the Court's appellate jurisdiction, including cases involving contempt of Congress.[54] The bill quietly died in committee as cooler heads prevailed.

Three days after the *Watkins* decision the House Un-American Activities Committee held hearings in San Francisco. A friendly witness had named the journalist John M. Eshelman among fifty-five men and women named as Communists.[55] A reporter at Hearst's *San Francisco Examiner*, Eshelman had previously worked as a copy editor at Hearst's *Los Angeles Call-Bulletin* in the late 1940s. "I believe that this committee, under the First Amendment, has no right to inquire into anyone's political associations, past or present," he testified. "I am not a Communist nor in sympathy with it [communism], nor am I in sympathy with the rightwing subversion."[56] Within a few hours the *Examiner* fired him and told readers in the next day's edition that the *Examiner* had fired him after his appearance before the committee.[57] The Newspaper Guild took the firing to a federal arbitration board but the outlook was bleak.[58] Arbitrator Carl R. Schedler took nearly a year to release his decision. In what had become a familiar refrain, he held for the *Examiner* in a June 13, 1958, ruling that Eshleman's "conduct had terminated his usefulness and was detrimental" to his newspaper. "A newspaper may at times desire to be controversial and it is obvious that the issue of Communism today is to some controversial, but it should be the decision of the paper itself whether, when and as to what to be controversial about," Schedler wrote.[59]

But the *Watkins* decision had an immediate effect on Seymour Peck's conviction because he had responded to questions in a manner similar to Watkins's. Days after the *Watkins* decision came down, a federal appellate court ordered Peck's case returned to Judge Youngdahl with stern instructions to dismiss the indictment or order a new trial.[60] Youngdahl reviewed the case and found the circumstances "indistinguishable in scope or nature from those the Supreme Court condemned in *Watkins*" and voided Peck's conviction. "Although he did not use the word 'pertinency,' [Peck] informed the Subcommittee that he did not believe that it possessed the authority to ask the particular questions involved," Youngdahl wrote.[61]

The other three journalists would not be so fortunate because they had not challenged the Eastland committee in the same manner, and as a result their circumstances were not so clearly influenced by the *Watkins* decision. As the political uproar about *Watkins* continued to swirl, the Supreme Court agreed to consider a similar appeal by Lloyd Barenblatt, a university professor who had refused to answer questions before HUAC.[62] When the Court agreed to hear Barenblatt's appeal, similar cases were put on indefinite hold, including the convictions of Shelton, Price, and Whitman.

The appeals process continued until June 1959 when the Supreme Court appeared to back down from the constraints imposed by its *Watkins* decision by upholding Barenblatt's conviction.[63] The most important aspect of the new decision, as far as the journalists were concerned, was Barenblatt's claim that the First Amendment protected academic freedom, a legal argument that was only a short distance from the journalists' freedom of the press argument. Writing for the majority in *Barenblatt v. United States*, Justice Harlan Stone wrote:

> The protections of the First Amendment, unlike a proper claim of the privilege against self-incrimination under the Fifth Amendment, do not afford a witness the right to resist inquiry in all circumstances. . . . We conclude that the balance between the individual and the governmental interests here at stake must be struck in favor of the latter, and that therefore the provisions of the First Amendment have not been offended.[64]

With *Barenblatt* now established as the guiding precedent for all other cases, a federal appeals court upheld the convictions of Shelton and Price, ruling that the Eastland committee had not violated their First Amendment rights or the constitutional safeguards for the press. Wrote Warren Burger, who then sat on the Court of Appeals for the District of Columbia:

> The important right of the press to be free and independent is not impaired by an inquiry into possible abuse of the right which is directed at destroying the very freedom the First Amendment assures. Indeed in the Barenblatt opinion in response to a similar argument the Court sharply pointed out that "investigative power" in this domain is not to be denied Congress solely because the field of education is involved.[65]

In the summer of 1960 Whitman's lawyers suggested that the Newspaper Guild file a legal brief supporting their client. The guild quickly rejected the request. Whitman's lawyers also recognized that there was little prospect that the American Newspaper Publishers Association would agree to support him. "While it would be refreshing if the newspaper publishers would take this position, they have in the past shown themselves to be such gutless wonders that it hardly seems worthwhile even to raise the question with them," wrote Van Arkel.[66] In July the appeals court upheld Whitman's conviction, saying:

> Given the presently considered conspiratorial nature of the Party, a common belief of which Whitman does not claim ignorance, it would seem that the questions ... were pertinent to an investigation of subversive activities as manifested by the organization of members of the press into Communist Party cells in the period following World War II, and such an inquiry was not without relevance to Party activities in 1956, when the Subcommittee questioned Whitman.[67]

Although the appeals process had been a humiliating and demoralizing experience for the journalists, their fortunes began to shift the following March when the Supreme Court agreed to review Shelton's conviction. Lawyers for Whitman and Price scrambled to file their own appeals, arguing the same issues that the Court had previously rejected, only now they were able to cite more favorable recent precedents that had begun to rein in the investigative powers of Congress.[68] The New York Civil Liberties Union (NYCLU) filed a brief on Whitman's behalf, arguing that the First Amendment argument that had been brushed aside. "Without outright prohibition but nevertheless effectively, the [Eastland] committee diminished the guarantee of free expression," argued the NYCLU's Nanette Dembitz. "If the questions had any pertinence, their 'slim semblance of pertinency' was insufficient to justify the severe interference they worked in First Amendment freedoms."[69]

Five months later the Court handed down its decision, reversing each conviction in a 5–2 decision. The key, and common to all the cases, was a single, narrow legal technicality that required grand jury indictments to specify the "subject under inquiry" by investigative committees. That technicality conveniently permitted the Court to undo the committee's handiwork but without addressing the more important issue for the journalists: their rights under the First Amendment. Justice William O. Douglas, a consistent supporter of First Amendment freedoms, seized the opportunity to address their concerns in a powerful concurring opinion. He wrote:

> Under our system of government, I do not see how it is possible for Congress to pass a law saying whom a newspaper or news agency or magazine shall or shall not employ. I see no justification for the Government investigating the capacities, leanings, ideology, qualifications, prejudices or politics of those who collect or write the news. It was conceded on oral argument

that Congress would have no power to establish standards of fitness for those who work for the press. It was also conceded that Congress would have no power to prescribe loyalty tests for people who work for the press. Since this investigation can have no legislative basis as far as the press is concerned, what then is its constitutional foundation?[70]

Upon their exoneration by the courts Whitman sent a note to Sulzberger thanking him "immeasurably" for his support.[71] Retired by then and in poor health, the publisher drafted a response. "The era in which charges were brought against you was a disgrace to our country. I am glad that the position we took was sustained by our highest court," he said.[72] But the draft generated considerable controversy at the newspaper. Orvil Dryfoos, a descendant of the patriarchal Ochs family, considered it tantamount to a ringing endorsement of Whitman's defiance and engineered a second note. The revised version read: "Thank you for your pleasant letter of May 22nd. It was good of you to write as you did. Faithfully yours, [initialed AHS]."[73]

Within a few weeks Whitman received an ominous telephone call from Anthony Lewis, who was covering the Supreme Court for the *Times*; he warned that conservative critics might pressure the Justice Department to reindict Whitman.[74] Fearing the worst, Whitman's lawyers turned to the *Times*, but their request for help was quickly brushed aside. "I have, of course, no way of knowing whether a re-indictment of these persons would be prejudicial to the interests of the Times, or if it is thought that it may be, what if any action might be proper," Van Arkel wrote.[75] The response from the *Times* showed that the newspaper's sentiment on the Communist issue had not changed appreciably since 1955. "Mr. Whitman has suffered enough," the *Times* told Van Arkel. "I don't see what The New York Times can do in this matter, and rather doubt that The New York Times should do anything."[76]

The most stunning development of all came three months later, in September 1962, when Attorney General Robert Kennedy directed the Justice Department to reindict each of the plaintiffs cleared by the *Russell* decision, including the three journalists.[77] James Wechsler of the *New York Post*, who understood firsthand the vulnerability of journalists who were former party members, excoriated Kennedy on his newspaper's editorial page. "Probably most Americans have by now forgotten what the cases were about," he wrote. "But the targets and their families have not. The U.S. press should be especially concerned; several of those under fire were plainly selected by the Eastland committee for punishment because they worked for a newspaper called The New York Times, which had been a harsh critic of Mr. Eastland's works."[78] Wechsler understood that although President Kennedy remained neutral on the Communist issue when he served in the Senate, his brother Robert had briefly worked on McCarthy's staff during the early 1950s before a bitter spat erupted over Roy Cohn's promotion to committee counsel.[79] Although Robert Kennedy was regarded as a liberal, he continued to admire McCarthy, whom his father had supported with generous campaign contributions during the 1950s. RFK continued to support the anti-Communist campaign after his brother named him attorney general.[80] Although the Fifth Amendment prohibits trying a defendant twice for the same crime, as the Shelton case illustrated there are numerous exceptions that leave government prosecutors free to seek another trial.[81] The Kennedy administration was no more willing to pick a fight with Congress on this matter than the Supreme Court had been years before.

Back to the Beginning

In late 1962 the ACLU agreed to underwrite a renewed defense of both Whitman and Shelton. "The contempt citations are a relic of McCarthyism which did such disservice to the principle of free speech and association embedded in our First Amendment," the organization said.[82] Whitman faced the additional problem of losing his lawyer, who had been exhausted by the appeals. Lawrence Speiser, director of the ACLU's Washington office, agreed to take the case. Speiser had successfully challenged a California law that required veterans to take a loyalty oath in order to qualify for a property tax exemption. Before moving to Washington, D.C., he successfully defended Allen Ginsberg in the late 1950s when the government prosecuted him for obscenity in connection with his poem *Howl*.[83]

The new trials began in October 1962, and they closely paralleled the trials of five years earlier. Shelton's case centered more intently on the mysterious "Finbar" letter described at the first trial, and his attorney insisted on having the letter brought to court, prompting another protest by Assistant U.S. Attorney William Hitz. "It no longer exists," Hitz told the court. Joseph Rauh, Shelton's attorney, made no attempt to hide his annoyance when he called Sourwine to the witness stand.

> RAUH: Did you know that this case was pending in the Supreme Court and the defense depended on this letter?"
> SOURWINE: Certainly, I knew about the conviction and the appeal. I could not deny that I was aware that it was going to the Supreme Court.

RAUH: Were you aware that we had subpoenaed that letter in the first trial?

SOURWINE: I testified in that trial. . . . I knew about it.

RAUH: Yet you permitted it to be destroyed?

SOURWINE: I did, yes.[84]

Two weeks later, on January 30, 1963, Eastland took the stand to testify, an appearance that required another Senate resolution, and he proved to be even less forthcoming than at the first trial. In response to dozens of questions he answered, "I don't remember," or "I can't recall."[85]

In February Shelton and Whitman were convicted for a second time, triggering another lengthy round of appeals. Whitman had become exhausted by the strain, but Shelton vowed to fight. By now the courts had amassed a considerable number of decisions that enabled lawyers to base their appeals on the technicalities that were most likely to sway the courts. In September 1963 Shelton's lawyers managed to tip the balance of the divided appeals court by winning a 2–1 decision in his favor. In March 1964 the thirteen-page opinion found that Sourwine had violated Shelton's rights by breaking the committee's own rules governing subpoenas, but the appellate judges but left the First Amendment questions unanswered. Anthony Lewis reported in the *Times* that the decision added up to "a warning that the courts will demand the strictest procedural fairness of Congressional committees before sustaining contempt charges—and especially in cases that have dragged on for years."[86] The decision also offered an illuminating commentary on the difficult constitutional issue raised by the case. Appellate judge J. Skelly Wright wrote: "We are asked to balance Congress' need to know against the right of the individual and the press to be let alone. We shrink from this awesome task and adopt a narrower disposition of this case which will not require the resolution of the constitutional problem presented." As justification, the court pointed to the 1952 Supreme Court decision that had reversed the conviction of Edward Rumely after he refused to testify before HUAC. "The Supreme Court indicated that even a strained interpretation of the congressional resolution was preferable to deciding the case on a constitutional basis," the appellate court said.[87]

Shelton's victory cleared the way for an appeal by Whitman; however, in a surprise announcement from Nicholas Katzenbach's Justice Department in late 1964, government lawyers filed motions to dismiss the cases against both Whitman and Price. The legal entanglements of Whitman's case would not be resolved completely until the following year.[88] By then he had worked at the *New York Times* for fourteen years. He had spent nearly ten of those years trying to vindicate himself and remove the stigma attached to his social activism during the 1930s. Whitman and the other embattled journalists managed to avoid jail, but luck played a decisive role. The circumstances surrounding their cases suggest that if they had waged their legal battles earlier in the period known as the McCarthy era, and had staged a hard-line defense of press freedom against government encroachment, they would have faced the more severe punishment meted out to the Hollywood Ten, who had raised similar issues nearly a decade earlier.

CHAPTER TEN

Living with the Legacy

T HE McCARTHY ERA has influenced journalism for generations, playing a critical role in the economic well-being reporters and editors and their ability to defend themselves against government intrusion in the process of providing the public with information free of government censorship. Many journalists suspected that the Eastland committee hearings were aimed primarily at the *New York Times* in retribution for that newspaper's stand against the racial segregation that the Mississippi senator supported so adamantly. However, evidence suggests that the committee's main target was not the *Times* but the Newspaper Guild in retaliation for its efforts to unionize newsrooms. Despite the repeated denials by Senator Eastland and his colleagues, after the hearings ended Vlad Besterman, general counsel of the House Judiciary Committee, confided to Sydney Gruson of the *Times,* after the investigation ended, that the guild was indeed the primary target.[1]

As it had in other investigations, the FBI fueled the hunt for Reds in newsrooms. FBI documents do not account for every journalist subpoenaed by Congress, but the documents demonstrate that the FBI played a prominent role in determining who was called to testify, much as it did in the investigations of entertainment, education, the federal workforce, the legal profession, and organized labor.[2] The documents related to the guild and individual journalists show that investigative committees seeking guidance on which journalists to target needed to look no further than the voluminous files that the FBI had assembled during the 1940s.

J. Edgar Hoover held to a stereotypical view in believing that all Communists were puppets of a sinister regime that posed a grave danger to the security of the United States; whether they had access to sensitive information was irrelevant to him. His perspective would once again be prominent in U.S. politics after the terrorist attacks on the World Trade Center and the Pentagon in 2001, when Congress granted the FBI broad authority to keep suspected terrorists under surveillance. Although the enemy was different, the rationale behind the passage and reauthorization of the U.S.A. Patriot Act early in the twenty-first century was a clear echo of Hoover's point of view during the McCarthy era. But by 2006 more than half of Americans believed that the FBI and other federal agencies were "intruding on privacy" in the effort to fight terrorism.[3]

The public was less skeptical during the 1940s and 1950s when publishers readily fired suspected Communists, affirming the newspapers' patriotism but also lending legitimacy to fears that the newspaper industry had been infiltrated by Communists. At the same time the firings defused the militancy that had transformed the Newspaper Guild from a passive professional organization into a confrontational labor union during the 1930s and 1940s. Critics used Red-baiting as weapon for that weakened the guild and made it vulnerable.

Historians have shown that McCarthyism was a collaborative effort that was waged on many fronts against a variety of targets but particularly against organized labor, and this included the labor movement within the newspaper industry.[4] The Taft-Hartley Act pushed back many of the gains won by labor during the 1930s.[5] By banning secondary picketing, the act made it impossible for the guild to target advertisers in order to pressure publishers who refused to negotiate. Taft-Hartley also made it impossible for the guild to demand "closed shop" provisions, a primary objective of its drive to organize newsrooms during the 1930s. In addition, the requirement that union leaders sign affidavits swearing they were not members of the Communist Party effectively robbed the guild and other Left-led unions of many of their most forceful and creative leaders.[6]

McCarthyism perpetuated internal dissent that produced schisms that would haunt the guild for decades. The deep divisions diverted attention from the important business of organizing newsrooms during a critical period in the union's history. The rifts deepened after the guild loosened its membership requirements to bolster its rolls and build bargaining clout, allowing membership by office workers and elevator operators, for example. By the 1970s editorial workers, who had formed the guild's core for nearly four decades, had become a minority. The new majority proved to be less willing to engage in confrontation and more willing to grant concessions than their predecessors.[7]

Although guild membership rose to 30,000 in 1959, primarily because of the union's expanded membership criteria, the number hit a plateau in the early 1960s.[8] The number of contracts between guild locals and management also hit a plateau.[9] In the late 1980s the guild was jolted by a stream of defections by young journalists. They began to dismiss the guild as "a self-serving club for the professionally washed-up and over-the-hill, battle scarred veterans."[10] Moreover, technological advances robbed the guild of potential members. Electronic systems replaced elevator operators. Computers made dictationists and copy boys obsolete. Bargaining units in California, Montana, Washington, and Michigan voted to decertify after nearly four decades. Guild membership, which stood at 26,202 in 1992 (down by 832 from a year earlier), had not been so low since 1967. The guild responded by cutting back personnel and reducing the number of conventions and conferences it sponsored.[11]

By the mid-1990s automation had made it nearly impossible for the unions to shut down a newspaper. Disillusioned guild members complained of the decline in bargaining clout. "What's missing is a more aggressive stance," complained Bruce Meachum, administrator of the Denver local.[12] Important voices began to question the guild's relevance, setting the stage for its merger in 1996 with the 600,000-member Communication Workers of America. By 2004 the Internet was cutting deeply into newspaper advertising revenue.[13]

McCarthyism was not the sole cause of the guild's problems, but it left the union weakened to a point where it could not sustain its influence in the face of other challenges, such as technological advances that shrank its membership and therefore its influence in newsrooms. The guild was not alone as declines were seen throughout organized labor. In 1955, the year the CIO merged with the AFL, 95 percent of the nation's workforce belonged to a union; by 2004 that number stood at 53 percent.[14] As a succession of major unions dropped out of the once-powerful AFL-CIO, observers called it labor's "greatest upheaval since the Great Depression."[15] The Newspaper Guild now often accepted concessions that were unimaginable in the late 1930s and 1940s. "The Guild has been weakened by its inability to shut a newspaper down," wrote Randy Dotinga in *Editor and Publisher* in a 1998 story that has proved to be an enormous understatement.[16] At the *San Francisco Chronicle*, for example, newsroom negotiators accepted reduced vacations, fewer sick days, and fewer opportunities for part-time work. Both sides called the 2005 agreement "essential to the future" of the newspaper and its employees.[17] In Youngstown, Ohio, the *Vindicator* began to hire permanent replacements in 2005 after workers rejected a wage offer that barely kept up with inflation.[18] In York, Pennsylvania, newspaper negotiators proposed a contract that included no raises and banned disparagement of the company by employees, a position the owner later disavowed.[19] Newsroom cuts continued in 2006, including layoffs at some of the nation's leading newspapers, including the *New York Times, Washington Post, Los Angeles Times,* and *Time.* Facing sharp declines in circulation and advertising revenue, the *Philadelphia Inquirer* handed layoff notices to seventy-one newsroom employees in January 2007, firing about 17 percent of the paper's editorial staff, and the *Boston Globe* handed notices to nineteen in its newsroom.[20] The situation confronting guild members was poignantly expressed by journalist Ben Bagdikian ten years before the most recent wave of givebacks. "I was punished in the 1950s for joining a newsroom union," he wrote. "Forty years later, the attitude of publishers had not changed. Neither had underpayment of reporters."[21]

The Rights of Journalists

Another important legacy of the McCarthy era is caution in the newsroom in the face of government intimidation. It is not known how many quietly resigned from newspapers rather than face public humiliation in the 1950s. Moreover, it is difficult to know the degree to which news stories were molded to conform politically. It is impossible to know how many issues were ignored for fear of triggering backlash from readers and how many stories were shelved to avoid controversy. But journalists who lived through the investigation felt fear and timidity taking hold in the newsrooms. "The moment an actor or writer is attacked, he becomes a 'controversial personality,'" wrote John Oakes of the *New York Times* in a 1954 article on the lasting damage of McCarthyism. "All one would have to do to get rid of an actor or author one didn't like would be to start a rumor that he had a politically-questionable background."[22] By some accounts editors at the *Times* in the 1960s timidly avoided characterizations that would make the radical antiwar movement appear acceptable and downplayed stories that appeared to be excessively critical of government policies, lest the paper once again be accused of harboring Communist sympathies.[23] Many would argue that such journalistic timidity is exactly what the Founders had in mind in framing the First Amendment. But although the Constitution precludes Congress from "abridging freedom of speech, or of the press," the breadth and scope of that protection is subject to interpretation by the courts and has been slow to evolve.[24] Concern about government intimidation goes back to the colonial era when the trial of John Peter Zenger in 1735 focused public attention on the punishment facing newspaper publishers who dared to criticize the British government.[25] Under British common law seditious libel, as it was called, included anything "false, scandalous, or malicious" directed at the government, and violators could be fined, imprisoned, pilloried, and whipped. Andrew Hamilton's argument that Zenger had published truthfully prompted a jury to find Zenger innocent. Historians have argued that Zenger's case, as well as the British legal scholar William Blackstone's 1769 pronouncement that press freedom is measured in terms of prior restraint, prompted the framers of the Constitution to adopt the First Amendment to protect the free exchange of ideas.[26] Once the Fourteenth Amendment applied the Bill of Rights to the states in 1868, the stage was set for the Supreme Court to tackle the issue of prior restraint.[27] The first opportunity did not come until 1931 when the Court ruled, in *Near v. Minnesota,* that government officials could not prohibit newspapers from publishing by declaring them a public nuisance.[28] The Court expanded the protection in 1936 to include indirect attacks, ruling in *Grosjean v. American Press Company* that Louisiana governor Huey Long's tax on newspapers was unconstitutional.[29]

By the late 1930s the courts had established prior restraint as unconstitutional but had not addressed constraints on newsgathering. When journalists were called to testify before investigative committees in the 1950s, the extent of their protection was unclear. This lack of clarity, combined with the widespread fear of domestic communism following World War II, produced an atmosphere that left individual journalists ripe for exploitation. Framers of the First Amendment could not have foreseen the calculated manipulation and intimidation that characterized McCarthyism, nor could they have foreseen how journalism would develop from an adjunct function of colonial printers into a profession resting on the principle of social responsibility. Throughout the 1950s, when Congress used its contempt powers to compel witnesses not otherwise charged with any crime (such as advocating overthrow of the government) to divulge their political beliefs, embattled journalists made forceful arguments that intimidation of the men and women who gather and report the news is a violation of press freedom.[30] Journalists who stood on the First Amendment's press protections rather than the Fifth Amendment were particularly vulnerable, given the precedent set by the Hollywood Ten after the Supreme Court refused to recognize their claim for protection under the free speech/free expression clause of the First Amendment.

The McCarthy era presented newspapers with an opportunity to forcefully defend the rights of individual journalists under the Constitution's free press clause and protect the role of newspapers in American society. It represented a struggle between journalists who sought to defend the public's right to a free press and politicians who claimed to be defending national security, leaving the First Amendment caught in the middle. But during the McCarthy era the newspaper industry was fragmented and nearly paralyzed by fear of criticism and boycotts by readers and advertisers if they were accused of being "soft" on Communists. Publishers failed to recognize the journalists' refusal to cooperate with investigative committees as a dramatic act of civil disobedience against a dangerous assault on press freedom. Publishers also failed to recognize that the divide-and-conquer strategy used by political opportunists left journalism more vulnerable than before.[31] During the 1950s editors and publishers were more concerned with government restrictions on information than with the vulnerability of individual journalists to government intimidation.[32]

The most obvious threat that anti-Communists saw from Red journalists was their ability to infuse Communist propaganda into the news. Neither the FBI nor the investigative committees found any serious evidence that Red journalists were inserting propaganda in the news or editorial columns of mainstream newspapers. Indeed, Hoover showed no interest in systematically monitoring newspaper content, concentrating instead on discrediting individual journalists, frequently by spreading unsubstantiated rumors about them. Conservatives may argue that the anti-Communist campaign waged by Hoover and others put would-be infiltrators on notice that they faced grave consequences if they tampered with newspaper content. But the surveillance of newspapers during the 1940s, coupled with the investigative hearings during the 1950s, raised profound free press issues that were never addressed. One of those central questions was exactly what risk journalists who once belonged to the Communists Party actually posed for national security, absent any evidence of tampering with newspaper content. If journalists belonged to the party at some point in their lives, were they forever a threat?

The First Amendment arguments raised by journalists during the McCarthy era were not recognized by the courts until 1958, two years after the Eastland hearings, when actor-singer Judy Garland sued Marie Torre, a *New York Herald Tribune* reporter. Torre had quoted an unnamed CBS executive as describing Garland as overweight and "known for a highly developed inferiority complex."[33]

Broadly speaking, Garland's lawsuit revolved around a central issue of the McCarthy era: the government's power to compel a journalist to testify against her will. In her deposition Torre refused to divulge the name of the network executive she had quoted anonymously. Garland's attorneys asked the U.S. District Court to compel Torre to name the individual. The district court held for Garland and Torre appealed. Brushing aside Torre's claim of First Amendment protection, the Supreme Court refused to review her appeal, and she went to jail rather than reveal the source's name.[34]

The Supreme Court did not comment on the constitutional argument made by Torre until the early 1970s, after President Richard Nixon directed the Justice Department to indict Earl Caldwell of the *New York Times,* who had refused to testify at a grand jury investigation of threats against Nixon by the militant Black Panther Party.[35] A HUAC member during the late 1940s who was elected to the Senate in 1950, Nixon had maintained a tempestuous relationship with the press throughout his political career, flattering supportive outlets while castigating critics, a tactic reminiscent of Senator Joseph McCarthy's during the early 1950s.[36] After Nixon became president in 1968, he used a variety of tactics to silence his critics, including illegal break-ins and wiretaps to identify leaks from the White House, and he maintained an "enemies list" of hundreds of individuals, including a score of journalists.[37] In 1969 Vice President Spiro Agnew put journalism on the defensive when he characterized media critics of administration policies—particularly the *New York Times* and CBS News—as "nattering nabobs of negativism" that offered "a narrow and distorted picture of America."[38] During 1969 and 1970, Nixon's first two years in the White House, his administration served more than fifty subpoenas on the two largest television networks, CBS and NBC, seeking production notes and videotape they had not broadcast in an effort to gather information about the Black Panther Party.[39]

In 1971 the Court bolstered protection of newspapers and other media when it blocked the Justice Department from exercising prior restraint in its effort to prevent the *New York Times* and the *Washington Post* from publishing the "Pentagon Papers," an accurate history of the Vietnam War that the administration had buried until it was leaked by Daniel Ellsberg, an analyst for the Rand Corporation.[40] The Court had been willing since the 1930s to defend publishers under the First Amendment from potentially coercive tactics. However, it had been consistently unwilling to extend similar protection to individual journalists who faced similar tactics, including Marie Torre in the 1950s and Earl Caldwell, who was convicted of contempt of court in the early 1970s after he resisted the government's demands.

When Caldwell's appeal reached the Supreme Court in 1972, the issue was a newspaper's rights to protect its confidential sources, not the rights of journalists to avoid questions about their thoughts and political beliefs, which had been the question twenty years earlier as various congressional committees investigated domestic communism. After the Court combined Caldwell's with two similar cases, professional organizations and news outlets rallied to the defense of all the journalists whose testimony the government had sought to compel. News organizations recognized the need to leave the 1950s. The *Times,* the Newspaper Guild, and the American Newspaper Publishers Association, among others, all filed briefs supporting the reporters in the case now known as *Branzburg v. Hayes.*[41] In June 1972, twelve days before the Watergate break-in, a 5–4 ruling by the Court made it clear that journalists were like any other citizen and have no First Amendment right—under free press or free speech—to withhold information (such as the identities of their sources) from a grand jury investigating a criminal matter. However, the Court stipulated that government prosecutors could not use the subpoena power for "official harassment of the press," an acknowledgment of the violation of civil liberties that had defined McCarthyism in the 1950s.[42] In a dissenting opinion Justice William O. Douglas took note of the connection between newsgathering and freedom of the press. "The press has a preferred position in our constitutional scheme, not to enable it to make money, not to set newspapermen apart as a favored class, but to bring fulfillment of the public's right to know," he wrote.[43] In a separate dissent, Justice Potter Stewart and two of his colleagues placed a heavy burden on the government to prove its need for such testimony and became a widely used standard in the lower courts. What is noteworthy here is that Stewart's dissent reflected a rationale that he had expressed earlier as a circuit judge sitting on the Court of Appeals that ruled against Torre in the late 1950s.[44] Although *Branzburg* provided limited protection for journalists, it failed to clearly define the central issue confronting the press during the McCarthy era regarding the government's power to compel journalists to testify.

Unfinished Business

After *Branzburg* the press and government prosecutors maintained a mutual understanding that journalists would be called to testify only as a last resort. Throughout the 1970s and 1980s state legislatures adopted so-called shield laws to protect journalists; even so, a cloud of uncertainty left journalists vulnerable, and several were jailed, including *New York Times* reporter Myron Farber, who served forty days in 1978 after refusing to reveal his sources during a criminal trial. Author Vanessa Leggett served five months in 2001 after refusing to reveal her sources for an article about a homicide investigation.[45] Several other journalists attracted public attention during the 1970s and 1990swhen they refused to answer questions before congressional committees seeking to learn their sources. Although the reporters were threatened with contempt charges, the committees ultimately backed down.[46]

The cases of Farber, Leggett, and the others were hardly anomalies. Indeed, it would be a mistake to dismiss the issues confronting the press during the 1950s as relics of the Cold War. A 1993 report by the Reporters Committee for Freedom of the Press, an organization of journalists formed in response to the *Branzburg* case, said that more than half of the nine hundred news organizations it had surveyed had been targets of subpoenas for unpublished photographs, reporters' notes, and testimony from journalists; however, the survey also showed that imaginative lawyers were able to have more than 70 percent of the orders quashed, suggesting that the subpoenas had been issued more as a nuisance than to obtain otherwise unavailable information.[47]

Only the year before a committee had subpoenaed three journalists to testify about their sources. Committee members called *Newsday* reporter Timothy Phelps and National Public Radio correspondent Nina Totenberg were summoned to testify about stories they had written related to sexual harassment allegations made by Anita Hill against Supreme Court nominee Clarence Thomas. Separately, *Washington Times* reporter Paul Rodriguez was asked to name his source for a story involving an ethics investigation of five senators who had business dealings with savings and loan executive Charles Keating. "In the McCarthy era, dozens of people were sent up for refusing to testify about their own political beliefs or those of their friends," the *Nation* said in a 1992 editorial. "Many more lost their jobs or suffered other indignities for daring to exercise First Amendment rights. In most cases, the Senate or House committees had all the information they wanted. The whole point of bringing witnesses to the inquisitors of the day was to force them into 'contempt' and its consequences."[48] The committees ultimately dropped their threats to hold the reporters in contempt. As a result, issues surrounding the government's power to compel journalists to testify were again left unresolved, as they had been since the Eastland investigation. Despite all the court cases and the ongoing conflicts between the government and the media since the 1950s, the central issue that arose during the heyday of anticommunism has never been taken up by the Supreme Court.

The debate took an especially dramatic twist in 2005 in the Plame case. The attention of a special counsel appointed to find the leaker quickly focused on Matthew Cooper of *Time* and Miller, even though Miller had written no article using Plame's name.[49] Indeed, newspaper headlines in 2005 and the 1950s were strikingly similar to headlines during the McCarthy era: "Two Reporters Now Face Prison for Contempt," "How Media Split under Pressure in the Leak Probe," and "Support Wanes for Reporter in CIA Leak."[50] And much as the *New York Times* had allowed the Eastland committee to serve subpoenas in its newsroom in 1955, *Time* agreed to surrender Cooper's notes on the eve of his having to enter jail, after his source consented to be named before a grand jury. *Time*'s editor-in-chief, Norman Pearlstine, a lawyer by training, echoed the rationale expressed by newspaper publishers in the 1950s when he characterized refusal to comply as "detrimental to our journalistic principle to think of ourselves as above the law."[51] Miller, on the other hand, refused and began serving a jail sentence in July 2005 where she remained for eighty-five days until her source, I. Lewis "Scooter" Libby, consented to disclosure of his name.[52]

In September 2006 Richard Armitage, deputy secretary of state, revealed that he had been Robert Novak's source but was unaware at the time that Plame was a covert operative, a key element in the law against naming CIA agents, and his admission essentially ended the controversy. In the end, the greatest repercussions had been felt by a journalist who had not written a story about the affair. Victoria Toensing, a former deputy attorney general, described the government's three-year probe into the leak as "one of the most factually distorted investigations in history."[53]

Miller's jailing stoked the decades-long dispute about reporters' rights, although the profession was now in the hands of a generation that had no direct experience with the McCarthy era. Again, the newspaper industry stood divided. The most biting criticism of *Time* came when the *Salt Lake Tribune* described it as "corporate cowardice."[54] The Newspaper Guild described Miller's jailing as "a major setback to one of the nation's core democratic principles."[55] And for the first time in the organization's history, the American Society of Newspaper Editors endorsed the concept of a national shield law to protect reporters. But some news outlets condemned the press's attempts to resist the government.[56] The *Wall Street Journal* criticized "liberal" newspapers, most notably the *New York Times*, for demanding that a special prosecutor be appointed in the Plame case.

The *Journal* argued that by appealing what it deemed to be Miller's legally weak case to the Court of Appeals, "the *Times* probably left everyone in the media less able to protect sources against future prosecutorial raids."[57] Prosecutors noted the divisions among the press and attempted to bolster their argument for compelling Miller and other journalists to testify by pointing to editorials in the *Chicago Tribune* and the *Los Angeles Times,* and to comments by Anthony Lewis, the *Times*'s Supreme Court reporter for thirty-two years, as examples of those who recognized appropriate limits to First Amendment protection for the press.[58]

The conflict cannot be pinned solely on the newspaper industry's failure to confront McCarthyism, but the echoes are unmistakable. The Miller episode carried an air of theatricality. After her credibility became an issue, she resigned from the *Times,* which further obscured the central question of the government's power to compel testimony from journalists where it is not clear that any crime has been committed.[59] Although it is the duty of the courts to interpret the scope and meaning of the First Amendment, it is the duty of newspapers to defend the First Amendment protection of the press against government encroachment. *Times* publisher Arthur Sulzberger Jr., grandson of the publisher during the McCarthy era, remarked in 2005 that fear of losing a case is not a good reason not to fight it. "If you don't stand for what you believe in, don't risk a decision because you think you might lose, I think that is a short-sighted approach," he said.[60]

John Peter Zenger represented the courage of a single individual to challenge arbitrary use of government powers to intimidate the press. Journalists who stood their ground during the McCarthy era closely paralleled Zenger's stance, but their defiance was interpreted as un-American and disloyal because of the stigma attached to domestic communism. "I established the principle that the *Times* does not fire people who invoke the Fifth Amendment," Melvin Barnet reflected in the late 1990s. "I won and I lost."[61] Alden Whitman reached a similar conclusion following the *Branzburg* decision. "Ten years for nothing," he said. "What [Eastland] really wanted to do was to embarrass Mr. Sulzberger and to embarrass the *Times* by showing the *Times* carried on its payroll a number of former Communists. While he couldn't find a current one, he did find a number of former ones."[62] Years after the hearings Whitman and Seymour Peck reserved much of their bitterness for colleagues who had failed to support them. "They felt they would be tainted if they came to the defense of people who had admitted to having been Communists in the past," said Peck. "They wanted to be kosher and safe."[63]

Epilogue

J OURNALISTS WHO STOOD on moral principle and refused to answer questions before investigative committees during the McCarthy era suffered both economic and psychological hardships. They had been easy targets because the newspaper industry, like the movie industry in the late 1940s, was full of ex-radicals whose political activities during the 1930s could be exploited by conservatives. They lost in the courts, and arbitration panels held the journalists to a higher standard than workers in other industries because of their influence on public opinion. Where the firing of a pipe fitter would be overturned, journalists consistently found themselves out of luck and out of work, and each decision made it more difficult for journalists to prevail in the next case.[1] In ruling against John Eshelman in his case against Hearst's *San Francisco Examiner* in 1958, for example, the arbitrator cited earlier decisions against Melvin Barnet and Jack Shafer at the *New York Times* and Theodore Polumbaum at United Press, not the recalcitrant pipe fitter who was ordered to be reinstated.[2]

Most Americans held little sympathy for those who refused to cooperate. The general attitude was that witnesses who got into trouble had brought their fates on themselves by refusing to purge themselves and affirm their loyalty to America.[3] With only a few exceptions—the three at the *New York Times* and one at the *San Francisco Chronicle*—journalists who resisted the investigative committees were fired. Most never again worked in daily journalism. Melvin Barnet, for example, tried but failed to find work at other New York newspapers. At one point he thought the *New York Post* would take him on, but even the liberal *Post* recognized that a journalist who had been tainted by the investigative committees represented a public relations nightmare. He harvested oranges in Florida and worked as a cook on a shrimp boat to support himself during the 1960s until he became an editor at the trade newspaper *Medical Tribune,* along with Jack Shafer, who also had been fired by the *Times.* Barnet was the associate editor when he retired in 1978. He died in June 1998 at eighty-three.[4] Jack Shafer eventually retired to Florida and refused to discuss the McCarthy era or his career at the *Times.* Nathan Aleskovsky worked for cartoonist Walt Kelly, the creator of the cartoon strip *Pogo,* and joined a New York public relations firm in 1959. Ten years later he was killed in an automobile accident outside New York at age fifty-six.[5] William Price became active in New York City politics but continued to be hounded by the FBI. In the early 1980s he was awarded $10,000 in a suit he filed against the FBI related to illegal wiretaps, burglaries, and mail openings.[6] Thomas Buchanan, who was fired in 1948 by the *Washington Star,* eventually moved to Paris with his wife and five children and worked in the computer industry. He later wrote several books, including one on the John F. Kennedy assassination.[7] David Gordon was eighty-three when he died in New York City in December 1997. A family-written notice in the *New York Times* said that he had been "among a group of courageous News York City newspaper men" who lost their jobs when they refused to cooperate with the Eastland committee.[8]

A few of the embattled journalists managed to salvage their journalism careers. Elliott Maraniss, for example, worked at several left-wing newspapers after he was fired by the *Detroit Times.* He later joined the *Capital Times,* a daily in Madison, Wisconsin, with a long history of anti-McCarthyism. He worked his way through the newsroom hierarchy to become a revered city editor and eventually editor.[9] At his request his 2004 obituary made no mention of his clash with HUAC. One of the first reporters he had hired paid tribute, saying, "He enlarged the paper's role as a voice against social injustices, large and small."[10]

Beyond the financial and professional strains, the victims' families also suffered the trauma. The daughter of Alden Whitman, the *New York Times* copy editor who was convicted of contempt of Congress in 1956, found herself ostracized by her friends when a local newspaper reported the news of her father's testimony on its front page. Her father blamed the breakup of his marriage on the social strains that resulted from his appearance before the Eastland committee.[11] The family of Seymour Peck, also of the *Times,* endured threatening letters and harassing telephone calls. "Nuts would call you up at 3 in the morning and scream things at you, or not say anything at all," he said. "The newspaper in Queens played up every story and gave our home address so I got all kinds of hate mail."[12] Peck became the editor of the *Times Book Review* after his court battles ended in 1957. In the early morning hours of January 1, 1985, he was killed while returning home from a New Year's Eve party after his car collided with another. The driver of the second car was charged with driving while intoxicated. Peck's obituary was written by his friend Herbert Mitgang, a *Times* reporter who was questioned by the Eastland committee during a closed session but not in public. Peck was sixty-seven.[13]

McCarthyism's newsroom casualties were far fewer than its victims in other professions—teachers, government employees, entertainers. Nearly three thousand civilians were dismissed from government jobs between 1947 and 1956, nearly three hundred radio artists were blacklisted, the Hollywood Ten went to prison, and several witnesses committed suicide after they received a subpoena or after they appeared to testify.[14] What makes the journalists stand out from others who were targets during the McCarthy era is that they worked in an industry specifically protected by the Bill of Rights. But, as they learned, it offered scant protection to individual journalists. Their treatment, both outside the newspaper industry and inside, provided a graphic warning for their colleagues to guard against expressing views or participating in organizations that might later be used against them.

Several of the journalists were hounded by the FBI well after their congressional appearances. Janet Scott, for example, was pursued well into the 1960s, although she had been fired by the *Knickerbocker News* after her appearance before HUAC in 1953. FBI agents tracked her employment, her home address, and her travels.[15] The FBI also tracked Whitman. Several weeks before the 1972 election the FBI alerted the Secret Service to Whitman's Communist background, although it is difficult to understand how an obituary writer posed a threat to the president or national security.[16] Whitman's relegation to the obit disk revolutionized newspaper obituary writing as he became the celebrated practitioner of the form, turning the worst job on most newspapers into an art. In the early 1970s he interviewed Supreme Court Justice William O. Douglas for the *Times*'s obituary files. At the end of a full day of interviewing, Whitman mentioned his court case. "I didn't want to say this at the beginning, but I can't leave without saying I want to thank you for having voted for me," Whitman said, referring to Douglas's vote in his case.

"I knew who you were before you came," Douglas responded. "How has it been?"[17]

Whitman's obituary for Douglas ran in the *Times* four years after Whitman's retirement, and it noted that Douglas had "strong convictions on individual rights that often generated controversy."[18]

Whitman also wrote an admiring obituary for the attorney who represented him in the earliest phase of his court challenge, Thurman Arnold, who died in 1969. Neither Arnold's nor Douglas's obituary mentioned the men's roles in freeing Whitman. However, Arnold's obit did note that he had defended many leftists and suspected Communists during the McCarthy era with little or no payment. "He relished the fact that his firm's corporate clients were, in effect, paying the freight for his attacks on McCarthyism," Whitman noted.[19] Whitman retired from the *Times* in 1976 and died in September 1990 after suffering a stroke in Monte Carlo, where he was attending a celebration of the seventieth birthday of former *Times* food editor Craig Claiborne. Whitman's body was cremated and the ashes strewn at his favorite places in Paris. A *Times* obituary written by a group of his former colleagues noted that he had transformed obituary writing into an art, and as a tribute to his work they attached no byline to the announcement of his death.[20]

Robert Shelton wrote for the *Times* culture desk after his court cases ended. There, during the 1960s and 1970s, he helped launch the careers of a score of musicians and singers, including Janis Ian, Bob Dylan, Janis Joplin, Judy Collins, the Mothers of Invention, Peter, Paul and Mary, and others. In the late 1960s Shelton had moved to Britain, where he died in December 1995 at age sixty-nine.[21]

Janet Scott moved to New York City after she was fired by the *Knickerbocker News*. She worked as a sales representative at Advance Printing Company for more than twenty-five years. In 1981 she was given a gold pin by the Newspaper Guild for her service. "She raised hell," commented R. Victor Stewart, president of the Albany Guild. She was eighty-eight when she died in July 1992.[22]

James Wechsler remained editor of the liberal *New York Post* following his appearance before the McCarthy committee. In 1961 he became editor of the newspaper's editorial page and wrote a regular column. In 1980, four years after media baron Rupert Murdoch bought the *Post* and shifted the newspaper to a conservative stance, Wechsler stepped down as editorial editor but continued to write his column "to provide a dissenting view for readers" of the *Post*. He died of cancer in New York City in September 1983.[23]

Winston Burdett, the CBS correspondent who unleashed the 1955 Senate investigation, appeared to escape the social and professional penalties that confronted other informers. Many witnesses who named names and were seen as patriots in the 1950s later found themselves subjected to scorn and retribution after their testimony came to be regarded as a betrayal of friends and colleagues.[24] In 1966 Burdett received the prestigious "Outstanding Achievement" award from Sigma Delta Chi, the journalist organization that later became the Society of Professional Journalists. He was seventy-nine when he died in Rome in May 1993.[25]

Harvey Matusow served forty-four months of a five-year prison term for perjury in 1956. He settled in a commune in Utah where he worked to help impoverished Native Americans. He later moved to New Hampshire and died at seventy-five in January 2002 from injuries suffered in an automobile crash.[26]

James Eastland of Mississippi served in the U.S. Senate for thirty-six years, including twenty-two years as chairman of the Judiciary Committee. As president pro tem of the Senate from 1972 to 1978, he had been third in line to succeed three presidents: Richard Nixon, Gerald R. Ford, and Jimmy Carter. After retiring from the Senate in 1978, he returned to his huge cotton plantation in Sunflower County where he died of pneumonia in 1986 at age eighty-one. His obituary in the *Times* briefly mentioned the investigation of the press, noting that it had been "abandoned."[27]

Julien G. Sourwine retired from the Senate Internal Security Subcommittee in 1976 and died ten years later at a nursing home in Reno, Nevada. He was seventy-eight. His obituary in the *New York Times* noted that he and Senator Eastland had denied that the *Times* was singled out during the investigation in the 1950s.[28]

Joseph McCarthy was forty-seven when he died four months after his censure by the Senate in 1956. A front-page obituary in the *Times* noted that between 1950 and 1954, he "wielded more power than any other Senator." The Senate voted to condemn his tactics in December 1956. Then-senator Richard Nixon told the *Times*: "Years will pass before the results of his [Senator McCarthy's] work can be objectively evaluated, but his friends and many of his critics will not question his devotion to what he considered to be the best interests of his country." Although the article gave the cause as "a liver ailment," others blamed excessive drinking.[29]

When J. Edgar Hoover died of heart failure in 1972 at seventy-seven, newspaper obituaries that pointed to his controversial reign only scratched the surface. The *Times* observed that he had "built [the FBI] into a dominant and controversial force in law enforcement. The newspaper noted that he had "molded the FBI in his own image—efficient, incorruptible and rigid."[30] As a symbolic tribute, members of Congress voted to allow his body to lie in state in the Capitol rotunda, a gesture that is traditionally reserved for former presidents. In 2005, as Hoover's legacy became better understood, Laurence H. Silberman, a conservative federal judge on the U.S. Circuit Court of Appeals for the District of Columbia, made headlines when he called for Hoover's name to be removed from the J. Edgar Hoover FBI building in downtown Washington, D.C. Having reviewed previously secret documents from Hoover's reign at the FBI, Silberman complained that the former director had "allowed—even offered—the bureau to be used by presidents for nakedly political purposes."[31]

Attorney Morris Ernst gained a national reputation as a liberal advocate for literary and artistic freedom despite his desire to punish Communists and former Communists. His seemingly conflicting positions on political and social issues made him one of the most complicated figures in the anti-Communist movement. During the 1930s he defended the rights of the Newspaper Guild to bargain collectively for journalists. In the 1940s and 1950s he worked to oust Communists from the guild, as he had worked to oust Communists at the American Civil Liberties Union in the 1930s. In later years his law practice specialized in defending literary figures against censorship. He died in New York in May 1976 at age eighty-seven. His obituary in the *New York Times,* written by Alden Whitman, said that Ernst favored "due process of the law and procedure for (any) person, Communist or other."[32]

Republican Rep. Harold Velde of Illinois succeeded J. Parnell Thomas of New Jersey as chairman of the Un-American Activities Committee after Thomas was convicted of taking kickbacks in late 1949 and sent to jail. Ironically, he was held at the same Danbury, Connecticut, penitentiary that housed the convicted members of the Hollywood Ten. After his parole in September 1950 Thomas bought three New Jersey weeklies and became a newspaper publisher. The Newspaper Guild added his name on its "Dishonor Roll" of public officials. Velde, on the other hand, remained on HUAC until his retirement in 1974 when he moved to Arizona. He died in 1985 at age seventy-five.[33]

HUAC turned its attention to the civil rights movement in the 1960s and the antiwar movement in the 1970s. After it became the target of protests, it was abolished in 1975, a relic that was no longer effective. The Senate shut down the Internal Security Subcommittee two years later.[34]

Notes

Introduction

1. Sen. William E. Jenner, R-Ind., speech delivered to the Inland Daily Press Association, February 27, 1956, Chicago, "Newspapers, Miscellaneous" folder, box 183, Senate Internal Security Subcommittee Papers, National Archives.

2. In January 2003 the Bush administration sent U.S. armed forces into Iraq to topple Saddam Hussein's regime, claiming Iraq had stockpiled biological and chemical weapons and had acquired components for building nuclear weapons. Miller had written numerous articles that gave credence to those claims but, after the U.S. invaded Iraq, it quickly became clear that Iraq had no such weapons. In early July 2003 former U.S. ambassador Joseph Wilson, who opposed the war in Iraq, published an op-ed article in the *New York Times* in which he described how the Bush administration had sent him to investigate claims that Iraq had acquired uranium for nuclear weapons from Niger. Wilson said that he found no evidence in Niger to back up the claims but that the White House continued nonetheless to cite the Niger rumor as fact as Bush made his case for war. The article embarrassed the White House, and it appeared that administration officials had set out to discredit Wilson. Those officials, later identified as I. Lewis "Scooter" Libby, Karl Rove, and Richard Armitage, told reporters anonymously that Wilson's wife, Valerie Plame, worked for the CIA and had exerted her influence to have her husband selected to probe the Niger rumor. The implication was that Plame wanted her husband for the job because he opposed invading Iraq, as she did, and could be counted on to discredit the Niger information.

3. Several journalists agreed to testify after those informants waived their confidentiality agreements with the reporters, but Judith Miller refused to testify, saying such waivers could not be trusted because their signing might have been coerced by the government (Joe Hagan, "U.S. Prosecutor Says Reporters Deserve Jail," *Wall Street Journal,* July 5, 2005, B-1; Don Van Natta Jr., Adam Liptak, and Clifford J. Levy, "The Miller Case: A Notebook, a Cause, a Jail Cell and a Deal," *New York Times,* October 16, 2005, 1; Jeffrey Toobin, "Name That Source," *New Yorker,* January 16, 2006, 7–16; Anne Marie Squeo and Sarah Ellison, "Court Cases Raise New Issues about Shielding News Sources," *Wall Street Journal,* April 19, 2006, A-5).

4. James Bandler, "Contempt Orders Are Upheld on Reporters in CIA Leak Case," *Wall Street Journal*, February 16, 2005, A-2; Evan Perez, "As Libby Goes to Trial, Case Appears Weakened," *Wall Street Journal*, January 12, 2007, A-6.

5. Larne Manly, "A Difficult Moment, Long Anticipated," *New York Times*, July 7, 2005, A-16; Anne Marie Squeo and John D. McKinnon, "Top Cheney Aid Charged in Leak Inquiry," *Wall Street Journal*, October 29, 2005, 1; Eric Lichtblau, "Journalists Said to Figure in Strategy in Leak Case," *New York Times*, November 16, 2005, A-20.

6. Leonard W. Levy, *Freedom of Speech and Press in Early American History: Legacy of Suppression* (New York: Harper, 1963), 18–87; John Lofton, *The Press as Guardian of the First Amendment* (Columbia: University of South Carolina Press, 1980), 1–19.

7. Ralph H. Johnson and Michael Altman, "Communists in the Press: A Senate Witch-Hunt of the 1950s Revisited," *Journalism Quarterly* 55 (1978): 487–93; David Caute, *The Great Fear: The Anti-Communist Purge under Truman and Eisenhower* (New York: Simon and Schuster, 1978), 449–53; James Aronson, *The Press and the Cold War* (New York: Monthly Review Press, 1970), 75–77, 139–52.

8. "Staff: Senate Investigation" file, series 2, C/D, Turner Catledge Papers, Special Collections, Mitchell Memorial Library, Mississippi State University.

9. Arthur Gelb, *City Room* (New York: G. P. Putnam's Sons, 2003), 262.

10. Frank J. Donner, *The Un-Americans* (New York: Ballantine, 1961), 54–97.

11. Kenneth O'Reilly, *Hoover and the Un-Americans: The FBI, HUAC, and the Red Menace* (Philadelphia: Temple University Press, 1983), 94–100.

12. Caute, *Great Fear*, 21; Ellen Schrecker, *No Ivory Tower: McCarthyism and the Universities* (New York: Oxford University Press, 1986), 308–37.

13. Caute, *Great Fear*, 21; Schrecker, *No Ivory Tower*, 308–37.

14. Richard Gid Powers, *Not without Honor: The History of American Anticommunism* (New Haven, Conn.: Yale University Press, 1995), 227–46, Ralph S. Brown, *Loyalty and Security: Employment Tests in the United States* (New Haven, Conn.: Yale University Press, 1958), 176–82; Caute, *Great Fear*, 515; Ellen Schrecker, *The Age of McCarthyism: A Brief History with Documents* (Boston: Bedford, 1994), 39; Ronald Goldfarb, *The Contempt Power* (New York: Columbia University Press, 1963), 197.

15. Robert K. Carr, *The House Committee on Un-American Activities, 1945–1950* (Ithaca, N.Y.: Cornell University Press, 1952), 364–405; Donner, *Un-Americans*, 147–63.

16. Jim Tuck, *McCarthyism and New York's Hearst Press: A Study of Roles in the Witch Hunt* (Lanham, Md.: University Press of America, 1995); David Nasaw, *The Chief: The Life of William Randolph Hearst* (Boston: Houghton Mifflin, 2000), 502–506; Aronson, *The Press and the Cold War*, 75–77.

17. Kenneth O'Reilly: *Hoover and the Un-Americans: The FBI, HUAC, and the Red Menace* (Philadelphia: Temple University Press, 1983), 34–36.

18. Caute, *Great Fear*, 79; Ted Morgan, *Reds: McCarthyism in Twentieth-Century America* (New York: Random House, 2003), 514–16; William Preston Jr., *Aliens and Dissenters: Federal Suppression of Radicals, 1903–1933* (New York: Harper Torchbooks, 1963), 152–207.

19. Daniel Leab, *A Union of Individuals: The Formation of the American Newspaper Guild, 1933–1936* (New York: Columbia University Press, 1970), 267–68; Sam Kuczun, "History of the American Newspaper Guild" (Ph.D. diss., University of Minnesota, 1970, 190–92.

20. Richard M. Fried, *Nightmare in Red: The McCarthy Era in Perspective* (New York: Oxford University Press, 1990), 43–45.

21. Larry Ceplair and Steven Englund, *The Inquisition in Hollywood: Politics in the Film Community, 1930–1960* (New York: Anchor, 1980); Merle Miller, *The Judges and the Judged* (New York: Doubleday, 1952; John Cogley, *Report on Blacklisting II: Radio-Television* (New York: Fund for the Republic, 1956).

22. Victor S. Navasky, *Naming Names* (New York: Penguin, 1991), 319–22.

23. Ceplair and Englund, *Inquisition in Hollywood,* 345–50; Haig Bosmajiam, *The Freedom Not to Speak* (New York: New York University Press, 1999), 198–205.

24. Ellen Schrecker, *Many Are the Crimes: McCarthyism in America* (New York: Little, Brown, 1998), xi.

25. Arthur M. Schlesinger Jr., *The Vital Center: The Politics of Freedom* (Boston: Houghton Mifflin, 1949), 3.

26. Sidney Lens, *Radicalism in America* (New York: Thomas Y. Crowell, 1969), 5–24; Preston, *Aliens and Dissenters,* 11–34.

27. Joseph R. Starobin, *American Communism in Crisis, 1943–1957* (Cambridge, Mass.: Harvard University Press, 1972), 108–14; David A. Shannon, *The Decline of American Communism* (New York: Harcourt Brace, 1959), 92–97; Guenter Lewy, *The Cause That Failed: Communism in American Political Life* (New York: Oxford University Press, 1990), 307–308; Navasky, *Naming Names,* 26.

28. Leab, *A Union of Individuals,* 267–68; Kuczun, "History of the American Newspaper Guild," 190–92.

29. John Earl Haynes and Harvey Klehr, *Venona: Decoding Soviet Espionage in America* (New Haven, Conn.: Yale University Press, 1999), 57–92.

30. See generally Harvey Klehr, John Earl Haynes, and Fridrikh Igorevich Firsov, *The Secret World of American Communism* (New Haven, Conn.: Yale University Press, 1995); Harvey Klehr, John Earl Haynes, and Kyrill M. Anderson, *The Soviet World of American Communism* (New Haven, Conn.: Yale University Press, 1998); Herbert Romerstein and Eric Breindel, *The Venona Secrets: Exposing Soviet Espionage and America's Traitors* (Washington, D.C.: Regnery, 2000); Allen Weinstein and Alexander Vassiliev, *The Haunted Wood: Soviet Espionage in America—The Stalin Era* (New York: Modern Library, 2000).

31. Haynes and Klehr, *Venona,* 7.

32. Kuczun," History of the American Newspaper Guild," 190–91.

33. David L. Potess and others, *The Journalism of Outrage: Investigative Reporting and Agenda Building in America* (New York: Guilford, 1991), 29–42; Judith Serrin and William Serrin, eds., *Muckraking! The Journalism That Changed America* (New York: New Press, 2002), ixx–xxii.

34. Upton Sinclair, *The Autobiography of Upton Sinclair* (New York: Harcourt, Brace, 1962), 224, 268–77.

35. Aileen S. Kraditor, *"Jimmy Higgins": The Mental World of the American Rank-and-File Communist, 1930–1958* (Westport, Conn.: Greenwood, 1988), 226; Fraser M. Ottanelli, *The Communist Party of the United States: From the Depression to World War II* (New Brunswick, N.J.: Rutgers University Press, 1991), 76; Harvey Klehr, *The Heyday of American Communism: The Depression Decade* (New York: Basic Books, 1984), 91–92, 173.

36. See Michael Emery, Edwin Emery, and Nancy L. Roberts, *The Press and America: An Interpretative History of the Mass Media,* 9th ed.(Boston: Allyn and Bacon, 2000); Frank Luther Mott, *American Journalism: A History, 1690–1960* (New York: Macmillan, 1962); William David Sloan and James D. Startt, *The Media in America: A History* (Northport, Ala.: Vision Press, 1996); Sterling Kittross, *Stay Tuned: A Concise History of American Broadcasting,* 3rd ed. (Mahwah, N.J.: Lawrence Erlbaum Associates, 2002). Jean Folkerts and Dwight L. Teeter Jr., *Voices of a Nation: A History of Mass Media in the United States* (Boston: Allyn and Bacon, 2002), 458.

37. Edwin R. Bayley, *Joe McCarthy and the Press* (New York: Pantheon, 1981); Lawrence N. Strout, *Covering McCarthyism: How the* Christian Science Monitor *Handled Joseph R. McCarthy, 1950–1954* (Westport, Conn.: Greenwood, 1999).

38. Edward M. Alwood, "The Hunt for Red Writers: The Senate Internal Security Subcommittee Investigation of Communists in the Press, 1955–56" (Ph.D. diss., University of North Carolina, 2000); Ralph H. Johnson and Michael Altman, "Communists in the Press:

A Senate Witch-Hunt of the 1950s Revisited," *Journalism Quarterly* 55 (1978): 487–93; Aronson, *Press and the Cold War,* 139–52; Harrison Salisbury, *Without Fear or Favor: The New York Times and Its Times* (New York: Times Books, 1980), 483–92; Gelb, *City Room,* 252–56; Susan E. Tifft and Alex S. Jones, *The Trust: The Powerful Family behind the New York Times* (Boston: Little, Brown, 1999), 263–70.

39. Haynes and Klehr, *Venona,* 339–94.

40. "Strange New Pals in the K.G.B.," *New York Times,* August 13, 1992, A22; Jacob Weisberg, "Cold War without End," *New York Times,* November 28, 1999, 120; Alan M. Jalon, "This Gadfly's Ghost Won't Remain Still," *Los Angeles Times,* December 7, 2003, E-4; Cassandra Tate, "Who's Out to Lunch Here?" *Columbia Journalism Review,* November–December 1992, 13–14.

41. Haynes and Klehr, *Venona,* 14–18; Christopher John Girard, "A Program of Cooperation: The FBI, the Senate Internal Security Subcommittee, and the Communist Issue, 1950–54" (Ph.D. diss., Marquette University, 1993), 354–57; O'Reilly, *Hoover and the Un-Americans,* 194–95.

Chapter One: Awakening the Newsroom

1. Frances Rockmore, "Three Days' Work in Sweatshop for $2.63 Pay," *Brooklyn Daily Eagle,* March 16, 1933, M-1.

2. Donald Paneth, "The Newspaper Guild," *Encyclopedia of American Journalism* (New York: Facts on File Publishers, 1983), 331.

3. Kenneth Stewart, *News Is What We Make It: A Running Story of the Working Press* (Westport, Conn.: Greenwood, 1943), 48; Frederick Lewis Allen, *Since Yesterday: The Nineteen-Thirties in America* (New York: Bantam, 1939), 218.

4. Alfred McClung Lee, *The Daily Newspaper in America: The Evolution of a Social Instrument* (New York: Octagon, 1973), 670–77.

5. Daniel J. Leab, *A Union of Individuals: The Formation of the American Newspaper Guild, 1933–1936* (New York: Columbia University Press, 1970), 4–25.

6. Lee, *Daily Newspaper in America,* 214–15; Alfred McClung Lee, "The Basic Newspaper Pattern," *Annals of the American Academy of Political and Social Science* (January 1942): 52; Frank Luther Mott, *American Journalism: A History, 1690–1960* (New York: Macmillan, 1962), 645; David Nasaw, *The Chief: The Life of William Randolph Hearst* (Boston: Houghton Mifflin, 2000), 314–21.

7. Leab, *A Union of Individuals,* 33–40.

8. Heywood Broun, "It Seems to Me," *New York World-Telegram,* August 7, 1933, 13.

9. Dale Kramer, *Heywood Broun: A Biographical Portrait* (New York: Current Books, 1949), 38–40.

10. Ibid., 94.

11. Ibid., 112.

12. Heywood Broun, "It Seems to Me," *New York World,* August 5 and 6, 1927, 11.

13. Stewart, *News Is What We Make It,* 52.

14. Kramer, *Heywood Broun,* 173–83.

15. Heyward Broun, "It Seems to Heywood Broun," *Nation,* May 9, 1928, 532.

16. *New York World,* May 5, 1928, 11.

17. Kramer, *Heywood Broun,* 191–92.

18. Ibid., 204–21.

19. Ibid., 225.

20. Heywood Broun, "It Seems to Me," *New York World-Telegram,* April 29, 1933, 11.

21. Stewart, *News Is What We Make It,* 131–33.

22. Heywood Broun, "It Seems to Me," *New York World-Telegram,* August 7, 1933, 13.

23. "*World* Asks Court to Let Scripps-Howard Buy It; Rival Bid by Paul Block," *New York Times*, February 25, 1931, 1.

24. Leab, *A Union of Individuals*, 67–69.

25. Sol Jacobson, "The Fourth Estate: A Study of the American Newspaper Guild" (Ph.D. diss., New School for Social Research, 1960), 23–25.

26. Robert Bordner, "Why We Organized!" *Quill*, October 1933, 6.

27. Edwin Emery, *History of the American Newspaper Publishers Association* (Westport, Conn.: Greenwood, 1970), 230.

28. "Reporters Organizing," *Editor and Publisher*, December 9, 1933, 22.

29. Leab, *A Union of Individuals*, 114–16.

30. Ibid., 39–40, 69–76.

31. C. C. Nicolet, "The Newspaper Guild," *American Mercury*, October 1936, 188–89.

32. Irving Howe and Lewis Coser, *The American Communist Party: A Critical History* (New York: Frederick A. Praeger, 1957), 372; Ellen Schrecker, *Many Are the Crimes: McCarthyism in America* (Boston: Little, Brown, 1998), 49.

33. James Aronson, *The Press and the Cold War* (New York: Monthly Review Press, 1970), 10–19.

34. "Humiliating Failure," *Editor and Publisher*, September 15, 1934, 24.

35. "Publication of Ledger Resumed; Guild Is Still on Strike," *Editor and Publisher*, December 1, 1934, 8.

36. Leab, *A Union of Individuals*, 171.

37. Ibid., 125, 190.

38. Ibid., 689.

39. Nasaw, *Chief*, 483–84.

40. Richard O'Connor, *Heywood Broun: A Biography* (New York: G. P. Putnam's Sons, 1975), 186–87.

41. *Associated Press v. National Labor Relations Board*, 301 U.S. 103 (1937), 132.

42. Leab, *A Union of Individuals*, 137–42.

43. Elizabeth Dilling, *The Red Network: A "Who's Who" and Handbook of Radicalism for Patriots* (Kenilworth, Ill.: Elizabeth Dilling, 1934), 268.

44. Dale Kramer, *Heywood Broun: A Biographical Portrait* (New York: Current Books, 1949), 254.

45. "A.F. of L. Affiliation: What Would It Mean to Strength of Guild?" *Guild Reporter*, March 15, 1935, 1. Eddy served as the top executive of the New York local before becoming the national guild's first paid executive.

46. Leab, *A Union of Individuals*, 205–15.

47. Ibid., 250–55.

48. Jacobson, "Fourth Estate," 50.

49. Leab, *A Union of Individuals*, 270–75.

50. Jacobson, "Fourth Estate," 50–55.

51. "Seattle Strike Is Won; Big Gains Elsewhere," *Guild Reporter*, December 1, 1936, 1.

52. "News Guild Backs Enlarging Court," *New York Times*, June 11, 1937, 8.

53. "ANG to CIO," *Time*, June 21, 1937, 60–61.

54. "Newspaper Guild Voted to Join C.I.O.," *New York Times*, June 8, 1937, 5.

55. Leab, *A Union of Individuals*, 129–33.

56. "Firm Stand against Guild Closed Shop Voted by Eleven Newspaper Groups," *Editor and Publisher*, July 3, 1937, 1.

57. "Red Herring Brought In," *Guild Reporter*, August 1, 1937, 1.

58. "Broun Called Communist 'Stooge,'" *Washington (D.C.) Herald*, July 19, 1937, 4; "Broun Denies Link to Russia, Assails Green," *New York Post*, July 20, 1937, 3; Jacobson,

"Fourth Estate," 93–100. Green later led a campaign to oust Reds from the AFL and to join the anti-Communist crusade to expose them in CIO-affiliated unions (Bert Cochran, *Labor and Communism: The Conflict That Shaped American Unions* [Princeton, N.J.: Princeton University Press, 1977], 67–71).

59. Dulles, *Labor in America*, 268–71.

60. Harvey Klehr, *The Heyday of American Communism: The Depression Decade* (New York: Basic Books, 1984), 223–33.

61. Melvin W. Reder, *Labor in a Growing Economy* (New York: John Wiley, 1957), 70; Foster Rhea Dulles, *Labor in America: A History* (New York: Thomas Y. Crowell, 1949), 288–98.

62. O'Connor, *Heywood Broun: A Biography*, 186.

63. Sam Kuczun, "History of the American Newspaper Guild" (Ph.D. diss., University of Minnesota, 1970), 189–90.

64. Morris Ernst, *The Best Is Yet . . .* (New York: Harper, 1945), 85; O'Connor, *Heywood Broun: A Biography*, 188.

65. Klehr, *Heyday of American Communism*, 216, 243.

66. "Daily Worker Writer Recalls Broun Urging Reds in Union," *Editor and Publisher,* June 25, 1955, 62.

67. Stewart, *News Is What We Make It*, 211.

68. Howe and Coser, *American Communist Party*, 385n; Joanne Lisa Kenen, "White Collars and Red-Baiters: Communism and Anti-Communism in the American Newspaper Guild, 1933–1956" (senior thesis, Harvard University, 1980), 26–28.

69. Jacobson, "Fourth Estate," 48, 86.

70. Ibid., 86–113.

71. M. J. Heale, *American Anticommunism: Combating the Enemy Within, 1830–1970* (Baltimore: John Hopkins University Press, 1990), 129.

Chapter Two: The Politics of Anticommunism

1. Frank J. Donner, *The Un-Americans* (New York: Ballantine, 1961), 12.

2. Ibid., 13–16.

3. M. J. Heale, *American Anticommunism: Combating the Enemy Within, 1830–1970* (Baltimore: John Hopkins University Press, 1990), 115; Walter Goodman, *The Committee: The Extraordinary Career of the House Committee on Un-American Activities* (New York: Farrar, Straus and Giroux, 1968), 49.

4. House Special Committee on Un-American Activities, *Investigation of Un-American Propaganda Activities in the United States,* 75th Cong., 3rd sess., November 7, 1938 (Washington, D.C.: GPO, 1938), 100 (hereafter cited as the Dies Committee hearings).

5. Richard Gid Powers, *Not without Honor: The History of American Anticommunism* (New Haven, Conn.: Yale University Press, 1995), 172.

6. Dies Committee hearings, August 20, 1938, 880–81.

7. Ibid., August 22, 1938, 919.

8. Ibid.

9. Ibid., 938.

10. August Ogden, *The Dies Committee: A Study of the Special House Committee for the Investigation of Un-American Activities, 1938–1944* (Washington, D.C.: Catholic University of America Press, 1945), 65.

11. Testimony of Margaret A. Kerr, Dies Committee hearings, August 18, 1938, 977.

12. Testimony of Ray E. Nimmo, Dies Committee hearings, October 24, 1938, 1776.

13. Dies Committee hearings, November 7, 1938, 2167.

14. Testimony of Benjamin Gitlow, Dies Committee hearings, September 11, 1939, 4713.

15. Testimony of Joseph Zack, Dies Committee hearings, September 30, 1939.

16. Testimony of Maurice L. Malkin, Dies Committee hearings, October 13, 1938, 5774.

17. "Dies 'Open-Minded'"; Gives Broun 1 Minute," *Guild Reporter*, August 38, 1.

18. Ibid.

19. Dies Committee hearings, January 3, 1940, 12–13.

20. "Heywood Broun, 51, Columnist, Is Dead," *New York Times*, December 19, 1939, 23.

21. Ibid., 1.

22. "3,000 Mourn Broun at St. Patrick Mass," *New York Times*, December 21, 1939, 23.

23. "Broun's Successor," *Time*, January 22, 1940, 38–39.

24. Westbrook Pegler, "Fair Enough," *Washington Post*, December 9, 1939, 11.

25. Dale Kramer, *Heywood Broun: A Biographical Portrait* (New York: Current Books, 1949), 249.

26. William F. Buckley Jr., "Rabble-Rouser," *New Yorker*, March 1, 2004, 48.

27. Westbrook Pegler, "Fair Enough," *Washington Post*, June 1, 1940, 7.

28. Ibid., July 3, 1940, 7.

29. "Text of National Guild Constitution," *Editor and Publisher*, December 23, 1933, 6.

30. "Broun's Successor," 38.

31. "The Guild's New President," *Guild Reporter*, January 15, 1940, 1.

32. Daniel J. Leab, *A Union of Individuals: The Formation of the American Newspaper Guild, 1933–1936* (New York: Columbia University Press, 1970), 266–67.

33. Westbrook Pegler, "A Trojan Foal," *Washington Post*, June 19, 1940, 7; Pegler, "Fair Enough," June 1, 1940, *New York World-Telegram*, June 1, 1940, 7; Pegler, "Fair Enough," *World-Telegram*, June 5, 1941, 21; Pegler, "Fair Enough," *Washington Post*, June 11, 1940, 9; Pegler, "Fair Enough," *World-Telegram*, February 1, 1941, 13; Pegler, "Fair Enough," *World-Telegram*, June 31, 1940, 28; Pegler, "The V.F.W. Plan," *Washington Post*, July 2, 1940, 9; Pegler, "'Cunning Mantraps,'" *Washington Post*, July 3, 1940, 7.

34. Drew Pearson and Robert S. Allen, "Washington Merry-Go-Round," *Washington (D.C.) Times Herald*, June 10, 1940, 14.

35. Campaign flyer, October 23, 1940, "Elections—Anti-Red Slate, 1939–1940," box 12, Newspaper Guild, Local 3 Collection, Robert F. Wagner Labor Archives, Tamiment Institute Library, New York University.

36. "Battle's On," *Guild Reporter*, June 1, 1940, 3.

37. Blanche Wiesen Cook, *Eleanor Roosevelt: The Defining Years, 1933–1938* (New York: Penguin, 1999), 290, 302, 424; "Mrs. Roosevelt to Fight Communists in N.Y. Guild," *Editor and Publisher*, August 10, 1940, 5; "Mrs. Roosevelt Backs Anti-Red Guild Candidates," *Editor and Publisher*, December 14, 1940, 9.

38. "Sullivan Is New President," *Guild Reporter*, July 19, 1940, 1; Sam Kuczun, "History of the American Newspaper Guild" (Ph.D. diss., University of Minnesota, 1970), 207.

39. "Sullivan Is New President."

40. "Guild Bars Move to Denounce Isms," *New York Times*, July 12, 1940, 13.

41. "The Guild Elects," *Editor and Publisher*, July 20, 1940, 22.

42. Hodding Carter, "Showdown in Memphis," *Nation*, July 20, 1940, 48–49.

43. "Guild Still Split over Issue of Communism," *Editor and Publisher*, September 20, 1940, 6; "The Motions for Referendum," *Guild Reporter*, October 1, 1940, 2; "News Guild Bars 'ISMS,'" *New York Times*, February 28, 1941, 21; Sol Jacobson, "The Fourth Estate: A Study of the American Newspaper Guild" (Ph.D. diss., New School for Social Research, 1960), 130–35.

44. "News Guild Bars 'ISMS.'"

45. "Official Vote Listed in Newspaper Guild's First Direct Election," *Washington Post,* October 17, 1941, A-2.

46. Kuczun, "History of the American Newspaper Guild," 190–93.

47. Jacobson, "Fourth Estate," 136–39.

48. James A. Wechsler, "The Fourth Estate at Detroit," *Nation,* July 5, 1941, 7; James A. Wechsler, *The Age of Suspicion* (New York: Random House, 1953), 167; Victor S. Navasky, *Naming Names* (New York: Penguin, 1991), 58–59; Edwin Emery, *The Press and America,* 5th ed. (Englewood Cliffs, N.J.: Prentice Hall, 1984), 694.

49. Athan G. Theoharis and John Stuart Cox, *The Boss: J. Edgar Hoover and the Great American Inquisition* (Philadelphia: Temple University Press, 1988), 56.

50. Powers, *Not without Honor,* 23–31; Athan Theoharis, *The FBI and American Democracy* (Lawrence: University Press of Kansas, 2004), 29–31.

51. Athan G. Theoharis, *Spying on Americans: Political Surveillance from Hoover to the Huston Plan* (Philadelphia: Temple University Press, 1978), 255n8.

52. Ibid., 68.

53. Regin Schmidt, *Red Scare: FBI and the Origins of Anticommunism in the United States, 1919–1943* (Copenhagen: Museum Tusculanum Press, 2000), 362–65.

54. Theoharis, *FBI and American Democracy,* 48.

55. Theoharis, *Spying on Americans,* 42.

56. Ibid., 255n8.

57. The unit was later renamed the Special War Policies Unit and undertook analysis and evaluation of FBI intelligence reports and the review of names placed on the FBI's Custodial Detention List.

58. Tamm to Hoover, December 17, 1940, FBI 100-7326-1. Citations for FBI documents use the string of numbers that the FBI assigned to all investigative documents. The first set of numbers designates the branch of the FBI where the document is stored, the second set indicates the folder where the document was filed, and the third identifies the specific memorandum or report. The number 100 references FBI headquarters in Washington, D.C. The number 7326 was assigned to the Newspaper Guild file.

59. Hoover to Lawrence M.C. Smith, December 20, 1940, FBI 100-7326-1. Smith became a member of the Franklin D. Roosevelt administration in 1933 and worked as general coordinator of the legal division of the National Recovery Administration. During World War II he became chief of the Neutrality Laws Unit at the Justice Department.

60. Smith to Hoover, January 13, 1941, FBI 100-7326-3.

61. B. E. Sacket to Hoover, February 17, 1941, FBI 100-7326-5. In response to my July 2004 request under the Freedom of Information Act for files on Heywood Broun, the FBI said it could find "no records pertinent" to the request. However, Natalie Robins claims in her 1992 book that the FBI had assembled a "one-page file" on Broun. After I appealed the denial, the FBI furnished three documents, dated more than a decade after Broun's death, that mentioned his name, including an April 1957 report on the American Lithuanian Workers Literary Association. None of the documents indicated that Broun was ever the subject of an FBI investigation (David M. Hardy to author, March 16, 2005; Natalie Robins, *Alien Ink: The FBI's War on Freedom of Expression* [New Brunswick, N.J.: Rutgers University Press, 1992], 418).

62. Unsigned, "American Newspaper Guild—C.I.O.," November 25, 1941, FBI 100-7326-18X.

63. Hoover to SAC, New York, February 26, 1942, FBI 100-7325-17.

64. [Name deleted], report, March 27, 1942, FBI 100-7326-19.

65. War Department, Military Intelligence Division, unsigned memorandum sent to the FBI, January 31, 1942. FBI 100-7326-17. Hoover relayed the memo to the New York field office on February 26, 1942.

66. Ibid.

67. John Earl Haynes and Harvey Klehr, *Venona: Decoding Soviet Espionage in America* (New Haven, Conn.: Yale University Press, 1999), 76–77.

68. Ibid., 4–7.

69. March 27, 1942, FBI report.

70. Hoover to SAC New York, April 11, 1942, FBI 100-7326-20; Hoover to SAC New York, May 15, 1942, FBI 100-7326-22; [name deleted], memo to SAC Cleveland, April 6, 1943, 1200-7326-106; D. M. Ladd to Hoover, May 3, 1943, FBI 100-7326-171.

71. Hoover to Smith, October 7, 1942, FBI 100-732-638.

72. Smith to Hoover, November 17, 1942, FBI 100-7326-41.

73. For a history of the American Newspaper Guild from 1933 to 1936, see Leab, *A Union of Individuals*; for a history of the guild from its founding through the late 1950s, see Kuczun, "History of the American Newspaper Guild."

74. The Office of Navel Intelligence (ONI) forwarded my request for files on the Newspaper Guild to the Naval Criminal Investigative Service (NCSI) of the Department of the Navy. The NCSI responded that it was unable to identify any files related to the guild (Gina Watson, ONI, to author, July 29, 2004; Linda M. Riddle, information and privacy coordinator, NCSI, to author, August 10, 2004).

75. Hoover to SAC, Telex message, Grand Rapids, date deleted, FBI 100-7326-86.

76. McFarlin to Hoover, April 6, 1943, FBI 100-7326-115; Ladd to Hoover, May 3, 1943, FBI 100-7326-111.

77. Report by [name deleted], April 13, 1944, FBI 100-7326-183.

78. Jacobson, "Fourth Estate," 194; Fraser M. Ottanelli, *The Communist Party of the United States: From the Depression to World War II* (New Brunswick, N.J.: Rutgers University Press, 1991), 192–93.

79. Hoover to SAC, New York, 20 August 1942, FBI 100-7326-27.

80. Hoover to Agents in Charge, January 25, 1943, FBI 100-7326-69.

81. Report by [name deleted], April 26, 1943, FBI 100-7326-100.

82. Report by [name deleted], September 7, 1943, FBI 100-7326-147.

83. Theoharis, *Spying on Americans,* 43–44.

84. Ibid., 42, 255n8.

85. E. G. Fitch to Ladd, August 2, 1944, FBI 100-7326-207.

86. SAC Milwaukee to Hoover, August 15, 1944, FBI 100-7326-216.

87. On FBI eavesdropping see Theoharis, *Spying on Americans,* 94–96; Schmidt, *Red Scare,* 367; Theoharis, *Chasing Spies,* 112–14, 142–55; Theoharis, *FBI and American Democracy,* 4–6, 58–60; Theoharis and Cox, *Boss,* 11–13; Robins, *Alien Ink,* 140–41; Steve Rosswurm, "The Wondrous Tale of an FBI Bug: What It Tells Us about Communism, Anti-Communism, and the CIO Leadership," *American Communist History* 2, no. 1 (2003): 3–20.

88. G. B. Norris to Hoover, February 17, 1943, FBI 100-7326-62; report from SAC St. Louis to Hoover, March 1, 1943, FBI 100-7326-62; J. B. Wilcox to Hoover, June 17, 1944, FBI 100-7326-19.

89. Report by [name deleted], October 25, 1944, FBI 100-7326-226.

90. Report by [name deleted], December 15, 1944, FBI 100-7326-227.

91. Unsigned report, "American Newspaper Guild—CIO," n.d., FBI 100-7326-227.

92. Report by [name deleted], April 13, 1944, FBI 100-7326-183.

93. Report by [name deleted], March 20, 1945, FBI 100-7326-240. Philip S. Foner was one of sixty faculty fired by City College of New York in 1941 after a witch hunt by the New York State legislature's Rapp-Coudert Committee. See Ellen Schrecker, *No Ivory Tower: McCarthyism and the Universities* (New York: Oxford University Press, 1986), 50, 82.

94. Report by [name deleted], December 18, 1944, FBI 100-7326-229.

95. Report by [name deleted], January 25, 1945, FBI 100-7326-232.

96. Donald L. Miller, *The Story of World War II* (New York: Simon and Schuster, 2001), 489–652; Walter LaFeber, Richard Polenberg, and Nancy Woloch, *The American Century: A History of the United States since 1941,* 5th ed. (Boston: McGraw-Hill, 1998), 294–312.

97. Theoharis, *FBI and American Democracy,* 67–68.

Chapter Three: Prelude to an Investigation

1. John Lewis Gaddis, *The United States and the Origins of the Cold War, 1941–1947* (New York: Columbia University Press, 1972), 309–12.

2. Richard M. Fried, *Nightmare in Red: The McCarthy Era in Perspective* (New York: Oxford University Press, 1990), 62.

3. Louis J. Halle, *The Cold War as History* (New York: Harper and Row, 1967), 103–108.

4. Athan Theoharis, *The FBI and American Democracy* (Lawrence: University Press of Kansas, 2004), 67–68.

5. Report of [name deleted], November 14, 1946, FBI 100-7326-285.

6. "No Contract–No Work Forces Hearst Paper in Los Angeles to Suspend," *Guild Reporter,* September 13, 1946, 1; "Los Angeles Back at Work," *Guild Reporter,* December 13, 1946, 1.

7. Edwin Emery, *History of the American Newspaper Publishers Association* (Westport, Conn.: Greenwood, 1970), 238–39.

8. "Stern Reveals Sale of His 3 Papers Was No Sudden Whim," *Guild Reporter,* February 14, 1947, 1, 3.

9. Hoover to D. M. Ladd and L. B. Nichols, March 11, 1947, FBI 100-7326-290.

10. Ladd to Hoover, March 14, 1947, FBI 100-7326-289.

11. Kenneth O'Reilly: *Hoover and the Un-Americans: The FBI, HUAC, and the Red Menace* (Philadelphia: Temple University Press, 1983), 64–79.

12. Ibid., 91–94.

13. Ibid., 37–48, 94–100.

14. House Committee on Education and Labor, *Amendments to the National Labor Relations Act,* 80th Cong., 1st sess., March 15, 1947 (Washington, D.C.: GPO, 1947), 5:3739 (hereafter cited as Labor Relations hearing).

15. Ibid., 3622.

16. David Caute, *The Great Fear: The Anti-Communist Purge under Truman and Eisenhower* (New York: Simon and Schuster, 1978), 58.

17. Labor Relations hearing, 3763.

18. "Guild Here Red-Run Says National Head," *New York Times,* March 16, 1947, 35.

19. "Statements on Murray Charges of 'Communism,'" *Guild Reporter,* March 28, 1947, 6.

20. "Ryan Silent on Party Ties," *New York Times,* March 16, 1947, 35.

21. "Brodie Calls Charge Political," *New York Times,* March 16, 1947, 35.

22. David McCullough, *Truman* (New York: Touchstone, 1992), 565–66; Alonzo L. Hamby, *Man of the People: A Life of Harry S. Truman* (New York: Oxford University Press, 1995), 422–25.

23. Foster Rhea Dulles, *Labor in America: A History* (New York: Thomas Y. Crowell, 1949), 373–76; Emery, *History of the American Newspaper Publishers Association,* 243; Gerard D. Reilly, "The Legislative History of the Taft-Hartley Act," *George Washington Law Review* 29 (December 1960): 285–300.

24. Harry A. Millis and Emily Clark Brown, *From the Wagner Act to Taft-Hartley: A Study of National Labor Policy and Labor Relations* (Chicago: University of Chicago Press, 1950), 537–41, 545–60.

25. "Murray and Carey Refuse to Sign Anti-Red Affidavit," *Guild Reporter,* September 12, 1947, 8.

26. "If the Taft-Hartley Bill Becomes Law, Here Is What You Are in For," *Guild Reporter,* June 13, 1947, 1.

27. Harvey A. Levenstein, *Communism, Anticommunism, and the CIO* (Westport, Conn.: 1981), 218–20.

28. John Earl Haynes, *Red Scare or Red Menace? American Communism and Anticommunism in the Cold War Era* (Chicago: Ivan R. Dee, 1996), 132; David J. Saposs, *Communism in American Unions* (New York: McGraw-Hill, 1959), 158–59.

29. M. J. Heale, *American Anticommunism: Combating the Enemy Within, 1830–1970* (Baltimore: Johns Hopkins University Press, 1990), 147–49.

30. "News Guild to Qualify," *New York Times,* November 4, 1947, 28.

31. "Red Charges Fly in Guild Election Fight," *Editor and Publisher,* December 13, 1947, 13.

32. "McManus, Ryan Ousted as N.Y. Guild Leaders," *Editor and Publisher,* December 27, 1947, 10.

33. "New Slate Elected by Newspaper Guild," *New York Times,* December 21, 1947, 42.

34. "New Officers' Statement," *Front Page,* January 1948, 3, General Files, 1935–50, folder 53, box 14, Newspaper Guild, Local 3 Collection, Robert F. Wagner Labor Archives, Tamiment Institute Library, New York University.

35. Walter Goodman, *The Committee: The Extraordinary Career of the House Committee on Un-American Activities* (New York: Farrar, Straus and Giroux, 1968), 39–45, 172–75.

36. Ibid., 161–62.

37. Ibid., 175–89.

38. Nancy Lynn Schwartz, *The Hollywood Writers' Wars* (New York: Alfred A. Knopf, 1982), 82–95; Ronald Radosh and Allis Radosh, *Red Star over Hollywood: The Film Colony's Long Romance with the Left* (San Francisco: Encounter Books, 2005), 44–60.

39. U.S. Congress, Senate, "Our Own First," Remarks of Robert R. Reynolds of North Carolina, 78th Cong., 2d sess., *Cong. Rec.* 90, pt. 8 (March 7, 1944): A1143–44.

40. Larry Ceplair and Steven Englund, *The Inquisition in Hollywood: Politics in the Film Community, 1930–1960* (New York: Anchor, 1980), 254–60.

41. Gladwin Hill, "Says Government Aided Film Reds," *New York Times,* May 17, 1947, 8.

42. Ceplair and Englund, *Inquisition in Hollywood,* 260.

43. U.S. Congress, House, "Communist Influences in the Motion-Picture Industry," remarks by J. Parnell Thomas of New Jersey, 80th Cong., 1st sess., *Congressional Record* 93, pt. 11 (June 6, 1947): A2687–88.

44. "Hollywood on the Hill," *Time,* November 3, 1947, 22; Patrick Goldstein, "Hollywood's Blackest Hour," *Los Angeles Times,* October 19, 1997, 8.

45. The Hollywood Ten were Alvah Bessie, Herbert Biberman, Lester Cole, Edward Dmytryk, Ring Lardner Jr., John Howard Lawson, Albert Maltz, Samuel Ornitz, Adrian Scott, and Dalton Trumbo.

46. Radosh and Radosh, *Red Star over Hollywood,* 153–62.

47. House Committee on Un-American Activities, *Hearings Regarding the Communist Infiltration of the Motion Picture Industry,* 80th Cong., 1st sess., October 27, 1947 (Washington: GPO, 1947), 291–95.

48. "Hollywood on the Hill," 22; "Tale of Two Cities," *Newsweek,* November 10, 1947, 17.

49. "Movies to Oust Ten Cited for Contempt of Congress," *New York Times,* November 26, 1947, 1.

50. "Loyalty Tests for Employment in the Motion Picture Industry," *Stanford Law Review* 6 (May 1954): 438–72.

51. Jay Walz, "Ten Film Men Cited for Contempt in Overwhelming Votes by House," *New York Times,* November 25, 1947, 1.

52. "Congress and Hollywood," *New York Times,* October 13, 1947, 24.

53. Anthony Leviero, "Inquiries by Congress Stir Much Indignation," *New York Times,* November 2, 1947, E-10; Hugh A. Fogarty, "Omaha," *New York Times,* November 2, 1947, E-6; Frank L. Kluckhorn, "Boston," *New York Times,* November 2, 1947, E-6.

54. Ceplair and England, *Inquisition in Hollywood,* 287–89.

55. Lauren Kessler, *Clever Girl* (New York: HarperCollins, 2003); Kathryn S. Olmsted, *Red Spy Queen: A Biography of Elizabeth Bentley* (Chapel Hill: University of North Carolina Press, 2002).

56. "Stand Up and Be Counted Out," *Time,* June 28, 1948, 42.

57. "Firing of Reporter as Red Stirs Debate by Newspaper Guild," *Washington (D.C.) Times-Herald,* June 30, 1948, 11.

58. Thomas Buchanan, "Stand Up and Be Counted," undated clipping found in filed labeled "Communist Party—Newspaper," House Committee on Un-American Activities, Investigative Organizational Files, series 1, box 6, National Archives.

59. Kenneth O'Reilly, *Hoover and the Un-Americans: The FBI, HUAC, and the Red Menace* (Philadelphia: Temple University Press, 1983), 80.

60. Ibid.

61. Buchanan, "Stand Up and Be Counted."

62. "Guild Won't Aid Ousted Reds," *Washington Post,* May 18, 1948, 3.

63. "Washington to Vote on Whether to Fight Grievance of Member Fired for Being a Communist," *Guild Reporter,* May 28, 1948, 6.

64. "Move to Press Buchanan's Case Again Defeated," *Guild Reporter,* September 10, 1948, 4.

65. "Contract Pattern Set by Newspaper Guild," *New York Times,* July 3, 1948, 28.

66. "It Seems to Us," *Guild Reporter,* August 13, 1948, 6.

Chapter Four: Reds in the Newsroom

1. Louis J. Halle, *The Cold War as History* (New York: Harper and Row, 1967), 71–76, 163–67, 210–14; "Truman Statement on Atom," *New York Times,* September 24, 1949, 1.

2. Virginia Carmichael, *Framing History: The Rosenberg Story and the Cold War* (Minneapolis: University of Minnesota Press, 1993), 88–91; George E. Simmons, "The Communist Conspiracy Case: Views of 72 Daily Newspapers," *Journalism Quarterly* 27, no. 1 (March 1950): 3–11; Dozier C. Cade, "Witch-Hunting, 1952: The Role of the Press," *Journalism Quarterly* 29, no. 4 (Fall 1952): 396–407.

3. David Caute, *The Great Fear: The Anti-Communist Purge under Truman and Eisenhower* (New York: Simon and Schuster, 1978), 41–45.

4. Stephen J. Whitfield, *The Culture of the Cold War,* 2nd ed. (Baltimore: Johns Hopkins University Press, 1996), 21, 66, 134. Twelve Communist Party leaders were tried in January 1949 under the 1940 Smith Act, which made it illegal to advocate or teach forcible overthrow of the government. They were Eugene Dennis, Arno Gus Halberg, Gus Hall, Robert Thompson, Gil Green, Carl Winter, Benjamin Davis Jr., Henry Winston, John Williamson, John Gates, Jack Stachel, and William Foster. Eleven were found guilty in one of the longest trials in U.S.

history and jailed. Foster, the party's national chairman, became ill and died before he could stand trial (Ted Morgan, *Reds: McCarthyism in Twentieth-Century America* [New York: Random House, 2003], 312–20).

5. Arthur M. Schlesinger Jr., *The Vital Center: The Politics of Freedom* (Boston: Houghton Mifflin, 1949), 202–204.

6. Robert K. Carr, *The House Committee on Un-American Activities, 1945–1950* (Ithaca, N.Y.: Cornell University Press, 1952), 168–69.

7. Walter Goodman, *The Committee: The Extraordinary Career of the House Committee on Un-American Activities* (New York: Farrar, Straus and Giroux, 1968), 272–73.

8. Caute, *Great Fear*, 85; Carr, *House Committee on Un-American Activities*, 404.

9. Caute, *Great Fear*, 85.

10. Ibid., 500–14.

11. George Brown Tindall, *America: A Narrative History*, 2nd ed. (New York: W. W. Norton), 1271–72; Richard M. Fried, *Nightmare in Red: The McCarthy Era in Perspective* (New York: Oxford University Press, 1990), 117.

12. Caute, *Great Fear*, 104–108.

13. Frank J. Donner, *The Un-Americans* (New York: Ballantine, 1961), 147–62.

14. "Fight Must Continue on Communist Conspiracy," *Guild Reporter*, July 8, 1949, 13.

15. "Final Firing Wave Marks Merger of Field's Chicago Sun with the Times," *Guild Reporter*, February 13, 1948, 1.

16. "Strike Closes N.Y. World-Telegram and Sun; IEB Mobilizing Full Support for Strikers," *Guild Reporter*, June 23, 1950, 1.

17. "Truman Lauds Guild Efforts to Improve Conditions," *Guild Reporter*, 14 July 1950, 5.

18. Report by [name deleted], July 11, 1950, FBI 100-7326-326.

19. John Earl Haynes and Harvey Klehr, *Venona: Decoding Soviet Espionage in America* (New Haven, Conn.: Yale University Press, 1999), 247–49.

20. On the allegations against Stone see Ann Coulter, *Treason: Liberal Treachery from the Cold War to the War on Terrorism* (New York: Crown Forum, 2003), 97; Myra MacPherson, *All Governments Lie: The Life and Times of Rebel Journalist I. F. Stone* (New York: Scribner's, 2006), 285–306. On the defense of Stone see Cassandra Tate, "Who's out to Lunch Here?" *Columbia Journalism Review*, November–December 1992, 13; "Strange New Pals in the K.G.B.," *New York Times*, August 13, 1992, A-22.

21. Myra MacPherson, *All Governments Lie: The Life and Times of Rebel Journalist I. F. Stone* (New York: Scribner, 2006), 307–28.

22. Report by [name deleted], May 12, 1950, FBI 100-7326-324.

23. New York Field Office to Hoover June 20, 1950, FBI 100-7326-325.

24. U.S. Congress, House, Rep. Richard Vail speaking on "American Press," 82nd Cong., 1st sess., *Cong. Rec.* 97, pt. 1 (February 8, 1951): 1172; "Vail for Company Unions and against 'Outsiders,'" *Guild Reporter*, February 23, 1951, 3.

25. "Vail Asserts His Bill to Undermine Bargaining Strength of Guild Is Not Prompted by the Record," *Guild Reporter*, February 23, 1951, 3.

26. U.S. Congress, House, speech of Richard B. Vail, 82nd Cong., 1st sess., *Cong. Rec.* 97, pt. 1 (August 16, 1951): 10190–94.

27. Michael J. Ybarra, *Washington Gone Crazy: Senator Pat McCarran and the Great American Communist Hunt* (Hanover, N.H.: Steerforth Press, 2004), 569–605.

28. Larry Ceplair and Steven England, *The Inquisition in Hollywood: Politics in the Film Community, 1930–1960* (New York: Anchor, 1980), 361–97; Victor S. Navasky, *Naming Names* (New York: Penguin, 1991), 314–18.

29. Goodman, *Committee*, 313–14.

30. Ceplair and England, *Inquisition in Hollywood,* 255–58; Navasky, *Naming Names,* 314–18.

31. William Wheeler to Thomas Beale, August 9, 1955, "Communist Party—Newspaper," Investigative Organizations Files, series 1, box 6, House Committee on Un-American Activities, National Archives; Gerald Horne, *Class Struggle in Hollywood, 1930–1950* (Austin: University of Texas Press, 2001), 19–22, 42–44, 62–68.

32. Goodman, *Committee,* 313.

33. House Committee on Un-American Activities, *Communist Activities among Professional Groups in the Los Angeles Area,* 82nd Cong., 2nd sess., January 21–26 and April 9, 1952, pt. 1 (Washington, D.C.: GPO, 1952), 2459–85.

34. House Committee on Un-American Activities, *Communist Activities among Youth Groups,* 82nd Cong., 2nd sess., February 6, 1952 (Washington, D.C.: GPO, 1952), 3314; House Committee on Un-American Activities, *Annual Report of the Committee on Un-American Activities,* January 3, 1953 (Washington, D.C.: GPO, 1953), 69–71.

35. House Committee on Un-American Activities, *Communist Activities among Professional Groups,* May 22 and July 8, 1952, pt. 2 (Washington, D.C.: GPO, 1952), 3551–66.

36. Ibid., 3570.

37. Ibid., 3573.

38. Ibid., 3575–96.

39. "Discharge for CP Affiliation in Arbitration," *Editor and Publisher,* July 12, 1952, 12.

40. Los Angeles Daily News and American Newspaper Guild, Los Angeles Newspaper Guild (CIO), 19 Lab. Arb. Rep. (BNA) 39 (1952) (Dodd, Arb.).

41. Ibid.

42. Report by [name deleted], September 7, 1943, FBI 100-7326-147.

43. House Committee on Un-American Activities, *Communist Activities among Professional Groups,* April 7–8, 1953, pt. 4 (Washington, D.C.: GPO, 1953), 717–85.

44. "Oliver Quits LA Job after Red Quizzing," *Guild Reporter,* April 24, 1953, 4.

45. Dorothy Frank, "I Was Called Subversive," *Collier's,* March 28, 1953, 68; "To Take the Pressure Off," *Time,* April 27, 1953, 50.

46. "To Take the Pressure Off"; "Editor Loses Job, Charges a 'Smear,'" *New York Times,* April 18, 1953, 9.

47. "News Guild Head Assails Inquiries," *New York Times,* June 30, 1953, 21.

48. Report by [name deleted], September 10, 1946, FBI 100-7326-282.

49. House Committee on Un-American Activities, *Communism in the Detroit Area,* 82nd Cong., 2nd sess., February 26, 1952, pt. 1 (Washington, D.C.: GPO, 1952), 2757–64.

50. Elie Abel, "Artist Called Red Loses Job on Paper," *New York Times,* February 29, 1952, 11.

51. "3 Detroit Newsmen Called 'Reds' Seek Local Guild Protection," *Guild Reporter,* March 14, 1952, 4.

52. House Committee on Un-American Activities, *Communism in the Detroit Area,* 2947.

53. Mary Maraniss, interview by author, July 13, 2004 (telephone).

54. Steve Rosswurm, "The Catholic Church and the Left-Led Unions: Labor Priests, Labor Schools, and the ACTU," in Steve Rosswurm, ed., *The CIO's Left-Led Unions* (New Brunswick, N.J.: Rutgers University Press, 1992), 119–37.

55. Douglas P. Seaton, *Catholics and Radicals: The Association of Catholic Trade Unionists, and the American Labor Movement, from Depression to Cold War* (East Brunswick, N.J.: Associated University Presses, 1981), 75–97.

56. House Committee on Un-American Activities, *Communism Methods of Infiltration,* 82nd Cong., 2nd sess., April 21, 1953, pt. 3 (Washington, D.C.: GPO, 1953), 988–1012.

57. Ibid., 83rd Cong., 1st sess., April 21–22, 1953, pt. 3, 987–1012.

58. "Polumbaum Case Is Referred to Grievance Body," *Guild Reporter*, June 12, 1953, 8.

59. "Bias Is Held Cause to Dismiss Writer," *New York Times*, July 2, 1954, 7.

60. "Loyalty and Private Employment: The Right of Employers to Discharge Suspected Subversives," *Yale Law Journal* 62 (May 1953): 954–84.

61. "Local 34 Founder Recollects," *Guilder*, January 1982, 3.

62. Report from [name deleted], August 12, 1943, FBI 100-226300-1.

63. Report by [name deleted], December 15, 1944, FBI 100-7326-227; memorandum, SAC Albany, to director, FBI, August 17, 1954, FBI 1-226300-36.

64. House Committee on Un-American Activities, *Hearings Regarding Communism in Labor Unions in the United States*, 80th Cong., 1st sess., July 25, 1947 (Washington, D.C.: GPO, 1947), 223.

65. House Committee on Un-American Activities, *Investigation of Communist Activities in the Albany, N.Y., Area*, 83rd Cong., 1st sess., July 13–14, 1953, pt. 1 (Washington, D.C.: GPO, 1953), 223.

66. "Janet Scott Given Notice of Discharge," *Knickerbocker News*, July 16, 1953, 1.

67. "Reporter Fired for Misconduct after Albany Commie Hearing," *Guild Reporter*, July 24, 1953, 1.

68. "Tri-City Guild Reverses Action in Janet Scott Discharge Case," *Guild Reporter*, January 22, 1954, 5.

69. "Reporter's 5th Amendment Plea Viewed as Misconduct," *Editor and Publisher*, December 19, 1953, 7.

70. Janet Scott, "How Crazy Can They Get?" *Nation*, December 12, 1953, 509–10.

71. House Committee on Un-American Activities, *Investigation of Communist Activities in the San Francisco Area—Part 4*, 83rd Cong., 1st sess., December 4, 1953 (Washington, D.C.: GPO, 1954), 3392–3400.

72. "Copy Reader's Silence in Quiz No Bar to Job," *Editor and Publisher*, December 19, 1953, 7.

73. James Benet, interview by author, June 23, 1998 (telephone).

74. Jack Gould, "TV Play Canceled in Fight on Actress," *New York Times*, August 28, 1950, 1; Jack Gould, "'Aldrich' Show Drops Jean Muir; TV Actress Denies Communist Ties," *New York Times*, August 29, 1950, 1.

75. "Warner Cautions Employees on Reds," *New York Times*, September 2, 1950, 11.

76. Sig Mickelson, *The Decade That Shaped Television News: CBS in the 1950s* (Westport, Conn.: Praeger, 1998), 64–65.

77. Unsigned memorandum, "American Newspaper Guild—C.I.O.," November 25, 1941, FBI 100-7326-18X.

78. Report, [name deleted], February 5, 1944, FBI 100-7326-175.

79. Edward Bliss Jr., *Now the News: The Story of Broadcast Journalism* (New York: Columbia University Press, 1991), 203–204.

80. Erik Barnouw, *Tube of Plenty: The Evolution of American Television*, 2nd ed. (New York, Oxford University Press, 1990), 130.

81. Joseph E. Persico, *Edward R. Murrow: An American Original* (New York: McGraw-Hill, 1988), 333.

82. John Cogley, *Report on Blacklisting: Radio-Television* (New York: Fund for the Republic, 1956), 123.

83. "Why Columbia Waives the Rule," *Variety*, December 27, 1950, 19.

84. A. M. Sperber, *Murrow: His Life and Times* (New York: Freundlich Books, 1986), 366.

85. Howard K. Smith, *Events Leading up to My Death: The Life of a Twentieth-Century Reporter* (New York: St. Martin's Press, 1996), 224.

86. "Control of Radio for Defense Urged," *Los Angeles Times*, December 20, 1950, 2.

87. William S. Paley, *As It Happened* (New York: Doubleday, 1979), 281.

88. "Peabody Awards Given in Radio, TV," *New York Times*, April 27, 1951, 33.

89. "Pledges Asked," *Broadcasting/Telecasting*, February 5, 1951, 43; "Loyalty in Pennsylvania," *Broadcasting/Telecasting*, March 5, 1951, 75; "Discharge over Loyalty," *New York Times*, June 14, 1950, 40.

90. "Discharge over Loyalty."

91. According to Merle Miller, McCaffery may have been the only exception CBS made among its twenty-five hundred employees. See Merle Miller, *The Judges and the Judged* (New York: Doubleday, 1952), 193.

92. Whitfield, *Culture of the Cold War*, 166.

93. Jack Gould, "Conspiracy of Silence," *New York Times*, April 22, 1951, II-9.

94. Quoted by Miller, *Judges and the Judged*, 217.

95. Navasky, *Naming Names*, 206–209.

96. House Committee on Un-American Activities, *Investigation of Communist Activities, New York Area*, 84th Cong., 1st sess., August 17–18, 1955, pt. 7 (Washington, D.C.: GPO, 1955), 2435–47. Kraber was a well-known folk singer with several albums to his credit. After his television career he made films, including the award-winning documentary *Boundary Lines*, and appeared on the New York stage. He died in September 1986 at age 81 ("Tony Kraber Dead at Age 81; An Actor, Singer and Director," *New York Times*, September 12, 1986, D-20).

97. The Federal Communications Commission withheld the license renewal of a television station in Erie, Pennsylvania, in 1954 after station owner Edward Lamb was accused of membership in the Communist Party ("TV License Held up on New Red Charge," *New York Times*, March 13, 1954, 21).

Chapter Five: The Specter of McCarthy

1. David Caute, *Great Fear: The Anti-Communist Purge under Truman and Eisenhower* (New York: Simon and Schuster, 1978), 85–110.

2. Senate Committee on the Judiciary, Subcommittee to Investigate the Administration of the Internal Security Act and Other Internal Security Laws, *Communist Domination of Union Officials in Vital Defense Industry—International Union of Mine, Mill, and Smelter Workers*, 82nd Cong., 2nd sess., October 6–9, 1952 (Washington, D.C.: GPO, 1952), 162.

3. Thomas C. Reeves, *The Life and Times of Joe McCarthy: A Biography* (New York: Stein and Day, 1982), 224.

4. "Reds Infiltrate Government, Educational, Cultural Agencies, Ex-Communist Declares," *Great Falls Tribune*, October 15, 1952, 8.

5. Senate Subcommittee, *Communist Domination of Union Officials*, 162; David M. Oshinsky, *A Conspiracy So Immense: The World of Joe McCarthy* (New York: Free Press, 1983), 183.

6. "Weighing in the Balance," *Time*, October 22, 1951, 21–24.

7. Harvey Matusow, *False Witness* (New York: Cameron and Kahn, 1955), 25.

8. Senate Committee on the Judiciary, Subcommittee to Investigate the Administration of the Internal Security Act and Other Internal Security Laws, *Strategy and Tactics of World Communism*, 84th Cong., 1st sess., February 21, 1955, pt. 1 (Washington, D.C.: GPO, 1955), 39.

9. Robert M. Lichtman and Ronald D. Cohen, *Deadly Farce: Harvey Matusow and the Informer System in the McCarthy Era* (Urbana: University of Illinois Press, 2004), 32.

10. Matusow, *False Witness*, 30.

11. Ibid., 33.

12. Harvey Matusow, "Secret FBI Man Reveals: 3,500 Students Recruited Here for Red Fifth-Column," *New York Journal American*, February 5, 1952, 1.

13. "Brownell Drops Informant Plan," *New York Times,* April 16, 1955, 8.

14. Richard H. Rovere, *The American Establishment and Other Reports, Opinions, and Speculations* (New York: Harcourt, Brace and World, 1962), 113–32.

15. "Data Fail to Jar Red Trial Witness," *New York Times,* July 26, 1952, 14.

16. Richard C. Reeves, *The Life and Times of Joe McCarthy: A Biography* (New York: Stein and Day, 1982), 430.

17. Jean Franklin Deaver, "A Study of Senator Joseph R. McCarthy and 'McCarthyism' as Influences upon the News Media and the Evolution of Reportorial Method" (Ph.D. diss., University of Texas at Austin, 1970), 191.

18. Oshinsky, *A Conspiracy So Immense,* 183.

19. Laurence C. Eklund, "Editor Lashed by McCarthy," *Milwaukee Journal,* November 9, 1949, 1.

20. Oshinsky, *A Conspiracy So Immense,* 185.

21. W. A. Swanberg, *Luce and His Empire* (New York: Scribner's and Sons, 1972), 302.

22. Reeves, *Life and Times of Joe McCarthy,* 441.

23. "Matusow Termed 'Planted' Witness," *New York Times,* February 4, 1955, 8.

24. Affidavit Matusow provided to the *New York Times,* exhibit 7, Senate Subcommittee, *Strategy and Tactics of World Communism,* 84th Cong., 1st sess., February 22, 1955, pt. 2 (Washington, D.C.: GPO, 1955), 139–40.

25. "Walter Winchell of New York," *New York Mirror,* January 14, 1953, 10.

26. Joseph and Stewart Alsop, "Ex-Red Informers' Testimony Shaky, Alsops Find," *Louisville Courier-Journal,* January 19, 1953, 4.

27. Neal Gabler, *Winchell: Gossip, Power and the Culture of Celebrity* (New York: Alfred A. Knopf, 1994), 201.

28. D. M. Ladd to director, July 23, 1953, FBI 100-113-352.

29. Will Lissner, memorandum, March 14, 1969, 14–15, "Research Material," series 1, subseries A, Turner Catledge Papers, Special Collections, Mitchell Memorial Library, Mississippi State University (hereafter cited as Lissner memorandum).

30. Lichtman and Cohen, *Deadly Farce,* 78–80.

31. Report by [name deleted], July 11, 1950, FBI 100-7326-326.

32. "Behind Closed Doors," *Time,* May 11, 1953: 52; James A. Wechsler, *The Age of Suspicion* (New York: Random House, 1953), 167–85, 263.

33. Ferdinand Kuhn, "Vast Hunt on to Sift Reds out of Arts," *Washington Post,* April 24, 1953, 1.

34. Oliver Pilat and William V. Shannon, "The One-Man Mob of Joe McCarthy," *New York Post,* September 4, 1951, 2.

35. "N.Y. Guild Names Page One Winners," *Guild Reporter,* March 14, 1952, 3.

36. Senate Permanent Subcommittee on Investigations of the Committee on Government Operations, *State Department Information Program: Information Centers,* 83rd Cong., 1st sess., April 24, 1953, pt. 4 (Washington, D.C.: GPO, 1953), 253, 256 (hereafter cited as McCarthy hearings).

37. "Parnell Thomas Going to Enter Publisher Ranks," *Guild Reporter,* July 27, 1951, 3.

38. McCarthy hearings, pt. 4, 272.

39. Ibid., 276–77.

40. Wechsler, *Age of Suspicion,* 289–90.

41. Murray Marder, "Wechsler, McCarthy Clash after Secret Probe Hearing," *Washington Post,* April 25, 1953, 11.

42. McCarthy hearings, pt. 5, 289.

43. Wechsler, *Age of Suspicion,* 304.

44. Ibid., 250–51.

45. McCarthy hearings, pt. 5, 310–15.

46. "Freedom and Fear," editorial, *New York Times*, May 9, 1953, 18.

47. "No Threat to Freedom," editorial, *Washington Evening Star*, May 9, 1953, A-4.

48. Arthur Krock, "A Professional Survey of Press Freedom," *New York Times*, May 19, 1953, 28.

49. "Walters Refers Wechsler Protest to Special Group," *Editor and Publisher*, May 16, 1953, 9.

50. McCarthy hearings, pt. 6, 393; Matusow, *False Witness*, 220.

51. "The ASNE Report on the Wechsler Case," *Nieman Reports*, October 1953, 25–26.

52. "Additional Comment on the Wechsler Case," *Nieman Reports*, October 1953, 27–29.

53. "Editors Disagree in Wechsler Case," *New York Times*, August 13, 1953, 23.

54. "Intimidating the Press," editorial, *Washington Post*, August 13, 1953, 10.

55. *Proceedings, Twentieth Annual Convention, American Newspaper Guild*, June 29–July 3, 1953, 3. Published proceedings of Newspaper Guild conventions are available at the Tamiment Library, New York University, and Seeley-Mudd Library, Yale University.

56. Ibid., 72.

57. House Committee on Un-American Activities, *Guild to Subversive Organizations and Publications*, 84th Cong. 1st sess., January 2, 1957 (Washington, D.C.: GPO, 1957), 105.

58. Peter Kihss, "Robbins, Showman, Admits He Was Red," *New York Times*, May 6, 1953, 1.

59. John Earl Haynes and Harvey Klehr, *Venona: Decoding Soviet Espionage in America* (New Haven, Conn.: Yale University Press, 1999), 109–11, 342.

60. McCarthy hearings, pt. 6, 411; C. P. Trussell, "Two Editors Balk Inquiry on Reds," *New York Times*, May 15, 1953, 4.

61. Cedric Belfrage, *The American Inquisition, 1945–1960* (Indianapolis: Bobbs-Merrill, 1973), 185; Caute, *Great Fear*, 238–41.

62. R. E. Garst to Adler, October 1, 1953, "Senate Investigations: Personnel Testifying, 1956–1961," folder 1, Arthur Hays Sulzberger Papers, New York Times Archives.

63. A. H. Belmont to Ladd, October 8, 1953, FBI 100-400370-7.

64. Quoted in Susan E. Tifft and Alex S. Jones, *The Trust: The Private and Powerful Family behind the* New York Times (Boston: Little, Brown, 1999), 265.

65. Lichtman and Cohen, *Deadly Farce*, 88–90.

66. Harrison Salisbury, *Without Fear or Favor: An Uncompromising Look at the* New York Times (New York: Times Books, 1980), 486.

67. James Reston, "Stalin for Eisenhower Meeting; Tells the Times That He Favors New Approach to End Korea War," *New York Times*, December 25, 1952, 1.

68. James Reston, *Deadline: A Memoir* (New York: Random House, 1991), 217. McCarthy's description pointed directly at Knowles, although he would not be named publicly for two more years. Knowles is also identified in Susan E. Tifft and Alex S. Jones, *The Trust: The Private and Powerful Family behind the* New York Times (Boston: Little, Brown, 1999), 266–67.

69. Daniel J. Leab, *A Union of Individuals: The Formation of the American Newspaper Guild, 1933–1936* (New York: Columbia University Press, 1970), 137–42.

70. Senate Committee on the Judiciary, *Strategy and Tactics of World Communism*, 84th Cong., 2nd sess., January 4, 1956, pt. 17 (Washington: GPO, 1956), 1635–36.

71. Lissner memorandum, 27–28.

72. Ibid., 31.

73. Clayton Knowles to Turner Catledge, September 26, 1955, "Staff: Senate Investigation" file, series II, C/D, Catledge Papers.

74. Lissner memorandum, 35.

75. "Text of National Guild Constitution," *Guild Reporter,* December 23, 1933, 6.

76. "Daily Worker Writer Recalls Broun Urging Reds in Union," *Editor and Publisher,* June 25, 1955, 62.

77. "Board Proposes Language to Bar Communist Members," *Guild Reporter,* February 25, 1955, 1; Ralph S. Brown Jr., *Loyalty and Security: Employment Tests in the United States* (New Haven, Conn.: Yale University Press, 1958), 154–56.

78. "Applause for Guild," *Editor and Publisher,* August 14, 1954, 38.

79. Campbell Watson, "Guild Builds Defenses; Red Ouster Policy Set," *Editor and Publisher,* August 14, 1954, 11.

80. Ibid.

81. On Murrow versus McCarthy, see Thomas Rosteck, *See It Now Confronts McCarthyism: Television Documentary and the Politics of Representation* (Tuscaloosa: University of Alabama Press, 1994); Daniel J. Leab, "'See It Now': A Legend Reassessed," in John O'Connor, ed., *American History/American Television: Interpreting the Video Past* (New York: Frederick Ungar, 1983), 1–32.

82. Sen. Herbert H. Lehman of New York speaking on the resolution of censure against the junior senator from Wisconsin, 83rd Cong., 2nd sess., *Cong. Rec.* 98, pt. 5 (July 31, 1954): 12903.

83. Edwin R. Bayley, *Joe McCarthy and the Press* (New York: Pantheon, 1981), 277–78.

84. Lichtman and Cohen, *Deadly Farce,* 77–82, 223–29.

85. Matusow, *False Witness,* 231.

86. Lichtman and Cohen, *Deadly Farce,* 96–97.

87. House Committee on Un-American Activities, *Communist Activities among Youth Groups,* 83rd Cong., 2nd sess., July 12, 1954, pt. 2 (Washington, D.C.: GPO, 1954), 3844 (hereafter cited as HUAC hearing); "Bishop Oxnam Hits Growing Political Use of 'Big Lie,'" *Washington Star,* June 7, 1954, B-1.

88. HUAC hearing, 5845–46; "Ex-Red Disputes Oxnam on 'Lies,'" *Washington Post and Times Herald,* July 13, 1954, 6; "Matusow Denies He Lied or Said to Oxnam He Did," *New York Herald Tribune,* July 13, 1954, 3.

89. HUAC hearing, 5843.

90. Lichtman and Cohen, *Deadly Farce,* 100.

91. Griffin Fariello, *Red Scare: Memories of the American Inquisition* (New York: W. W. Norton, 1995), 97–108.

92. "Matusow Sought Anti-Reds' Favor," *New York Times,* February 12, 1955, 10.

93. Robert M. Lichtman and Ronald D. Cohen, *Deadly Farce: Harvey Matusow and the Informer System in the McCarthy Era* (Urbana: University of Illinois Press, 2004), 122.

94. Senate Subcommittee, *Strategy and Tactics of World Communism,* 84th Cong., 1st sess., February 21, 1955, pt. 5 (Washington, D.C.: GPO, 1955), 455.

95. Senate Subcommittee, *Strategy and Tactics of World Communism: Significance of the Harvey Matusow Case,* 84th Cong., 1st sess., April 6, 1955, pt. 16 (Washington, D.C.: GPO, 1955), 88–89.

96. Senate Subcommittee to Investigate the Administration of the Internal Security Act, "Investigation of the Internal Security Act of 1950," *Annual Report for the Year 1955* (Washington, D.C.: GPO, 1956), 2.

97. Bayley, *Joe McCarthy and the Press,* 135–36.

98. Ibid., 216.

99. James Aronson, *The Press and the Cold War* (New York: Monthly Review Press, 1970), xii.

Chapter Six: Dark Clouds over the Newsroom

1. Walter Goodman, *The Committee: The Extraordinary Career of the House Committee on Un-American Activities* (New York: Farrar, Straus and Giroux, 1968), 510.

2. Ralph Roach to Alan Belmont, November 1, 1955, FBI ("Not Recorded").

3. The "Do Not File" stamp indicated that documents should not be incorporated into the FBI's central filing system (Athan Theoharis, *Chasing Spies: How the FBI Failed in Counterintelligence but Promoted the Politics of McCarthyism in the Cold War Years* [Chicago: Ivan R. Dee, 2002]), 142, 246).

4. SAC New York to Hoover, May 2, 1955, FBI 100-400370-29.

5. Jack Gould to Turner Catledge, March 10, 1955, "Senate Investigations:—Kraft, Charles J., 1954–1955," Arthur Hays Sulzberger Papers, New York Times Archives (hereafter cited as Sulzberger Papers); Will Lissner, memorandum, March 14, 1969, 80, "Research Material" file, series 1, subseries A, Turner Catledge Papers, Special Collections, Mitchell Memorial Library, Mississippi State University.

6. Lissner memorandum, 4-B.

7. Eugene Lyons, *The Red Decade* (New York: Arlington House, 1941), 340.

8. Benjamin Gitlow, *Whole of Their Lives* (New York: Charles Scribner's Sons, 1948), 7–15; Harvey Klehr, *Heyday of American Communism: The Depression Decade* (New York: Basic Books, 1984), 379.

9. "James Kieran Jr., Former Reporter," *New York Times,* January 11, 1952, 21.

10. "Newsmen Testify at Senate Inquiry," *New York Times,* January 5, 1956, 1.

11. Senate Subcommittee to Investigate the Administration of the Internal Security Act and Other Internal Security Laws, *Strategy and Tactics of World Communism,* 84th Cong., 2d sess., January 4–6, 1956, pt. 17 (Washington, D.C.: GPO, 1956), 1591.

12. Gould to Catledge, March 10, 1955.

13. Ibid., 79.

14. Lissner memorandum, 82–84.

15. Kraft to Catledge, January 18, 1955, "Senate Investigations: Charles J. Kraft, 1954–1955," Sulzberger Papers.

16. Catledge to Kraft, February 10, 1955, Sulzberger Papers. Documents describing Kraft's Communist connections were found among Catledge's papers, but Catledge did not divulge the association in his memoir, *My Life and the* Times.

17. "Senate Group Sets Espionage Inquiry Today," *Chicago Daily Tribune,* June 29, 1955, 17.

18. Alan Barth, "McCarran's Monopoly," *Reporter,* August 21, 1951, 5.

19. M. L. Barnet, "Probers and the Press," *Nation,* December 24, 1955, 552.

20. Richard Gid Powers, *Broken: The Troubled Past and Uncertain Future of the FBI* (New York: Free Press, 2004), 234–36.

21. Senate Committee, *Strategy and Tactics of World Communism,* 84th Cong., 1st sess., June 28–29, 1955, pt. 14 (Washington, D.C.: GPO, 1955), 1323.

22. Richard Burdett to author, May 20, 2003.

23. Larry Ceplair and Steven Englund, *The Inquisition in Hollywood: Politics in the Film Community, 1930–1960* (New York: Anchor Press/Doubleday, 1980), 334–56.

24. Raymond A. Schroth, *The Eagle and Brooklyn* (Westport, Conn.: Greenwood, 1974), 155–82.

25. Stanley Cloud and Lynne Olson, *The Murrow Boys: Pioneers on the Front Lines of Broadcast Journalism* (Boston: Houghton Mifflin, 1996), 174.

26. Schroth, Eagle *and Brooklyn*, 155–82; George Seldes, *Lords of the Press* (New York: Julian Messner, 1938), 173–76.

27. Cloud and Olson, *Murrow Boys*, 320. Donald L. Miller, *The Story of World War II*, rev. ed. (New York: Touchstone, 2001), 27–29.

28. Michael Emery, *On the Front Lines: Following America's Foreign Correspondents across the Twentieth Century* (Washington, D.C.: American University Press, 1995), 63; Schroth, *Eagle and Brooklyn*, 172.

29. SAC New York to director, FBI, May 4, 1955, FBI 100-37605-084.

30. Winston Burdett, "Lloyd's Made British Hold Fire on Bremen, War Reporter Told," *Brooklyn Eagle*, March 10, 1940, 1, Brooklyn Collection, Brooklyn Public Library (All *Brooklyn Eagle* stories cited may be found in the Brooklyn Collection); Martin Gilbert, *The Second World War*, rev. ed. (New York: Henry Holt, 1989), 31–43.

31. Report of [name deleted], December 7, 1951, FBI 100-376050-30; Emery, *On the Front Lines*, 18.

32. Winston Burdett, "Allies Hurled Back 25 Miles, Face Debacle in Norway War," *Brooklyn Eagle*, April 25, 1940, 1.

33. Winston Burdett, "Concerted Norse Drive Seen Sweeping Out Foe," *Brooklyn Eagle*, April 19, 1940, 1.

34. Winston Burdett, "Nazi Planes' Drone of Death Paralyzes Norse Civilians," *Brooklyn Eagle*, April 21, 1940, 1.

35. Edward Bliss Jr., *Now the News: The Story of Broadcast Journalism* (New York: Columbia University Press, 1991), 99.

36. Ibid., 99–111; Alexander Kendrick, *Prime Time: The Life of Edward R. Murrow* (Boston: Little, Brown, 1969), 189–90.

37. Maxine Block, ed., *Current Biography* (New York: H. W. Wilson, 1943), 89.

38. Associated Press, "Belgrade Phone, Radio Barred to Boro Reporter," *Brooklyn Eagle*, January 30, 1941, 10.

39. "CBS Tells of Burdett's Big Scoop," *New York Herald Tribune*, June 30, 1955, 9.

40. Cloud and Olson, *Murrow Boys*, 124.

41. "CBS Reporter's Wife Is Murdered in Iran," *New York Times*, April 27, 1942, 2; "Soviets, Iran Quash Kurdish Pillaging," *New York Times*, May 22, 1942, 11.

42. From a compact disk that accompanied Mark Bernstein and Alex Lubertozzi's *World War II on the Air: Edward R. Murrow and the Broadcasts That Riveted a Nation* (Naperville, Ill.: Sourcebooks, 2003), track 28.

43. Robert Desmond, *Tides of War: World News Reporting, 1931–1945* (Iowa City: University of Iowa Press, 1984), 327–28.

44. Bernstein and Lubertozzi, *World War II on the Air*, track 33.

45. Desmond, *Tides of War*, 452.

46. Cecil Brown, *Suez to Singapore* (New York: Random House, 1942), 8.

47. Sig Mickelson, *The Decade That Shaped Television News: CBS in the 1950s* (Westport, Conn.: Praeger, 1998), 67.

48. Cloud and Olson, *Murrow Boys*, 314.

49. Richard C. Hottelet, interview by author, January 29, 2005, Westport, Conn.

50. Walter Cronkite, interview by author, May 23, 2005, New York City.

51. Cloud and Olson, *Murrow Boys*, 125.

52. Winston Burdett, CBS Loyalty Oath, March 12, 1951, FBI 100-376050-17.

53. Joseph E. Persico, *Edward R. Murrow: An American Original* (New York: McGraw-Hill, 1988), 340–41; Cloud and Olson, *Murrow Boys*, 320.

54. Winston Burdett to J. Edgar Hoover, August 31, 1951, FBI 100-376050-17; M. A. Jones to Louis B. Nichols, September 7, 1951, FBI 100-376050-16.

55. Report by [name deleted], May 5, 1951, FBI 100-376050-6.

56. Jones to Nichols, September 7, 1951, FBI 100-376050-16; Report by [name deleted], May 5, 1951, FBI 100-376050-6.

57. Report of [name deleted], September 10, 1951, FBI 100-376050-11.

58. Report of [name deleted], October 27, 1951, FBI 100-376050-19.

59. Report of [name deleted], November 9, 1951, FBI 100-376050-22.

60. [name deleted] to Belmont, November 9, 1951, FBI 100-376050-22; Elizabeth Bentley, *Out of Bondage: The Story of Elizabeth Bentley* (New York: Devin-Adair, 1951), 157.

61. John Earl Haynes and Harvey Klehr, *Venona: Decoding Soviet Espionage in America* (New Haven, Conn.: Yale University Press, 1999), 236–49.

62. Bentley, *Out of Bondage,* 156.

63. Haynes and Klehr, *Venona,* 74.

64. Brother to Earl, September 13, 1939, Archive of the Secretariat of the Executive Committee of the Communist International, coded correspondence with the Communist Party U.S.A. (1933–43), Russian Center for the Preservation and Study of Documents and Recent History, 495-184-8 (1939 file), courtesy of John Earl Haynes, Library of Congress. The cable is believed to have been sent by George Dimitrov, head of the Comintern, to an unidentified asset of the New York KGB. See Haynes and Klehr, *Venona,* 343.

65. Haynes and Klehr, *Venona,* 79; Nigel West, *Venona: The Greatest Secret of the Cold War* (New York: HarperCollins, 1999), 279–80.

66. Report of [name deleted], December 7, 1951, FBI 100-376050-30.

67. Ibid.

68. Report of [name deleted], July 30, 1953, 59, FBI 100-376050-59.

69. [name deleted] to [name deleted], March 4, 1954, FBI 100-376050-64.

70. "Court Basis Cited in Passport Policy," *New York Times,* May 25, 1952, 29.

71. Caute, *Great Fear,* 245–47.

72. Stephen Whitfield, *The Culture of the Cold War* (Baltimore: Johns Hopkins University Press, 1991), 120–21.

73. Unnamed official of the Passport Office to Nichols at the FBI, June 9, 1954. The report is attached to a memo from Dennis A. Flinn, director of the Office of Security at the State Department, to Hoover, March 30, 1955, FBI 100-100-376050-73.

74. "Case of Winston Burdett," Department of State, RPS/ISP, June 9, 1954, FBI 100-376050-73.

75. Nichols to file, June 9, 1954, attached to memo, Flinn to Hoover, March 30, 1955, FBI 100-376050-73; SAC Washington Field Office to director, FBI, July 8, 1954, FBI 100-376050-65.

76. Affidavit of Winston Burdett, June 29, 1954, FBI 100-376050-65.

77. Belmont to L. V. Boardman, March 22, 1955, FBI 100-376050-71.

78. SAC New York to director, FBI, May 4, 1955, FBI 100-376050-84.

79. SAC New York to director, FBI, April 8, 1955, FBI 100-376050-81.

80. Signed Affidavit, Winston Burdett, April 8, 1955, FBI 100-376050-54.

81. Memo, Belmont to Boardman, March 24, 1955, FBI 100-3676050-73.

82. Mickelson, *Decade That Shaped Television News,* 67–68.

83. Harrison E. Salisbury, "The Strange Correspondence of Morris Ernst and John Edgar Hoover, 1939–1964, *Nation,* December 1, 1984, 575.

84. Daniel J. Leab, *A Union of Individuals: The Formation of the American Newspaper Guild, 1933–1936* (New York: Columbia University Press, 1970), 58–65; Morris Ernst, *The Best Is Yet . . .* (New York: Harper, 1945), 86–87.

85. Nichols to Clyde Tolson, April 7, 1955, FBI 100-376050-78. FBI redactors failed to expunge the name on the document, probably mistaking it for a reference to Morris Ernst, whose name the FBI did not redact, making it possible to deduce Robert Morris's role.

86. Nichols to Tolson, February 16, 1955, FBI 100-376050-66.

87. Nichols to Tolson, April 7, 1955, FBI 100-376050-78.

88. Mickelson, *Decade That Shaped Television News,* 144–51.

89. SAC to director, FBI, May 4, 1955, FBI 100-376050-84.

90. Nichols to Tolson, May 2, 1955, FBI 100-376050-83.

91. Ramon F. Adams, *Western Words: A Dictionary of the American West* (Norman: University of Oklahoma Press, 1968) 161.

92. Nichols to Tolson, May 17, 1955, FBI 100-376050-88.

93. Report by [name deleted], September 13, 1955, FBI 100-376050-105.

Chapter Seven: The Investigation

1. "The Eagle's Brood," *Time,* July 11, 1955, 19.

2. James Reston, "Strategist for Inquiry," *New York Times,* January 6, 1956, 7.

3. Senate Subcommittee to Investigate the Administration of the Internal Security Act and Other Internal Security Laws, *Strategy and Tactics of World Communism: Recruiting for Espionage,* 84th Cong., 1st sess., June 28–29, 1955, pt. 14 (Washington, D.C.: GPO, 1955), 1324 (hereafter cited as Eastland hearings, pt. 14).

4. Ibid., 1324.

5. Ibid., 1341.

6. Ibid.

7. Ibid., 1345–46.

8. Ibid., 1357.

9. Ibid., 1362.

10. "Eastland's Letter," *New York Herald Tribune,* June 30, 1955, 8.

11. "4 Statements on Inquiry," *Washington Post,* June 30, 1955, 8.

12. Eastland hearings, pt. 14, 1370–74.

13. Ibid., 1381.

14. Ibid., 1369.

15. *New York Herald Tribune,* June 30, 1955, 1; *Daily Mirror,* June 30, 1955, 1; *Chicago Daily Tribune,* June 30, 1955, 1; Max Lerner, "Spy Story," *New York Post,* July 1, 1955, 30; David Lawrence, "Lawrence Praises Winston Burdett for Confession," *Louisville Courier-Journal,* July 1, 1955, 6.

16. Arthur Hays Sulzberger to Louis Loeb, June 30, 1955, "Senate Investigations: 1954–1966," folder 7, Arthur Hays Sulzberger Papers, New York Times Archives.

17. Susan Dryfoos, *Iphigene: Memoirs of Iphigene Ochs Sulzberger of the* New York Times *Family* (New York: Dodd, Mead, 1981), 178.

18. "C.B.S. Man Admits He Was a Red Spy," *New York Times,* June 30, 1955, 1.

19. "4 Statements on Inquiry."

20. Senate Subcommittee to Investigate the Administration of the Internal Security Act and Other Internal Security Laws, *Strategy and Tactics of World Communism: Recruiting for Espionage,* 84th Cong., 1st sess., June 30, 1955, pt. 15 (Washington, D.C.: GPO, 1955), 1402 (hereafter cited as Eastland hearings, pt. 15).

21. Ibid., 1407.

22. "Russian Spies and American Conscience," *New York Post,* July 1, 1955, 30.

23. "Reporter in N.Y. Reveals He Once Was a Communist," *Chicago Sun-Times,* July 1, 1955, 8.

24. "No Security Breach Seen in 'Times' Korea Story," *New York Herald Tribune,* July 2, 1955, 7.

25. "Guild Wants 'Red' Record Cleared by Congress Unit," *Guild Reporter,* July 22, 1955, 1.

26. "Guild Senate Appearance Unnecessary after Eastland's Reply, Says Novak," *Guild Reporter,* August 26, 1955, 2.

27. Senate Subcommittee to Investigate the Administration of the Internal Security Act and Other Internal Security Laws, *Strategy and Tactics of World Communism: Recruiting for Espionage,* 84th Cong., 1st sess., July 13, 1955, pt. 16 (Washington, D.C.: GPO, 1955), 1490–91 (hereafter cited as Eastland hearings, pt. 16).

28. Griffin Fariello, *Red Scare: Memories of the American Inquisition* (New York: W. W. Norton, 1995), 356.

29. Report of [name deleted], January 31, 1964, FBI 100-420-207; SAC New York to director, February 14 1964, FBI 100-420207-2.

30. James Aronson, *The Press and the Cold War* (New York: Monthly Review Press, 1970), 151.

31. "Boudin Memorandum Re Melvin L. Barnet: Memorandum I," undated, "Cases—Private Industry: Barnet, Melvin—*New York Times,* 1955," folder 7, box 886, American Civil Liberties Union Papers, Mudd Library, Princeton University.

32. Melvin Barnet, interview by author, April 4, 1998, Brooklyn, New York.

33. Eastland hearings, pt. 16, 1497.

34. Melvin Barnet, interview by author, May 23, 1998, Brooklyn, New York.

35. Russell Porter, "Amnesty by Public Asked for Ex-Reds," *New York Times,* June 16, 1953, 20.

36. Eastland hearings, pt. 16, 1500.

37. Ibid.

38. "Boudin Memorandum III," undated, folder 7, box 886, ACLU Papers.

39. Arthur Hays Sulzberger to Melvin Barnet, July 13, 1955, from the files of Melvin L. Barnet.

40. "'News' Fires Reporter in Red Probe," *New York Herald Tribune,* July 15, 1955, 8.

41. Eastland hearings, pt. 16, 1572.

42. Ibid., 1573.

43. Sulzberger to Amory Bradford, November 23, 1955, Sulzberger Papers.

44. "*Times* Unit Grievance Committee's Recommendation to New York Newspaper Guild on Dismissal of Melvin L. Barnet," September 24, 1955, "Dismissal of Melvin Barnet, 1955," box T-3, Newspaper Guild, Local 3 Collection, Robert F. Wagner Labor Archives, Tamiment Institute Library, New York University.

45. "City Wide Bulletin," July 19, 1955, "Dismissal of Melvin Barnet, 1955," box T-3, Local 3 Papers.

46. Report of [name deleted], "Melvin L. Barnet," January 31, 1964, FBI 100-420207-3.

47. Barnet to *Times* Unit, September 21, 1955, Barnet files.

48. Special *Times* Unit Bulletin, October 14, 1955, "Staff: Senate Investigation" file, series 2, C/D, Catledge Papers.

49. "Court Sustains UP's Right to Fire Newsman Polumbaum," *Guild Reporter,* March 9, 1956, 8.

50. "Times Dismissal Held Arbitrable," *New York Times,* June 27, 1956, 25; "New York Votes to Drop Three '5th' Firing Cases," *Guild Reporter,* February 8, 1957, 2.

51. Anonymous to Reston, October 17, 1955, "Senate Investigations: Personnel Testifying, 1956–1961," Sulzberger Papers.

52. Anthony Lewis, interview by author, November 23, 1999 (telephone).

53. Reston to Catledge, November 4, 1955, "Staff: Senate Investigation" file, series II, C/D, Catledge Papers.

54. Erik Barnouw, *Tube of Plenty: The Evolution of American Television,* 2nd ed. (New York: Oxford University Press, 1990), 130; Joseph E. Persico, *Edward R. Murrow: An American Original* (New York: McGraw-Hill, 1988), 333.

55. Gay Talese, *The Kingdom and the Power* (New York: World, 1969), 288.

56. Christopher John Girard, "A Program of Cooperation: The FBI, the Senate Internal Security Subcommittee, and the Communist Issue, 1950–54" (Ph.D. diss., Marquette University, 1993), 357.

57. Herbert Mitgang, personal communication, December 13, 1999.

58. Talese, *Kingdom and the Power,* 288.

59. The New York Times Company and American Newspaper Guild, Local 3, Newspaper Guild of New York (AFL-CIO), 26 Lab. Arb. (BNA) 609 (1956) (Corsi, Arb.).

60. Alden Whitman, interview by Nora Sayre, n.d. Sayre conducted this and several other interviews of *Times* reporters in the 1980s as she was doing research for a book that later was published as *Previous Convictions: A Journey through the 1950s* (New Brunswick, N.J.: Rutgers University Press, 1995). She never used the material for her book and graciously gave me copies of the undated interviews from her files.

61. Catledge to file, November 16, 1955, "Senate Investigations: 1954–1966," Sulzberger Papers.

62. Seymour Peck, interview by Nora Sayre, n.d.

63. Turner Catledge, *My Life and the* Times (New York: Harper and Row, 1971), 233.

64. Catledge to file, November 16, 1955; SAC New York, to director, FBI, May 2, 1955, FBI 100-400370-79; Arthur Gelb, *City Room* (New York: G. P. Putnam's Sons, 2003), 254–59.

65. Herbert French to Louis Loeb, December 6, 1955, "Senate Investigations: 1954–1966," Sulzberger Papers.

66. New York Times and Local 3, Newspaper Guild of New York, 26 Lab. Arb. (BNA) 609 (1956) (Corsi, Arb.).

67. Aronson, *Press and the Cold War,* 140.

68. Senate Subcommittee to Investigate the Administration of the Internal Security Act and Other Internal Security Laws, *Strategy and Tactics of World Communism: Communist Activity in New York,* 84th Cong., 2nd sess., January 4–6, 1956, pt. 17 (Washington: GPO, 1956), 1761. (hereafter cited as Eastland hearings, pt. 17).

69. SAC New York to director, FBI, November 16, 1954, FBI 100-400370-18.

70. Catledge, *My Life and the* Times, 234.

71. Ibid., 234.

72. Draft statement (not issued), December 28, 1955, "Senate Investigations: 1954–1966," Sulzberger Papers.

73. Press release (not issued), draft 4, November 30, 1955, "Senate Investigations: 1954–1966," Sulzberger Papers.

74. Talese, *Kingdom and the Power,* 292; Harrison Salisbury, *Without Fear or Favor: The New York Times and Its Times* (New York: Times Books, 1980), 491.

75. Catledge, *My Life and the* Times, 227.

76. Aronson, *Press and the Cold War,* 139.

77. "Eastland Inquiry Off," *New York Times,* November 22, 1955, 17.

78. Drew Pearson, "N.Y. Times Target in Witch-Hunt," *Washington Post and Times Herald,* December 12, 1955, 43.

79. "The Untold Story," editorial, *New York Post,* December 7, 1955, 49.

80. I. F. Stone, "The *New York Times* Knuckles Under," *I. F. Stone's Weekly,* December 5, 1955, 1.

81. "Seeks to Limit Subscriptions," *Editor and Publisher,* December 17, 1955, 42; Robert C. Cottrell, *Izzy: A Biography of I. F. Stone* (New Brunswick, N.J.: Rutgers University Press, 1992), 174.

82. Anonymous letter, December 30, 1955, folder 67, box 5, Alden Whitman Papers, Manuscripts and Archives Division, New York Public Library.

Chapter Eight: Deeper Trouble

1. Drew Pearson, "Washington Merry-Go-Round," *Washington Post and Times Herald,* January 3, 1956, 37.

2. Lester Markel to Louis Loeb, August 17, 1955, "Senate Investigations: 1956–1961," folder 1, Arthur Hays Sulzberger Papers, New York Times Archives; John Desmond, "The Alger Hiss Case," *New York Times,* April 2, 1950, 183.

3. Susan E. Tifft and Alex S. Jones, *The Trust: The Powerful Family behind the* New York Times (Boston: Little, Brown, 1999), 276–77.

4. James Aronson, *The Press and the Cold War* (New York: Monthly Review Press, 1970), 139–40; Gay Talese, *The Kingdom and the Power* (New York: World Publishing, 1969), 289–90.

5. "Hearing on Reds Evokes Warning," *New York Times,* January 3, 1956, 15.

6. Murray Marder, "Red Probers Open Quiz of N.Y. Newsmen Today," *Washington Post and Times Herald,* January 4, 1956, 7.

7. Allen Drury, "Eastland Scores Critics of Inquiry," *New York Times,* January 4, 1956, 16.

8. The cartoon appeared in the *Washington Post* on January 4, 1956, p. 20.

9. William S. White, "Ruling to Figure in '54 Campaign," *New York Times,* May 18, 1954, 1; and "Eastland Offers Amendment," *New York Times,* May 25, 1954, 16.

10. "Eastland Inquiry," *New York Times,* January 8, 1956, IV-1; Harrison E. Salisbury, *Without Fear or Favor: An Uncompromising Look at the* New York Times (New York: Times Books, 1980), 489.

11. SAC New York to director, FBI, September 2, 1953, FBI 100-400370-8.

12. SAC New York to director, FBI, May 2, 1955, FBI 100-400370-29. Three years after the Eastland hearings, Drury published *Advise and Consent,* a novel about a presidential nominee who is railroaded during Senate confirmation hearings.

13. Senate Subcommittee to Investigate the Administration of the Internal Security Act and Other Internal Security Laws, *Strategy and Tactics of World Communism: Communist Activities in New York,* 84th Cong., 2nd sess., January 4–6, 1956, pt. 17 (Washington, D.C.: GPO, 1956), 1589 (hereafter cited as Eastland hearings, pt. 17).

14. Ibid., 1614.

15. Ibid., 1616.

16. Ibid., 1636.

17. Ibid., 1643.

18. Records of the Senate Subcommittee to Investigate the Administration of the Internal Security Act and Other Internal Security Laws, 1951–77, Investigative Subject Files, folder 3 ("Newspapers, New York"), box 183, Records Group 46, National Archives; Ellen Schrecker, *The Age of McCarthyism: A Brief History with Documents* (Boston: Bedford Books, 1994), 34.

19. Eastland hearings, pt. 17, 1663.

20. "Thin Ice," editorial, *Washington Post,* January 5, 1956, 12.

21. Special Committee of the U.S. Congress, *Maintenance of a Lobby to Influence Legislation on the Ship Purchase Bill,* 63rd Cong., 3rd sess., February 16, 1915 (Washington, D.C.: GPO, 1915), 387.

22. "The Voice of a Free Press," editorial, *New York Times,* January 5, 1956, 32.

23. Turner Catledge, *My Life and the* Times (New York: Harper and Row, 1971), 227.

24. Alden Whitman, interview by Nora Sayre, n.d.

25. Salisbury, *Without Fear or Favor*, 492n; Eleanor Roosevelt to Sulzberger, January 5, 1956, "Senate Investigations: 1954–1966," Sulzberger Papers.

26. On January 7 the *Times* printed excerpts from editorials in the *New York Post, Brooklyn Daily Independent, Newsday, Hartford Courant, (Providence, R.I.) Journal-Bulletin, Pittsburgh Post-Gazette, Wilmington (Del.) Morning News, Binghamton (N.Y.) Sun, Washington (D.C.) Evening Star, Louisville Courier-Journal, St. Louis Post-Dispatch, Milwaukee Journal*, and the *Denver Post*. The next day the paper excerpted comments from six more papers: the *New York Journal American, Quincy (Mass.) Patriot Ledger, Minneapolis Tribune, Washington Post and Times-Herald, Atlanta Journal*, and the *Kansas City Star*. The *Times* also noted the "political tone" of each of the newspapers—whether independent, Republican, or Democratic—based on the papers' entries in the *Editor and Publisher International Yearbook*.

27. Murray Kempton, "The Fly Swatter," *New York Post,* January 6, 1956, 5; Walter Lippmann, "Congress and the Press," *Herald Tribune,* January 10, 1956, 22; "Congressional Investigation," *Editor and Publisher,* January 14, 1956, 6.

28. Kempton, "Fly Swatter."

29. Eastland hearings, pt. 17, 1681.

30. Ibid., 1696.

31. Ibid., 1713.

32. Ibid., 1714.

33. "Guild Weighs Action in News Man's Firing," *New York Post,* January 6, 1956, 5.

34. "Mirror Dismisses Mahoney," *New York Mirror,* January 7, 1956, 2.

35. "C.L.U. Bids 'News' Reinstate Price," *New York Herald Tribune,* January 7, 1956, 4.

36. Eastland hearings, pt. 17, 1918.

37. Ibid., 1722–23.

38. Ibid., 1723.

39. D. M. Ladd to E. A. Tamm, October 18, 1941, FBI 100-406708, Alden Whitman Papers, Manuscripts and Archives Division, New York Public Library.

40. Hoover, to SAC New York, December 29, 1953, FBI 100-406708, Whitman Papers; Whitman interview.

41. Eastland hearings, pt. 17, 1735.

42. Ibid., 1738.

43. Ibid. 17, 1775–77.

44. Ibid. 17, 1783.

45. Ibid., 1778.

46. Ibid., 1780.

47. "6 Ousted from Newsroom Jobs by Eastland Committee Quiz," *Editor and Publisher,* January 14, 1956, 11.

48. "Two See Red Effort to Penetrate Press," *Chicago Sun-Times,* January 7, 1956, 4; "Eastland Committee Plans a New Inquiry," *New York Times,* January 8, 1956, 1.

49. "Eastland v. the Times," *Time,* January 16, 1956, 56.

50. Robert G. Spivack, "Probe of Press Over, Until Further Notice," *New York Post,* January 8, 1956, 5.

51. Gerald W. Johnson, "Not Red All Over," *New Republic,* January 16, 1956, 23. For more on Gerald W. Johnson, see Vincent Fitzpatrick, *Gerald W. Johnson: From Southern Liberal to National Conscience* (Baton Rouge: Louisiana State University Press, 2002).

52. "Sourwine Resigns to Run for Senate," *New York Times,* January 21, 1956, 12; James Reston, "Strategist for Inquiry," *New York Times,* January 6, 1956, 7. In the Democratic primary in September 1956, Sourwine came in fourth in a field of four and rejoined the Senate Internal

Security Subcommittee staff ("Bible Renominated in Race for Senate," *New York Times,* September 6, 1956, 26).

53. Sulzberger to Whitman, January 10, 1956, file 2, box 4, Whitman Papers.

54. Catledge, *My Life and the* Times, 235.

55. Senate Subcommittee to Investigate the Administration of the Internal Security Act and Other Internal Security Laws, *Scope of Soviet Activity in the United States,* 84th Cong., 2nd. sess., April 10, 1956, pt. 13 (Washington, D.C.: GPO, 1956), 716.

56. "Employee of Mirror Defies Senate Unit on Communist Tie," *New York Times,* April 11, 1956, 17; "N.Y. Reporter Pleads Fifth and Quits Job," *New York Herald Tribune,* April 13, 1956, 4.

57. "Congress, Communists, and the Press," editorial, *Chicago Daily Tribune,* January 14, 1956, 1, 8.

58. "Subverting the Press," editorial, *Washington Post,* January 7, 1956, 18.

59. "Slocum Urges Press to Fight for Freedom," *Editor and Publisher,* January 28, 1956, 56.

60. *Near v. Minnesota,* 283 U.S. 697 (1931).

61. Aronson, *The Press and the Cold War,* 147.

62. "Is Congressional Investigation of the Press a Threat to Freedom?" In *Problems of Journalism: Proceedings of the 1956 Convention of the American Society of Newspaper Editors* (Washington, D.C.: ASNE, 1956), 61.

63. Ibid., 69.

64. Russell Baker, "Senate Unit Asks Contempt Actions," *New York Times,* May 1, 1956, 11.

65. Whitman to Thurman Arnold, September 29, 1956, Whitman Papers.

Chapter Nine: Journalists and the First Amendment

1. Luther A. Huston, "6 Indicted by U. S. in Senate Inquiry," *New York Times,* November 27, 1956, 22. Two other people were indicted at the same time: Herman Liveright, a former television program director for WDSU in New Orleans, and Mary Knowles, a librarian in Plymouth Meeting, Pennsylvania.

2. Seymour Peck, interview by Nora Sayre, n.d.

3. Ellen Schrecker, *The Age of McCarthyism: A Brief History with Documents* (Boston: Bedford Books, 1994), 60.

4. Alden Whitman, "Thurman Arnold, Trust Buster, Dead," *New York Times,* November 8, 1969, 33.

5. Clifton Brock, *Americans for Democratic Action: Its Role in National Politics* (Washington, D.C.: Public Affairs Press, 1962), 45.

6. Norman Dorsen, "Summing Up a Remarkable Life," *Rights,* March–April 1990, a publication of the National Emergency Civil Liberties Committee, from the files of Melvin L. Barnet.

7. Richard Severo, "Telford Taylor, Who Prosecuted Nazis at Nuremberg War Crimes Trials, Is Dead at 90," *New York Times,* May 25, 1998, 13.

8. New York Civil Liberties Union, Board of Directors, Minutes, folder 4, box 488, September 11, 1956, 3, American Civil Liberties Union Papers, Mudd Library, Princeton University.

9. "4 Newsmen Warn of Peril in Contempt Citation," *Editor and Publisher,* June 9, 1956, 13.

10. Peck et al. to Joseph P. Murphy, n.d., folder 61, box 4, Alden Whitman Papers, Manuscripts and Archives Division, New York Public Library.

11. Michael Potoker to Whitman, June 29, 1956, folder 62, box 4, Whitman Papers.

12. Charles A. Perlik to Whitman, September 20, 1956, folder 61, box 4, Whitman Papers.

13. Whitman to Perlik, September 20, 1956, folder 62, box 4, Whitman Papers.

14. Perlik to Whitman, February 28, 1957, folder 62, box 4, Whitman Papers.

15. Carl Beck, *Contempt of Congress: A Study of the Prosecutions Initiated by the Committee on Un-American Activities, 1945–1957* (New Orleans: Hauser Press, 1959), 2–9.

16. *Kilbourn v. Thompson,* 103 U.S. 168 (1880). The case involved the arrest of Hallet Kilbourn after he refused to answer questions before a House committee. Following his release he sued the committee, the Speaker, and the sergeant at arms and was awarded $20,000 (Beck, *Contempt of Congress,* 7).

17. *McGrain v. Daugherty,* 237 U.S. 135 (1927). The case involved an investigation of the attorney general's office during the Teapot Dome scandal and demonstrated that a witness subpoenaed by the Senate is obliged to appear (Beck, *Contempt of Congress,* 8).

18. Beck, *Contempt of Congress,* 12–15.

19. *Lawson v. U.S.,* 176 F.2d 49 (D.C. Cir. 1949).

20. Harvey Klehr and John Earl Haynes, *The American Communist Movement: Storming Heaven Itself* (New York: Twayne, 1992), 191–94.

21. *U.S. v. Rumely,* 345 U.S. 41 (1953).

22. Ibid., 57.

23. *United States v. Lamont, United States v. Unger, United States v. Shadowitz,* 236 F.2d 312 (1956); *United States v. Kamin,* 136 F. Supp. 791 (1956).

24. *United States v. Robert Shelton,* 148 F. Supp. 926 (D.C. Cir. 1957), Transcript of Record, Supreme Court of the United States, October term, 1961, 49, 154.

25. Frank J. Donner, *The Age of Surveillance: The Aims and Methods of America's Political Intelligence System* (New York: Alfred A. Knopf, 1980), 146–47; Ronald Radosh and Joyce Milton, *The Rosenberg File: A Search for the Truth* (New York: Holt, 1983), 356–57.

26. Morris L. Ernst, "Why I No Longer Fear the FBI," *Reader's Digest,* December 1950, 135.

27. In the Senate this would be rule 26 of the Standing Rules of the Senate. Under this section a committee may vote to issue a subpoena or it may adopt a rule delegating the authority to a committee chairperson. The authority does not encompass committee staff. See, generally, John C. Grabow, *Congressional Investigations* (New York: Prentice Hall Law and Business, 1988), 80–85. See also Senate Committee on Rules and Administration, *Rules of Procedure for Senate Investigating Committees,* 84th Cong., 1st sess., 1955, Committee Report 2.

28. *Shelton,* Transcript of Record, 103.

29. James Reston, "Strategist for Inquiry," *New York Times,* January 6, 1956, 7.

30. *Shelton,* Transcript of Record, 105.

31. See the Court decisions in *Kilbourn; McGrain;* and *Sinclair v. United States,* 279 U.S. 263 (1929).

32. *Shelton,* Transcript of Record, 105.

33. Ibid., 154.

34. "Shelton, Robert, That Is, Found Guilty of Contempt," *Guild Reporter,* February 22, 1957, 8; "Librarian Jailed in Contempt Case," *New York Times,* January 19, 1957, 18; and "N.Y. Newsman Held Guilty of Contempt," *Washington Post,* January 19, 1957, A-2.

35. "Inquiry Is Accused," *New York Times,* March 13, 1957, 18.

36. *William A. Price v. United States,* 280 F.2d 715 (D.C. Cir. 1960).

37. Ibid., rev'd sub nom. *Russell v. United States,* 369 U.S. 749 (1962), Brief for the Petitioner, Supreme Court of the United States, October term, 1961, 37.

38. "Newsman Jailed in Contempt," *New York Times,* April 13, 1957, 9.

39. "Request by Senator Eastland for Permission to Testify in United States District Court in the Case of Seymour Peck, Charged with Contempt of the Senate," 85th Cong., 1st sess. *Cong. Rec.* 103, pt. 3 (March 21, 1957): 4135–36, 4140–47; Authorization for Senator Eastland to Testify in United States District Court in the Case of Seymour Peck, 85th Cong., 1st sess. *Cong. Rec.* 103, pt. 3 (March 21, 1957): 4202–13.

40. "Senator Eastland Testifies There Was Nobody But Us Chickens," *I. F. Stone's Weekly,* April 1, 1957, 3.

41. *Lawson v. United States* and *Trumbo v. United States,* 176 F.2d 49 (1949); cert. denied, 339 U.S. 934 (1950); rehearing denied, 339 U.S. 972 (1950).

42. "Newsman Guilty in Contempt Case," *New York Times,* March 27, 1957, 19.

43. Gerhard Van Arkel to Whitman, February 5, 1957, folder 49, box 4, Whitman Papers.

44. Van Arkel to Nanette Dembitz, March 28, 1957, folder 49, box 4, Whitman Papers.

45. Whitman to Van Arkel, February 28, 1957, folder 49, box 4, Whitman Papers.

46. Donald May, "He Despises the Informer," *Washington Daily News,* April 10, 1957, 10.

47. "Recent Decision in the United States District Court for the District of Columbia Again Rules Congress Has Power to Investigate Communist Party and Those Who Are Members Thereof," remarks of Senator Clyde Doyle of California, *Cong. Rec.* 103, pt. 1 (May 9, 1957): 6729.

48. "Reporter Denies He's a Red, Won't Talk about Past," *San Francisco Daily News,* June 21, 1957, 1.

49. New York Mirror Division, Hearst Corporation, and American Newspaper Guild, 27 Lab. Arb. (BNA) 811 (1956) (Turkus, Arb.).

50. Beck, *Contempt of Congress,* 161.

51. Arthur J. Sabin, *In Calmer Times: The Supreme Court and Red Monday* (Philadelphia: University of Pennsylvania Press, 1999), 106–14.

52. *Watkins v. United States,* 354 U.S. 178 (1957).

53. Sabin, *In Calmer Times,* 193–97; Beck, *Contempt of Congress,* 162–66.

54. "Federal Bar Convention," *U.S. Law Week,* October 1, 1957, 2161–62.

55. House Committee on Un-American Activities, *Hearings Held in San Francisco, Calif., June 18–21, 1957,* 58th Cong., 1st sess., June 21, 1957, pt. 2 (Washington, D.C.: GPO, 1957), 1280–81.

56. Ibid., 1280.

57. Lawrence E. Davies, "Walter Leaves Inquiry to G.O.P.," *New York Times,* June 22, 1957, 3; Los Angeles Daily News, 19 La. Arb. (BNA) 39 (1952); United Press Assn., 22 LA 679 (1954); The New York Times Company, 26 Lab. Arb. (BNA) 642 (1958) (Schedler, Arb.).

58. "SFONG to Contest Firing on '5th' Plea," *San Francisco Call-Bulletin,* June 28, 1957, 2.

59. Hearst Publishing Company, Inc., San Francisco Examiner Division and American Newspaper Guild, San Francisco–Oakland Newspaper Guild, Local 52, 30 Lab. Arb. (BNA) 642, 645 (1958) (Schedler, Arb.); "Guild Loses Case of Reporter Fired for Invoking Fifth," *People's World,* July 12, 1958, 2.

60. "Newsman Freed in Contempt Case," *New York Times,* July 12, 1957, 9.

61. *United States v. Peck,* 154 F. Supp. 603, 605 (D.C. Cir. 1957).

62. Beck, *Contempt of Congress,* 171–80.

63. Dean Alfange Jr., "Congressional Investigations and the Fickle Court," *University of Cincinnati Law Review* 30 (1961): 168–69.

64. *Barenblatt v. United States,* 360 U.S. 109, 126, 134 (1959).

65. *Shelton v. United States,* 280 F.2d 701, 707 (1960); *William A. Price v. United States,* 280 F.2d 715 (1960).

66. Van Arkel to A. H. Raskin, August 15, 1960, box 5, folder 72, Whitman Papers.

67. *Alden Whitman v. United States,* U.S. Supreme Court Records, Briefs, October term, 1961, 61.

68. *Russell v. United States,* 369 U.S. 749 (1962). The importance of establishing the pertinence of congressional inquiries was reflected in a series of cases during the mid- to late 1950s. These include *Watkins v. United States,* 354 U.S. 178 (1957), *Sacher v. United States,* 356 U.S. 576; *Barenblatt v. United States,* 360 U.S. 109 (1959); *Wilkinson v. United States,* 365 U.S. 399 (1960); *Braden v. United States,* 365 U.S. 431(1960); and *Deutch v. United States,* 367 U.S. 456 (1961). In *Watkins* the Court ruled that witnesses must be apprised of the relevance when they are called upon to respond to questions.

69. *Whitman,* New York Civil Liberties Union Brief, U.S. Supreme Court Records, 19–21.

70. *Russell v. United States,* 369 U.S. 749, 776 (1962).

71. Susan E. Tifft and Alex S. Jones, *The Trust: The Private and Powerful Family behind the New York Times* (Boston: Little, Brown, 1999), 816.

72. Sulzberger to Whitman (not sent), May 23, 1962, "Senate Investigations: 1954–1966," Arthur Hays Sulzberger Papers, New York Times Archives.

73. Sulzberger to Whitman, May 24, 1962, folder 62, box 4, Whitman Papers.

74. Whitman to Van Arkel, May 27, 1962, folder 50, box 4, Whitman Papers.

75. Van Arkel to Louis Loeb, June 7, 1962, folder 72, box 5, Sulzberger Papers.

76. Loeb to Van Arkel, June 12, 1962, folder 72, box 5, Sulzberger Papers.

77. Van Arkel to Whitman, September 21, 1962, folder 62, box 4, Whitman Papers.

78. James A. Wechsler, "Endless Trials," *New York Post,* September 24, 1962, 34.

79. Nicholas Von Hoffman, *Citizen Cohn: The Life and Times of Roy Cohn* (New York: Doubleday, 1988), 181–82.

80. David M. Oshinsky, *A Conspiracy So Immense: The World of Joe McCarthy* (New York: Free Press, 1983), 240–41.

81. Monroe G. McKay, "Double Jeopardy: Are the Pieces the Puzzle?" *Washburn Law Journal* 23 (1983): 1–23.

82. Press release, October 4, 1962, "Shelton, Robert—1963" folder, box 1689, ACLU Papers.

83. Samuel Walker, *In Defense of American Liberties: A History of the ACLU* (Carbondale: Southern Illinois University Press, 1990), 232, 245.

84. J. W. Maxwell, "Counsel Says He Destroyed Letter," *Washington Daily News,* January 17, 1963, 8.

85. "Eastland Testifies at Newsman's Trial," *New York Times,* January 31, 1963, 14.

86. Anthony Lewis, "Courts Settling 8 Contempt Cases," *New York Times,* March 22, 1964, 32.

87. *Shelton v. United States,* 327 F.2d 601, 606 (1963).

88. "U.S. Drops Contempt Case against a Times Newsman," *New York Times,* November 30, 1965, 28.

Chapter Ten: Living with the Legacy

1. Undated memo signed "SG" in "Staff: Senate Investigation" file, series 2, C/D, Turner Catledge Papers, Special Collections, Mitchell Memorial Library, Mississippi State University.

2. Ellen Schrecker, *Many Are the Crimes: McCarthyism in America* (Boston: Little, Brown, 1998), 76, 273.

3. Sheryl Gay Stolberg, "Patriot Act Revisions Pass House, Sending Measure to President," *New York Times,* March 8, 2006, A-20.

4. Ibid.; Schrecker, *Many Are the Crimes.*

5. Steve Rosswurm, "Introduction: An Overview and Preliminary Assessment of the CIO's Expelled Unions," in Rosswurm, ed., *The CIO's Left-Led Unions* (New Brunswick, N.J.: Rutgers University Press, 1992), 1–17.

6. Quoted in Stephen J. Simurda, "Sticking with the Union?" *Columbia Journalism Review,* March–April 1993, 25.

7. Richard M. Fried, *Nightmare in Red: The McCarthy Era in Perspective* (New York: Oxford University Press, 1990), 99–100; Haynes Johnson, "The Newspaper Guild's Identity Crisis," *Columbia Journalism Review,* November–December 1972, 44–48.

8. Sam Kuczun, "History of the American Newspaper Guild" (Ph.D. diss., University of Minnesota, 1970), 255–58.

9. Ibid., 363.

10. Daniel Lazare, "State of the Union," *Columbia Journalism Review,* January 1989, 43.

11. Gene Ruffini, "Who Needs the Guild?" *Editor and Publisher,* March 20, 1993, 48.

12. Simurda, "Sticking with the Union?" 25.

13. Jacques Steinberg, "At Other Tribune Papers, a Quandary of Where to Cut," *New York Times,* June 14, 2004, C-5.

14. Gary Fields, Kris Maher, and Ann Zimmerman, "Two Unions Quit AFL-CIO, Casting Cloud on Labor," *Wall Street Journal,* July 26, 2005, A-1.

15. "Union Disunity," *Christian Science Monitor,* July 27, 2005, 13.

16. Randy Dotinga, "Guild Still Standing Tall, Despite Loss," *Editor and Publisher,* July 25, 1998, 20.

17. Joe Garofoli, "Guild, Chronicle Reach Deal," *San Francisco Chronicle,* July 25, 2005, A-2.

18. "Youngstown Newspaper Strikers Turn Down Offer," *Pittsburgh Post-Gazette,* July 28, 2005, 1.

19. Joe Strupp, "One Paper, in Contract Proposal, Wants to Silence Criticism from Workers," *Editor and Publisher,* July 27, 2005, www.editorandpublisher.com.

20. Katharine Q. Seelye, "Times Company Announces 500 Job Cuts," *New York Times,* September 21, 2005, C-5; Katharine Q. Seelye, "Washington Post to Cut 80 Newsroom Jobs," *New York Times,* March 11, 2006, C-2; Katharine Q. Seelye, "Time Inc. to Cut 100 More Jobs as It Focuses on Web Business," *New York Times,* January 31, 2006, C-7; Sarah Ellison, "Clash of Cultures Exacerbates Woes for Tribune Co.," *Wall Street Journal,* November 10, 2006, 1A–29; Joann Loviglio, Associated Press, "Philadelphia Inquirer, Struggling with Circulation and Ad Declines, Lays Off 71 Staff," Findlaw.com, January 3, 2007, http://fsnews.findlaw.com/articles/ap/o/51/01-03-2007/d7a0000bfd145fcd.html; "New York Times to Cut Jobs in Boston, Worcester," *Wall Street Journal,* January 12, 2007, B-3.

21. Ben Bagdikian, *Double Vision: Reflections On My Heritage, Life, and Profession* (Boston: Beacon, 1995), 207.

22. John B. Oakes, "This Is the Real, the Lasting Damage," *New York Times,* March 7, 1954, SM-48.

23. Todd Gitlin, *The Whole World Is Watching: Mass Media in the Making and Unmaking of the New Left* (Berkeley: University of California Press, 1980), 75–76.

24. Anthony Lewis, "Privilege and the Press," *New York Review of Books,* July 14, 2005, 4–8.

25. Jackson Rurner Main, *The Antifederalists: Critics of the Constitution* (Chapel Hill: University of North Carolina Press, 1961), 255; Leonard W. Levy, "On the Origins of the Free Press Clause," *UCLA Law Review* 32 (1984): 202–208.

26. Thomas I. Emerson, *The System of Free Expression* (New York: Vintage, 1970), 99. The First Amendment was adopted in 1789, but it did not take effect until two years later, when it was ratified by the states.

27. Jeffrey Alan Smith, *Printers and Press Freedom: The Ideology of Early American Journalism* (New York: Oxford University Press, 1987), 59.

28. *Near v. Minnesota,* 283 U.S. 697 (1931).

29. *Grosjean v. American Press Co.,* 297 U.S. 233 (1936).

30. For example, testimony of Tom O'Connor, before House Committee on Un-American Activities, *Communist Activities among Professional Groups in the Los Angeles Area,* 82th Cong., 2nd sess., May 22 and July 8, 1952, pt. 2 (Washington, D.C.: GPO, 1952), 3573.

31. For example, Anthony Leviero, "'Book Burners' Are Assailed by President at Dartmouth," *New York Times,* June 15, 1953, 1.

32. Harold L. Cross, *The People's Right to Know: Legal Access to Public Records and Proceedings* (New York: Columbia University Press, 1953), 5.

33. Edward Ranzal, "Reporter Facing Jail in Contempt," *New York Times,* October 17, 1957, 30.

34. *Garland v. Torre,* 259 F.2d 545 (2nd Cir. 1958); Edward Ranzal, "Woman Reporter Gets Jail Term," *New York Times,* November 13, 1957, 30.

35. Margaret A. Blanchard, *Revolutionary Sparks: Freedom of Expression in Modern America* (New York: Oxford University Press, 1992), 396–401.

36. Michael Parenti, *Inventing Reality: The Politics of News Media,* 2nd ed. (New York: St. Martin's, 1993), 122; Stanley I. Kutler, *The Wars of Watergate: The Last Crisis of Richard Nixon* (New York: Alfred A. Knopf, 1990).

37. Israel Shenker, "Some Who Made 'Dean's List' Honored; Others Voice Outrage," *New York Times,* June 28, 1973, 38.

38. "Transcript of Address by Agnew Criticizing Television on Its Coverage of the News," *New York Times,* November 14, 1969, 24.

39. Douglas McCollam, "Attack at the Source," *Columbia Journalism Review,* March–April 2005, 36.

40. *New York Times Co. v. United States,* 713 U.S. 403 (1971).

41. *Branzburg v. Hayes,* 408 U.S. 665 (1972).

42. Ibid., 707.

43. Ibid., 721 (Douglas, dissenting).

44. *Garland v. Torre,* 259 F.2d 545, 550–51 (2nd Cir. 1958).

45. Howard Kurtz, "A Case Most Clearly Defined by Its Shadows," *Washington Post,* July 7, 2005, A-12.

46. See Jack Gould, "House Panel Bids C.B.S. Yield Films," *New York Times,* April 9, 1971, A-1; "Schorr Case Recalls Many Clashes between Press and Government Back to Start of the Nation," *New York Times,* March 15, 1976, 22; "Senate Counsel Loses Bid for Reporters' Testimony," *Washington Post,* March 26, 1992, A-1; "Senate Counsel Unable to Find Leaks," *Louisville Courier-Journal,* May 6, 1992, 8-A.

47. Reporters Committee for Freedom of the Press, *Agents of Discovery* (Arlington, Va.: Reporters Committee for Freedom of the Press, 1995).

48. "Indecent Disclosure," *Nation,* February 24, 1992, 1.

49. Howard Kurtz, "Justice Dept. Opposed Shield for Reporters," *Washington Post,* July 20, 2005, A-3.

50. Joe Hagan, "Two Reporters Now Face Prison for Contempt," *Wall Street Journal,* June 28, 2005, B-1; Laurie P. Cohen, Joe Hagan, and Anne Marie Squeo, "How Media Split under Pressure in the Leak Probe," *Wall Street Journal,* July 29, 2005, A-1; Joe Hagan, "Support Wanes for Reporter in CIA Leak," *Wall Street Journal,* October 24, 2005, B-1.

51. Joe Hagan, "Time Says It's Not Above the Law; Will Obey Court," *Wall Street Journal,* July 1, 2005, B-1.

52. "Judith Miller Goes to Jail," *New York Times,* July 7, 2005, A-22; David Johnston and Douglas Jehl, "Times Reporter Free from Jail; She Will Testify," *New York Times,* September 30, 2005, A-1.

53. Victoria Toensing, "What a Load of Armitage!" *Wall Street Journal,* September 15, 2006, A-12.

54. "Freedom of the Press: Communications Giant Puts Profit over Principle," *Salt Lake City Tribune,* July 1, 2005, 12.

55. "The Newspaper Guild Scores Federal Government for Journalists' Prosecution," *PR Newswire,* June 27, 2005.

56. "ASNE Endorses National Shield Law," American Society of Newspaper Editors Press Release, July 6, 2005.

57. "Jailing Reporters," editorial, *Wall Street Journal,* July 1, 2005, A-8.

58. Government Memorandum, Case No. 04-MS-407, October 7, 2004, U.S. District Court for the District of Columbia, n.d., 8–13. Lewis argued that the risk to the press of alienating the public by claiming special privileges was greater than any dangers posed by government encroachment. He argued that press privilege should be qualified, with "judges balancing the interests" (Lewis, "Privilege and the Press," 4).

59. Dan Froomkin, "Miller's Big Secret," Washingtonpost.com, September 30, 2005; Howard Kurtz, "The Judith Miller Story: Not Ready Yet," *Washington Post,* October 13, 2005, C-1.

60. Quoted in McCollam, "Attack at the Source," 35.

61. Melvin Barnet, interview by author, May 23, 1998, Brooklyn, New York.

62. Alden Whitman, interview by Nora Sayre, n.d.

63. Seymour Peck, interview by Nora Sayre, n.d.

Epilogue

1. An arbitrator in 1957 ordered Republic Steel Corporation to reinstate a pipe fitter who had invoked the Fifth Amendment before HUAC (Republic Steel Corporation, Corrigan-McKinney Plant and United Steelworkers of America, Hearst Publishing Company, Inc., San Francisco Local 1098, 28 Lab. Arb. [BNA] 811 [1957] [Platt, Arb.]).

2. Hearst Publishing Company, Inc., San Francisco Examiner Division and American Newspaper Guild, San Francisco–Oakland Newspaper Guild, Local 52, 30 Lab. Arb. (BNA) 642 (1958) (Schedler, Arb.).

3. Ellen Schrecker, *Many Are the Crimes: McCarthyism in America* (Boston: Little, Brown, 1998), xiv, 273.

4. Michael T. Kaufman, "Melvin Barnet, 83, Times Editor Fired after Charge of Communism," *New York Times,* June 19, 1998, C-19; Michael Cross-Barnet, "The New York Times Shafted My Father," *Los Angeles Times,* June 26, 2005, M-3; Michael Cross-Barnet, interview by author, October 27, 2002 (telephone).

5. Nathan Aleskovsky, "In Public Relations," *New York Times,* November 12, 1969, 47.

6. Peter Kihss, "5 Gain Settlements for F.B.I. Acts in 70s," *New York Times,* March 16, 1981, 1.

7. "Books–Authors," *New York Times,* October 1, 1964, 32; Robert H. Estabrook, "'Why' of 'Who Killed Kennedy?'" *Washington Post,* May 8, 1964, A-20.

8. "David Alex Gordon," *New York Times,* December 15, 1997, B-7.

9. "Retired Cap Times Editor Maraniss Dies at 86," *(Madison, Wisc.) Capital Times,* May 3, 2004, 5-A.

10. Ibid.

11. Alden Whitman, interview by Nora Sayre, n.d.

12. Seymour Peck, interview by Nora Sayre, n.d.

13. Herbert Mitgang, "Seymour Peck, Times Editor for 32 Years, Killed in Crash," *New York Times,* January 2, 1985, B-10.

14. Larry Ceplair and Steven Englund, *The Inquisition in Hollywood: Politics in the Film Community, 1930–1960* (New York: Anchor, 1980), 265–66; David Caute, *The Great Fear: The Anti-Communist Purge under Truman and Eisenhower* (New York: Simon and Schuster, 1978), 530; Ralph S. Brown Jr., *Loyalty and Security: Employment Tests in the United States* (New Haven, Conn.: Yale University Press, 1958), 487–97; Schrecker, *Many Are the Crimes,* 361.

15. Special Agent in Charge, New York, to Hoover, August 15, 1968. FBI 100-2230-59.

16. Hoover to director, U.S. Secret Service, March 23, 1971, FBI 100-406708, Whitman Papers, New York Public Library.

17. Whitman interview.

18. Alden Whitman, "William O. Douglas Is Dead at 81; Served 36 Years on Supreme Court," *New York Times,* January 20, 1980, 1.

19. Alden Whitman, "Thurman Arnold, Trust Buster, Dead," *New York Times,* November 8, 1969, 33.

20. "Alden Whitman Is Dead at 76; Made an Art of Times Obituaries," *New York Times,* September 5, 1990, D-23.

21. Jon Pareles, "Robert Shelton, 69, Music Critic Who Chronicled 60's Folk Boom," *New York Times,* December 19, 1995, 19.

22. Teresa Graham, "Janet Scott, 88, Longtime Albany Journalist," *(Albany, N.Y.) Times Union,* July 18, 1992, B-7.

23. Wolfgang Saxon, "James Wechsler, a Columnist and Ex-Editor of Post, Dies," *New York Times,* September 12, 1983, D-13.

24. Victor S. Navasky, *Naming Names* (New York: Penguin, 1991), 371–74.

25. Eric Pace, "Winston Burdett Is Dead at 79, Covered World and War for CBS," *New York Times,* May 21, 1993, 47; "Fraternity Cites 15 in Journalism," *New York Times,* April 17, 1955, 14.

26. Douglas Martin, "Harvey Matusow, 75, an Anti-Communist Informer, Dies," *New York Times,* February 4, 2002, B-7.

27. Marjorie Hunter, "James Eastland Is Dead at 81; Leading Senate Foe of Integration," *New York Times,* February 20, 1986, D-23.

28. "J. G. Sourwine, Ex-Senate Aide, Is Dead at 78," *New York Times,* July 22, 1986, A-20.

29. W. H. Lawrence, "McCarthy Is Dead of Liver Ailment, at Age 47," *New York Times,* May 3, 1957, 1.

30. Fred P. Graham, "J. Edgar Hoover, 77, Dies; Will Lie in State at the Capitol," *New York Times,* May 3, 1972, A-1.

31. Robert Novak, "For now, Hoover's Ghost Lives On," *Chicago Sun-Times,* December 1, 2005, 45.

32. Alden Whitman, "Morris Ernst, 'Ulysses' Cast Lawyer, Dies," *New York Times,* May 23, 1976, 40.

33. "H. H. Velde, Chief of Inquiry on Radicals," *New York Times,* September 6, 1985, B-6; "Parnell Thomas Going to Enter Publisher Ranks," *Guild Reporter,* July 27, 1951, 3.

34. Richard M. Fried, *Nightmare in Red: The McCarthy Era in Perspective* (New York: Oxford University Press, 1990), 196.

Selected Bibliography

Alfange, Dean Jr. "Congressional Investigations and the Fickle Court." *University of Cincinnati Law Review* 30, no. 2 (1961): 113–71.

Aronson, James. *The Press and the Cold War.* Indianapolis: Bobbs-Merrill, 1970.

Barnet, M. L. "Probers and the Press." *Nation* (1955): 552–54.

Barth, Alan. *Government by Investigation.* New York: Viking, 1955.

———. *The Loyalty of Free Men.* New York: Viking, 1951.

Bayley, Edwin R. *Joe McCarthy and the Press.* New York: Pantheon, 1981.

Beck, Carl. *Contempt of Congress: A Study of the Prosecutions Initiated by the Committee on Un-American Activities, 1945–1957.* New Orleans: Hauser Press, 1959.

Belfrage, Cedric. *The American Inquisition, 1945–1960.* Indianapolis: Bobbs-Merrill, 1973.

Belknap, Michal R. *Cold War Political Justice: The Smith Act, the Communist Party, and American Civil Liberties.* Westport, Conn.: Greenwood, 1977.

Blanchard, Margaret A. *Revolutionary Sparks: Freedom of Expression in Modern America.* New York: Oxford University Press, 1992.

Bliss, Edward Jr. *Now the News: The Story of Broadcast Journalism.* New York: Columbia University Press, 1991.

Brown, Ralph S. *Loyalty and Security: Employment Tests in the United States.* New Haven, Conn.: Yale University Press, 1958.

Cade, Dozier C. "Witch-Hunting, 1952: The Role of the Press." *Journalism Quarterly* 29, no. 4 (1952): 396–407.

Carr, Robert Kenneth. *The Constitution and Congressional Investigating Committees: Individual Liberty and Congressional Power.* New York: Carrie Chapman Catt Memorial Fund, 1954.

———. *The House Committee on Un-American Activities, 1945–1950.* Ithaca, N.Y.: Cornell University Press, 1952.

Catledge, Turner. *My Life and the* Times. New York: Harper and Row, 1971.

Caute, David. *The Great Fear: The Anti-Communist Purge under Truman and Eisenhower.* New York: Simon and Schuster, 1978.

Ceplair, Larry, and Steven Englund. *The Inquisition in Hollywood: Politics in the Film Community, 1930–1960.* New York: Anchor, 1980.

Chafee, Zechariah Jr. *Free Speech in the United States.* New York: Atheneum, 1969.

Cloud, Stanley, and Lynne Olson. *The Murrow Boys: Pioneers on the Front Lines of Broadcast Journalism.* Boston: Houghton Mifflin, 1996.

Cochran, Bert. *Labor and Communism: The Conflict That Shaped American Unions.* Princeton, N.J.: Princeton University Press, 1977.

Cogley, John. *Report on Blacklisting: Radio-Television.* New York: Fund for the Republic, 1956.

Cook, Fred. *The Nightmare Decade: The Life and Times of Senator Joe McCarthy.* New York: Random House, 1971.

Cray, Ed. *Chief Justice: A Biography of Earl Warren.* New York: Simon and Schuster, 1997.

Cushman, Robert E. *Civil Liberties in the United States.* Ithaca, N.Y.: Cornell University Press, 1956.

Deaver, Jean Franklin. "A Study of Senator Joseph R. McCarthy and 'McCarthyism' as Influences upon the News Media and the Evolution of Reportorial Method." Ph.D. diss., University of Texas at Austin, 1970.

Dembitz, Nanette. "Congressional Investigation of Newspapermen, Authors, and Others in the Opinion Field—Its Legality under the First Amendment." *Minnesota Law Review* 40 (1956): 517–60.

Diggins, John Patrick. *The Rise and Fall of the American Left.* New York: W. W. Norton, 1973.

Donner, Frank J. *The Un-Americans.* New York: Ballantine, 1961.

Draper, Theodore. *The Roots of American Communism.* New York: Viking, 1957.

Emerson, Thomas I. "Freedom of Association and Freedom of Expression." *Yale Law Journal* 74, no. 1 (1964): 1–35.

Emery, Edwin. *History of the American Newspaper Publishers Association.* Westport, Conn.: Greenwood, 1970.

Freeland, Richard M. *The Truman Doctrine and the Origins of McCarthyism: Foreign Policy, Domestic Politics, and Internal Security, 1946–1948.* New York: Alfred A. Knopf, 1972.

Fried, Richard. *Nightmare in Red: The McCarthy Era in Perspective.* New York: Oxford University Press, 1990.

Gelb, Arthur. *City Room.* New York: G. P. Putnam's Sons, 2003.

Gerard, Christopher John. "A Program of Cooperation: The FBI, The Senate Internal Security Subcommittee, and the Communist Issue, 1950–1956." Ph.D. diss., Cornell University, 1993.

Goldfarb, Ronald. *The Contempt Power.* New York: Columbia University Press, 1963.

Goldfield, Michael. *The Decline of Organized Labor in the United States.* Chicago: University of Chicago Press, 1987.

Goodman, Walter. *The Committee: The Extraordinary Career of the House Committee on Un-American Activities.* New York: Farrar, Straus and Giroux, 1968.

Griffith, Robert. *The Politics of Fear: Joseph R. McCarthy and the Senate.* Amherst: University of Massachusetts Press, 1987.

Halberstam, David. *The Fifties.* New York: Fawcett Columbine, 1993.

Haynes, John Earl. *Red Scare or Red Menace? American Communism and Anticommunism in the Cold War.* Chicago: Ivan R. Dee, 1966.

Haynes, John Earl, and Harvey Klehr. *Venona: Decoding Soviet Espionage in America.* New Haven, Conn.: Yale University Press, 1999.

Heale, M. J. *American Anticommunism: Combating the Enemy Within, 1830–1970.* Baltimore: Johns Hopkins University Press, 1990.

Hofstadter, Richard. *The Paranoid Style in American Politics and Other Essays.* Cambridge, Mass.: Harvard University Press, 1963.

Jacobson, Sol. "The Fourth Estate: A Study of the American Newspaper Guild." Ph.D. diss., New School for Social Research, 1960.

Johnson, Ralph H., and Michael Altman. "Communists in the Press: A Senate Witch-Hunt of the 1950s Revisited." *Journalism Quarterly* 55 (1978): 487–93.

Kendrick, Alexander. *Prime Time: The Life of Edward R. Murrow.* Boston: Little, Brown, 1969.

Klehr, Harvey. *The Heyday of American Communism: The Depression Decade.* New York: Basic Books, 1984.

Klehr, Harvey, John Earl Haynes, and Kyrill M. Anderson. *The Soviet World of American Communism.* New Haven, Conn.: Yale University Press, 1998.

Klehr, Harvey, John Earl Haynes, and Fridrikh Igorevich Firsov. *The Secret World of American Communism.* New Haven, Conn.: Yale University Press, 1995.

Kuczun, Sam. "History of the American Newspaper Guild." Ph.D. diss., University of Minnesota, 1970.

Leab, Daniel J. *A Union of Individuals: The Formation of the American Newspaper Guild, 1933–1936.* New York: Columbia University Press, 1970.

Lee, Alfred McClung. *The Daily Newspaper in America: The Evolution of a Social Instrument.* New York: Octagon, 1973.

Lens, Sidney. *Radicalism in America.* New York: Thomas Y. Crowell, 1969.

Levenstein, Harvey A. *Communism, Anticommunism, and the CIO.* Westport, Conn.: Greenwood, 1981.

Levy, Leonard W. *Emergence of a Free Press.* New York: Oxford University Press, 1985.

Lichtman, Robert M., and Ronald D. Cohen. *Deadly Farce: Harvey Matusow and the Informer System in the McCarthy Era.* Urbana: University of Illinois Press, 2004.

Liebovich, Louis. *The Press and the Origins of the Cold War.* New York: Praeger, 1988.

MacPherson, Myra. *"All Governments Lie": The Life and Times of Rebel Journalist I. F. Stone.* New York: Scribner, 2006.

Matusow, Harvey. *False Witness.* New York: Cameron and Kahn, 1955.

McAuliffe, Mary S. "Liberals and the Communist Control Act of 1954." *Journal of American History* 63, no. 2 (1976): 351–67.

Mickelson, Sig. *The Decade That Shaped Television News: CBS in the 1950s* Westport, Conn.: Praeger, 1998.

Miller, Merle. *The Judges and the Judged.* New York: Doubleday, 1952.

Mitgang, Herbert. *Dangerous Dossiers: Exposing the Secret War against America's Greatest Authors.* New York: D. J. Fine, 1988.

Morgan, Ted. *Reds: McCarthyism in Twentieth-Century America.* New York: Random House, 2003.

Nasaw, David. *The Chief: The Life of William Randolph Hearst.* Boston: Houghton Mifflin, 2000.

Navasky, Victor. *Naming Names.* New York: Penguin, 1991.

Neville, John F. *The Press, the Rosenbergs, and the Cold War.* Westport, Conn.: Praeger, 1995.

O'Connor, Richard. *Heywood Broun: A Biography.* New York: G. P. Putnam's Sons, 1975.

Ogden, August Raymond. *The Dies Committee: A Study of the Special House Committee for the Investigation of Un-American Activities, 1938–1944.* Washington, D.C.: Catholic University of America Press, 1945.

O'Reilly, Kenneth. *Hoover and the Un-Americans: The FBI, HUAC, and the Red Menace.* Philadelphia: Temple University Press, 1983.

Oshinsky, David M. *A Conspiracy So Immense: The World of Joe McCarthy.* New York: Free Press, 1983.

Ottanelli, Fraser M. *The Communist Party of the United States: From the Depression to World War II.* New Brunswick, N.J.: Rutgers University Press, 1991.

Paley, William S. *As It Happened.* New York: Doubleday, 1979.

Pember, Don R. "The Smith Act as a Restraint on the Press." *Journalism Monographs* (1969): 1–32.

Preston, William Jr. *Aliens and Dissenters: Federal Suppression of Radicals, 1903–1933.* Cambridge, Mass.: Harvard University Press, 1963.

Pritchett, C. Herman. *Civil Liberties and the Vinson Court.* Chicago: University of Chicago Press, 1954.

———. *Congress versus the Supreme Court.* Minneapolis: University of Minnesota, 1961.

Romerstein, Herbert, and Eric Breindel. *The Venona Secrets: Exposing Soviet Espionage and America's Traitors.* Washington, D.C.: Regnery, 2000.

Rosswurm, Steve. "The Catholic Church and the Left-Led Unions: Labor Priests, Labor Schools, and the ACTU." In Rosswurm, ed., *The CIO's Left-Led Unions.* New Brunswick, N.J.: Rutgers University Press, 1992.

———. "The Wonderous Tale of an FBI Bug: What It Tells Us about Communism, Anti-Communism, and the CIO Leadership." *American Communist History* 2, no. 1 (2003): 3–20.

Schrecker, Ellen. *Many Are the Crimes: McCarthyism in America.* Boston: Little, Brown, 1998.

Schwartz, Nancy Lynn. *The Hollywood Writers' Wars.* New York: Alfred A. Knopf, 1982.

Scott, Janet. "How Crazy Can They Get?" *Nation,* December 12, 1953, 509–10.

Simmons, George E. "The Communist Conspiracy Case: Views of 72 Daily Newspapers." *Journalism Quarterly* 27, no. 1 (1950): 3–11.

Taylor, Telford. *Grand Inquest.* New York: Simon and Schuster, 1955.

Theoharis, Athan G. *Seeds of Repression: Harry S Truman and the Origins of McCarthyism.* Chicago: Quadrangle, 1971.

———. *Spying on Americans: Political Surveillance from Hoover to the Huston Plan.* Philadelphia: Temple University Press, 1978.

Theoharis, Athan G., and John Stuart Cox. *The Boss: J. Edgar Hoover and the Great American Inquisition.* Philadelphia: Temple University Press, 1988.

Tifft, Susan E., and Alex S. Jones. *The Trust: The Private and Powerful Family behind the New York Times.* New York: Little, Brown, 1999.

Tuck, Jim. *McCarthyism and New York's Hearst Press: A Study of Roles in the Witch Hunt.* Lanham, Md.: University Press of America, 1995.

Wechsler, James. *Reflections of an Angry Middle-Aged Editor.* New York: Random House, 1960.

———. *The Age of Suspicion.* New York: Random House, 1953.

Index

EDWARD ALWOOD is Associate Professor of Journalism at Quinnipiac University and a former Correspondent for CNN. He is the author of *Straight News: Gays, Lesbians, and the News Media.*